MONSTERS IN THE MOVIES

▲ **Glenn Strange, Béla Lugosi, Lon Chaney, Jr.** in Abbott and Costello Meet Frankenstein [Charles Barton, 1948].

DK

▲ **Boris Karloff** in Abbott & Costello Meet Dr. Jekyll and Mr. Hyde [Charles Lamont, 1953].

Contents

Vampires	**4**
Dracula	16
A Stake Through the Heart!	18
In Conversation: Christopher Lee	20
Werewolves	**22**
In Conversation: Joe Dante	32
Zombies	**34**
Ghosts	**48**
Myths, Legends, & Fairy Tales	**58**
In Conversation: Ray Harryhausen	72
Dragons & Dinosaurs	**74**
Nature's Revenge	**86**
Space Monsters	**100**
Monstrous Machines	**118**
Human Monsters	**128**
Acknowledgments	144

Above: A one-sheet poster advertising a triple feature showing of *Frankenstein* [1931], *Dracula* [1931], and *The Wolf Man* [1941]. In the late '40s and early '50s, actor and cowboy Glenn Strange (who played the Frankenstein monster in both *House of Frankenstein* [1944] and *Abbott and Costello Meet Frankenstein* [1948]) would put on the costume and a rubber mask and, with other performers dressed as Dracula and the Wolf Man, rampage through the theater as the kids screamed with delight.

FROM THE COLLECTION OF BOB BURNS

Vampires

More films have been made featuring Dracula than almost any other fictional character. Tarzan is (forgive me) neck and neck.

Bram Stoker's novel *Dracula* appeared in 1897 and was an instant success. It was influenced by J. Sheridan Le Fanu's 1872 novel *Carmilla*, about a lesbian vampire who preys on young women—later the inspiration for the trilogy of Hammer films, *The Vampire Lovers* [Roy Ward Baker, 1970], *Twins of Evil* [John Hough, 1971], and *Lust for a Vampire* [Jimmy Sangster, 1971].

Varney the Vampire, a penny-dreadful serial by James Malcolm Rymer, preceded Le Fanu's *Carmilla*. And the first notion of the vampire as an aristocrat appeared in *The Vampyre* [1819], written by John Polidori on a holiday with Lord Byron and the poet Percy Bysshe Shelley. On that same holiday, Shelley's wife, Mary Shelley, wrote *Frankenstein*!

The first cinematic version of Stoker's *Dracula* was the German silent *Nosferatu* [F. W. Murnau, 1922] with the unforgettable Max Schreck as "Count Orlock." This beautiful film was, in fact, entirely ripped off from Stoker's book and Stoker's widow suppressed its release in the courts.

Bram Stoker's novel was adapted into a play by Hamilton Deane that toured England for three years before it opened in London's West End to tremendous acclaim. The play was heavily revised by John L. Balderston in 1927 for its debut on Broadway, where it was a sensation. Hungarian matinée idol Béla Lugosi played Dracula and veteran stage actor Edward Van Sloan portrayed Van Helsing. They reprised their roles in *Dracula* [Tod Browning, 1931], Universal Studios' follow-up to their smash hit *Frankenstein* [James Whale, 1931]. Lugosi was actually offered the role of the Monster in *Frankenstein* on the strength of his success in the play *Dracula*, but he felt the role of a non-speaking brute beneath an actor of his talent. The lead in a Hollywood adaptation of *Dracula* was another matter, however. The movie version followed the plot of the Balderston/Deane play rather than the novel.

▲ ***Varney the Vampire* or *The Feast of Blood*** An illustration from the 1847 "penny dreadful" pamphlet edition of James Malcolm Rymer's gothic vampire story. Many persistent vampire behaviors originated here.

Sadly, Lugosi's distinctive performance as the elegant Count typecast him for the rest of his career. Whenever movie work was scarce, Béla would go out on another theatrical tour of the play, eventually performing the role thousands of times.

Dracula is an early "talkie." Before sound dubbing, studios would often shoot different language versions of their movies on the same sets. Tod Browning shot during the day and a Spanish-language *Dracula* [George Melford, 1931], with Carlos Villarías as the vampire Count, shot on the same sound stages at night. Many believe this Spanish-language version to be superior to the English one.

Just as Universal capitalized on box-office powerhouse *Frankenstein* with *The Bride of Frankenstein* [James Whale, 1935] and *Son of Frankenstein* [Rowland V. Lee, 1939], so they soon followed *Dracula* with *Dracula's Daughter* [Lambert Hillyer, 1936]. Gloria Holden starred in the title role of a movie that is much better than it sounds. Keeping it in the family, the studio continued with *Son of Dracula* [Robert Siodmak, 1943], featuring a debonair Lon Chaney, Jr. as Count Alucard (Dracula spelled backwards).

Previous pages: Frances Dade as Lucy and Béla Lugosi as Count Dracula in *Dracula* [Tod Browning, 1931].
Opposite page: Christopher Lee as the Count in *Dracula Has Risen From the Grave* [Freddie Francis, 1968].

Lugosi played a Count Dracula lookalike named Count Mora in *Mark of the Vampire* [1935], Tod Browning's remake of his own *London After Midnight* [1927], the lost Lon Chaney silent. There is a nice twist at the end of *Mark of the Vampire*, which I will not spoil here.

Abbott and Costello Meet Frankenstein was Lugosi's last hurrah as Count Dracula for Universal. He is excellent in this well-mounted comedy. The fact that Béla ended up starring in Ed Wood movies does not dull his monumental contribution to Dracula lore.

Hammer's first Technicolor horror film introduced the world to a new, dynamic, sexy, and powerful Count Dracula: Christopher Lee. *Dracula* [*Horror of Dracula* in the US, Terence Fisher, 1958] also brought Lee's Dracula a worthy foe in Peter Cushing's driven Van Helsing. Both Lee and Cushing would go on to play these roles for decades although, unlike Lugosi, their wide range of character roles continued (and for Christopher Lee, continues) for the rest of their careers.

Hundreds of *Dracula* movies have been produced since then, including an excellent BBC adaptation starring Louis Jourdan as the Count and Frank Finlay as Van Helsing, and two big-budget feature productions: *Dracula* [John Badham, 1979], with Frank Langella as the Count and Laurence Olivier as Van Helsing, and *Bram Stoker's Dracula* [Francis Ford Coppola, 1992], starring Gary Oldman, with Anthony Hopkins as Van Helsing. Universal tried to milk this bat once again with the monster rally *Van Helsing* [Stephen Sommers, 2004], starring Hugh Jackman as an action-man Van Helsing, in an attempt to create a new franchise.

The folkloric rules of vampirism have been reinvented in almost every vampire film. Kathryn Bigelow's terrific *Near Dark* [1987] brought us a motley group of vampires trying to survive in the modern American west. Anne Rice's bestseller *Interview With the Vampire* was made into a lavish film [Neil Jordan, 1994] starring Tom Cruise and Brad Pitt, with the young Kirsten Dunst playing an older woman still in the body of the child she was when bitten. Her anger and frustration with her plight is identical to the vampire boy-child Homer in *Near Dark*, who is played by Joshua Miller with a raging intensity. The wonderful, Swedish, *Let the Right One In* [Tomas Alfredson, 2008] deals with a child vampire in a stark and poetic way.

Innocent Blood [John Landis, 1992] stars Anne Parillaud as Marie, a vampire who finds herself stranded in Pittsburgh alone and hungry. She refuses to take what she calls "innocent blood," and so must feed on criminals. Although she is careful not to create more bloodsuckers, by mistake she creates a vampire out of Sal "The Shark" Macelli (Robert Loggia), a vicious mafioso. She joins undercover cop Joe Gennaro (Anthony LaPaglia) to try and deal with a developing plague of monster mobsters. He falls in love with her, but isn't quite sure if he can trust a vampire, let alone make love to one.

In *30 Days of Night* [David Slade, 2007], a gang of vampires led by Danny Huston besiege an Alaskan town. *Daybreakers* [Michael and Peter Spierig, 2009] takes place in 2019, after a plague has turned the majority of the world's population into vampires.

Vampires continue to intrigue, scare, attract, repel, and entertain us. I'd like to end with a strange request in a book about movies: I urge you to read Stoker's original book. The story is told through letters and diaries and it's not only postmodern, it's really scary!

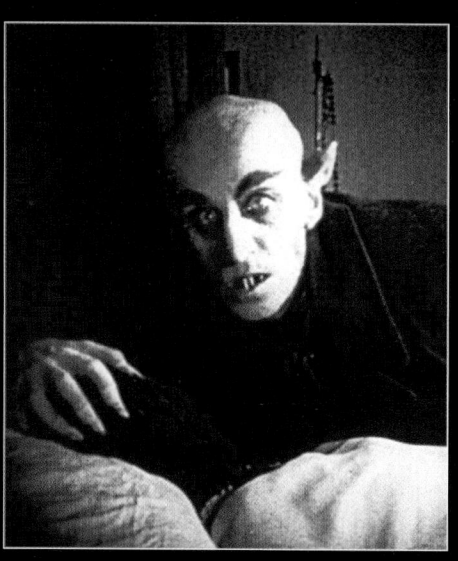

▲ **Nosferatu** [F. W. Murnau, 1922] Max Schreck as Nosferatu in this, the first (and unauthorized) screen version of Bram Stoker's novel *Dracula*. This German expressionistic silent was remade as *Nosferatu the Vampyre* by Werner Herzog in 1979.

Opposite page: (1) Carlos Villarías as "Conde Dracula" and Lupita Tovar as "Eva Stewart" in the Spanish language *Dracula* [George Melford, 1931], shot at night on the same sets as Browning's version. **(2) Brad Pitt** as Louis de Pointe du Lac, the vampire in Neil Jordan's 1994 film of Anne Rice's novel *Interview With the Vampire*. **(3) Andrew Stehlin** as Arvin, one of the vampires laying siege to an Alaskan town in *30 Days of Night* [David Slade, 2007]. **(4) Gloria Holden** as Countess Marya Zaleska in *Dracula's Daughter* [Lambert Hillyer, 1936], seen here burning her father's body in the hope that this will free her from the curse of vampirism.

VAMPIRES

◀ **Nosferatu**
[F. W. Murnau, 1922]
Max Schreck in the title role arrives in Wisborg; everyone else on board the ship is dead, apparently killed by a plague that leaves strange marks on the necks of victims.

▲ **Nosferatu the Vampyre**
[Werner Herzog, 1979] Klaus Kinski, in make-up based on Schreck's in Murnau's silent original, realizes too late that the sun is coming up. The beautiful Isabelle Adjani is Lucy Harker.

◀ **London After Midnight**
[Tod Browning, 1927]
In this movie mystery, the "vampires" are a red herring used to trap the real culprits. One of the most sought-after "lost films," mainly because of Lon Chaney's extraordinary make-up. Remade as *Mark of the Vampire* [Tod Browning, 1935] with Béla Lugosi as the "vampire."

> "You're not in London now, Dr. Garth, with your police. You're in Transylvania, in my castle!"
>
> Countess Marya Zaleska (Gloria Holden), *Dracula's Daughter*

▼ **Dracula's Daughter** [Lambert Hillyer, 1936] Universal Studios' first sequel to *Dracula* [Tod Browning, 1931] begins with Edward Van Sloan as Professor Abraham Van Helsing being taken to Scotland Yard and accused of Count Dracula's murder!

▲ *Vampyr* [Carl Theodor Dreyer, 1932] Allan Gray (Nicolas de Gunzberg) dreams that he sees himself in a coffin. Dreyer's haunting, dreamlike vampire film was disliked upon release, but its reputation has grown with time. Based on *In a Glass Darkly* [1872], J. Sheridan Le Fanu's collection of supernatural stories.

▲ **Mark of the Vampire** [Tod Browning, 1935] Carroll Borland as Luna and Béla Lugosi as Count Mora, her father, in this remake of *London After Midnight* [1927]. In the original, Lon Chaney played both the "vampire" and the Inspector from Scotland Yard. Lionel Atwill portrays the Inspector in this remake.

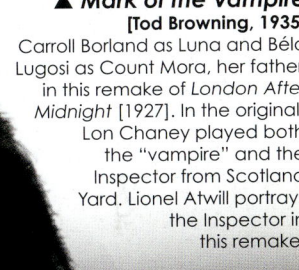

▲ **Son of Dracula** [Robert Siodmak, 1943] Lon Chaney, Jr. as Count Alucard holds Louise Allbritton as Katherine Caldwell in his power in this story, which brings the Transylvanian Count to New Orleans long before author Anne Rice had a similar idea.

▶ **Dracula** [Tod Browning, 1931] Béla Lugosi as Count Dracula about to bite Frances Dade as Lucy in the film that forever typecast the Hungarian actor as the vampire. Lugosi never wore fangs as Dracula.

VAMPIRES

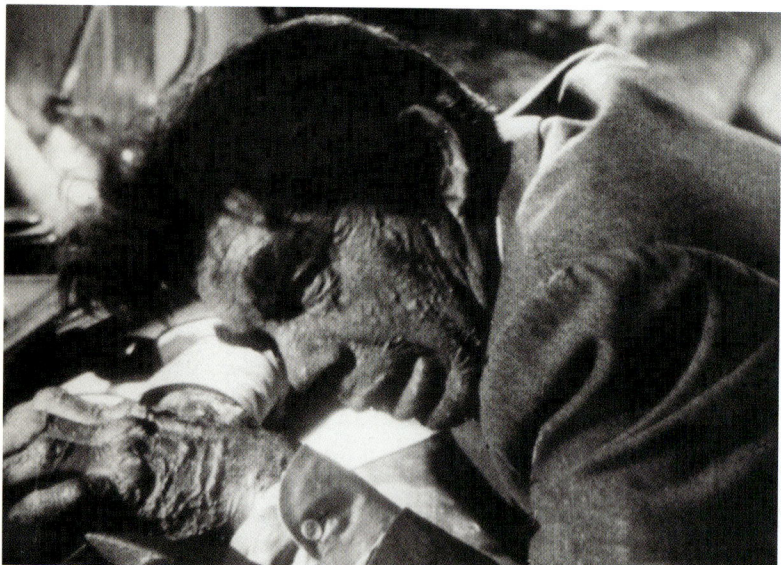

▲ *The Vampire* [Paul Landres, 1957] John Beal as Dr. Paul Beecher, a small town doctor who becomes addicted to the pills from another doctor's research with vampire bats. This could be a morality tale about drug addiction, but maybe it's just a B monster movie.

▲ *Dracula* [aka *Horror of Dracula*, Terence Fisher, 1958] The first time Christopher Lee played the Count in this international Hammer sensation. With a steadfast Peter Cushing as Van Helsing and in vivid Technicolor. Lee's powerful presence and sensual performance made a remarkable impact on movie audiences around the world. Here, the Count is about to indulge in a snack in this typical Hammer publicity shot.

▲ *House of Dracula* [Erle C. Kenton, 1945] The direct sequel to *House of Frankenstein* [Erle C. Kenton, 1944], this Universal "monster rally" features Wolf Man Larry Talbot (Lon Chaney, Jr.), and Dracula (John Carradine) asking Dr. Edlemann (Onslow Stevens) to cure their monstrous afflictions.

◀ *The Return of Dracula* [Paul Landres, 1958] Count Dracula (Francis Lederer) rises from his coffin in a small town where he tries to convince an all-American family that he is their cousin!

▲ *Plan 9 From Outer Space* [Ed Wood, 1959] A famously inept movie from Ed Wood, here is the exotic Vampira (Maila Nurmi) as a Vampire Girl from outer space!

▲ *Blood of Dracula* [Herbert L. Strock, 1957] A thrilling poster for a decidedly boring movie.

"Greetings, my friend. We are all interested in the future, for that is where you and I are going to spend the rest of our lives."

Criswell, *Plan 9 from Outer Space*

▲ *Blood and Roses* [Roger Vadim, 1960] One more movie based on Le Fanu's *Carmilla*. Vadim's film features the gorgeous Annette Vadim as Carmilla and the equally gorgeous Elsa Martinelli as her victim.

▶ *Atom Age Vampire* [aka *Seddok, l'erede di Satana*, Anton Giulio Majano, 1963] Alberto Lupo as the mutated Professor Alberto Levin needs blood!

VAMPIRES

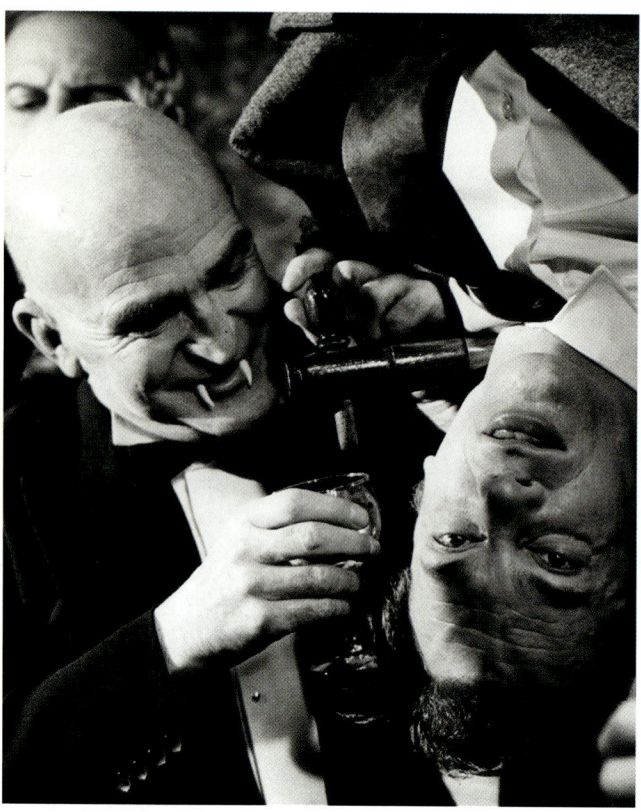

▲ **The Vault of Horror** [Roy Ward Baker, 1973] In another Amicus portmanteau movie, Daniel Massey discovers that he is on the menu when he enters a restaurant for vampires. Based on the EC comic book.

▲ **Kuroneko** [Kaneto Shindō, 1968] An amazing samurai vampire story set in the Sengoku period in Japan. This is Nobuko Otowa as Yone, the samurai's mother, who just wants her arm back. I first saw this at the Los Angeles County Museum of Art in a theater full of screaming people. Great!

▲ **The Fearless Vampire Killers** [aka *Dance of the Vampires*, Roman Polanski, 1967] Count von Krolock (Ferdy Mayne) abducts Sarah Shagal (Sharon Tate) from her bath in Polanski's vampire romp.

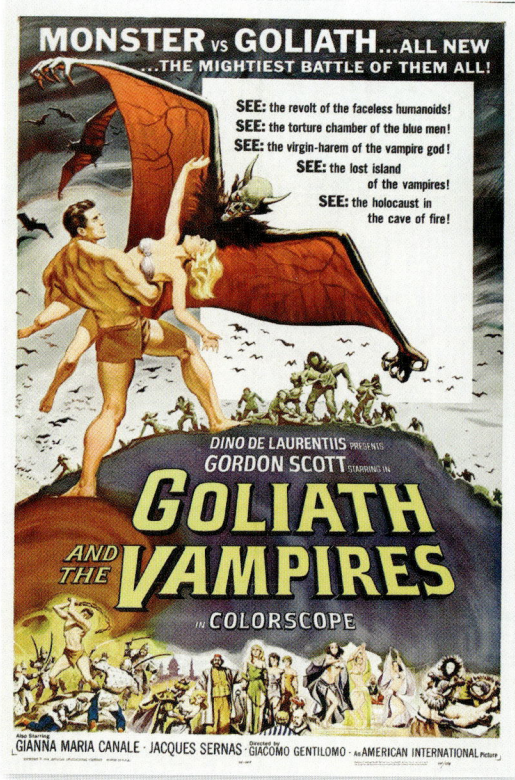

▲ **Goliath and the Vampires** [aka *Goliath and the Island of the Vampires*, Sergio Corbucci, Giacomo Gentilomo, 1961] Goliath faces a zombie who kidnaps women so his soldiers can drink their blood. As the poster says: "See: the virgin-harem of the vampire god!"

Dr. Van Helsing

◀ **Edward Van Sloan** [*Dracula*, 1931] Van Sloan also appeared in Universal's *Frankenstein* [1931] and *The Mummy* [1932] which makes him one of the classic Universal Monsters Players.

▼ **Peter Cushing** [*The Brides of Dracula*,1960] Cushing was not only one of the Hammer stock company, but always an outstanding presence in countless British and American films.

▲ **Black Sabbath** [Mario Bava, 1963] Bava's virtuoso direction makes this Italian anthology film a treat. Boris Karloff not only introduces the three stories, but stars in "The Wurdalak," based on a story by Tolstoy. As the loving grandfather who may be a Wurdalak, a vampire who feasts only on those he loves, Karloff is deeply frightening. The other two stories are equally scary. A Bava classic.

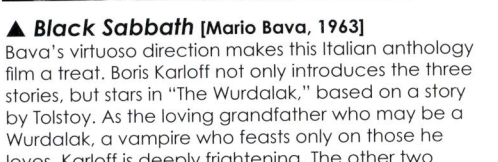

▲ **The Vampire and the Ballerina** [Renato Polselli, 1960] Black and white Italian horror schlock about a troupe of ballerinas who seek shelter in a spooky castle filled with vampires. The US prints have all of the nudity cut out, and since the nudity was the point of the whole exercise you can imagine the American audience's disappointment.

▶ **Anthony Hopkins** [*Bram Stoker's Dracula*, 1992] Van Helsing has killed Dracula's concubines, one of those heads was on a young Monica Bellucci.

▲ **Mel Brooks** [*Dracula: Dead and Loving It*, 1995] Brooks makes an excellent and believable Van Helsing.

▶ **Hugh Jackman** [*Van Helsing*, 2004] Indiana Jones he is not.

13

VAMPIRES

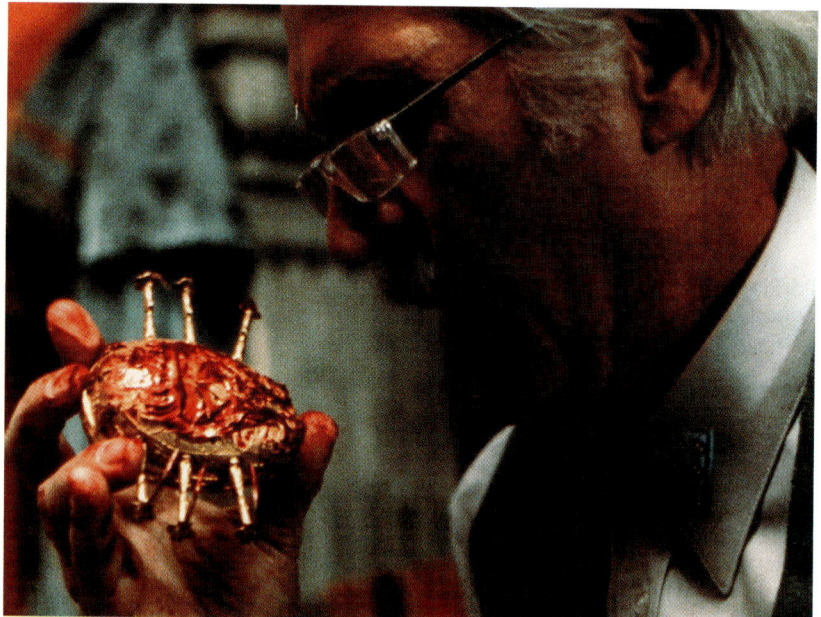

▲ **Cronos** [Guillermo Del Toro, 1993] Jesus Gris (Federico Luppi) examines the Cronos device which can give you youth and strength, but at a great price. The film that introduced the great Del Toro to an international audience. An original and haunting vampire story from Mexico.

▲ **Vampires** [aka *John Carpenter's Vampires*, John Carpenter, 1998] Sheryl Lee seems unaware of that guy on the ceiling behind her in Carpenter's vampire Western. James Woods is the head of a Vatican vampire hit squad who roams the West killing bloodsuckers.

▶ **Buffy the Vampire Slayer** [Fran Rubel Kuzui, 1992] Paul Reubens as Amilyn, one of the vampires Buffy (Kristy Swanson) slays in this teenage comedy/horror film that spawned a much more successful, long-running television series, starring Sarah Michelle Geller as Buffy.

◀ **The Little Vampire** [Uli Edel, 2000] Jonathan Lipnicki in the title role in this film based on the German children's book *Der kleine Vampir* by Angela Sommer-Bodenburg. With Richard E. Grant and Alice Krige.

▲▲ **From Dusk Till Dawn** [Robert Rodriguez, 1996] Salma Hayek as stripper Santanico Pandemonium before and just after she reveals her true vampiric nature. A fun grindhouse movie filled with famous actors having a good time.

▲ **Blade II** [Guillermo Del Toro, 2002] A sequel that is superior to the film it follows, as Del Toro continues the story of the half-human vampire killer played by Wesley Snipes and based on the Marvel Comics character.

▼▶ **Interview With the Vampire** [Neil Jordan, 1994] Brad Pitt, Kirsten Dunst, and Tom Cruise are all vampires in this big-budget movie version of the Anne Rice novel.

▶ **Vampire in Brooklyn** [Wes Craven, 1995] Eddie Murphy as Maximillian, who is a vampire in Brooklyn. Murphy also co-wrote and plays two other roles in the film.

"Lucy is not a random victim… She is the Devil's concubine!"

Van Helsing (Anthony Hopkins), *Bram Stoker's Dracula*

▶ **Bram Stoker's Dracula** [Francis Ford Coppola, 1992] Sadie Frost as Lucy is not too pleased to see that cross, in Coppola's imaginative retelling of *Dracula*.

VAMPIRES

DRACULA

▲▼ **Béla Lugosi** [*Dracula*, Tod Browning, 1931]
Lugosi's entrance: "I am Dracula. I bid you welcome." Below: some publicity person painted blood coming from the wounds on Frances Dade's neck from Lugosi's bite on this photo. The movie itself is entirely bloodless.

Bram Stoker's character Count Dracula has proven consistently popular since the novel was first published in 1897. He has been portrayed as handsome and suave, hideous and loathsome, and oftentimes all four. Here are just some of the actors who have donned the cape and fangs.

▲ **Christopher Lee** [*Dracula*, aka *Horror of Dracula*, Terence Fisher, 1958] Lee introduced both blood and fangs in his compelling and indelible portrayal of the vampire Count.

▲ **Robert Quarry** [*Count Yorga, Vampire*, Bob Kelljan, 1970]
Count Yorga is Count Dracula with another name.
The same director and star brought us *The Return of Count Yorga* the following year.

▲ **Louis Jourdan** [*Count Dracula*, Philip Saville, 1977] A BBC production, this film is one of the most faithful to the novel. Jourdan makes a fine, aristocratic Dracula with the stench of decay about him.

> "My, what a big bat!"
>
> John Harker (David Manners), *Dracula* [1931]

▲ **Lon Chaney, Jr.** [*Son of Dracula*, Robert Siodmak, 1943] Chaney, Jr. makes a strong physical presence work in his favor as the European bloodsucker in the American South.

◀ **Paul Naschy** [*El Gran Amor de Conde Dracula*, aka *Count Dracula's Great Love*, Javier Aguirre, 1974] Paul Naschy (Jacinto Molina) not only played Dracula, but a Wolf Man character named Waldemar Daninsky in 12 movies! Known as the "Spanish Lon Chaney," Naschy also played the Mummy, the Hunchback, Dr. Jekyll and Mr. Hyde, and any other horror icon that was laying around.

▶ **Shin Kishida** [*Lake of Dracula*, Michio Yamamoto, 1971] Perhaps the name Dracula was added for the Western release of this Japanese vampire movie, but he sure looks and acts like Dracula!

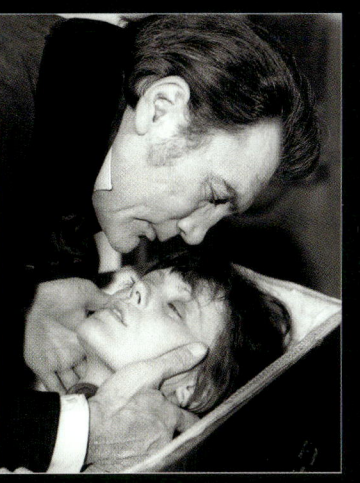
◀ **Jack Palance** [*Dracula*, aka *Dan Curtis' Dracula*, Dan Curtis, 1974] Seen here with Fiona Lewis as Lucy, Palance's Dracula was a ferocious and physically imposing figure of lust and power.

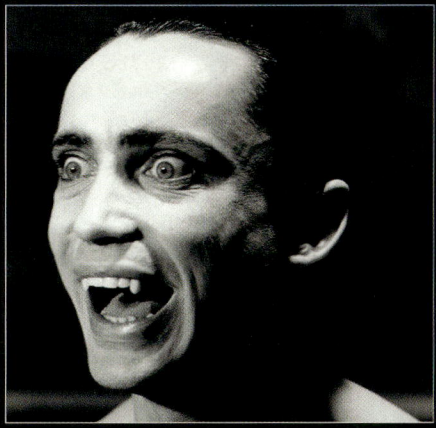
▲ **Udo Kier** [*Blood for Dracula*, aka *Andy Warhol's Dracula*, Paul Morrissey, 1974] Kier is funny and sad as a sickly Count Dracula who needs to travel from Transylvania for young virgin blood. He finds four lovely young girls in the house of their father (played by Italian film director Vittorio De Sica), but the estate's handyman (Joe Dallesandro) deflowers each one before Dracula can drink their blood. Very funny and rather elegant for such an outrageous plot. Roman Polanski shows up for a cameo.

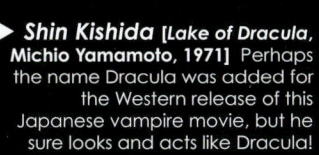
▲ **William Marshall** [*Scream, Blacula, Scream*, Bob Kelijan, 1973] AIP schlockmeister Sam Arkoff wanted a blaxploitation Dracula and somehow William Marshall gave the role dignity with his regal bearing and beautiful voice. A fun, crap movie, with Marshall rising above the fray.

▲ **Leslie Nielsen** [*Dracula: Dead and Loving It*, Mel Brooks, 1995] Nielsen, doing his best Lugosi, is actually quite dignified in this blood-soaked farce from Mel Brooks.

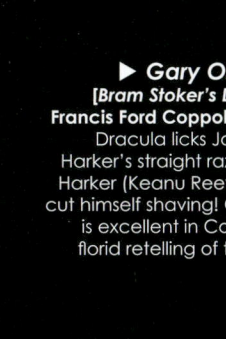
▶ **Gary Oldman** [*Bram Stoker's Dracula*, Francis Ford Coppola, 1992] Dracula licks Jonathan Harker's straight razor after Harker (Keanu Reeves) has cut himself shaving! Oldman is excellent in Coppola's florid retelling of the tale.

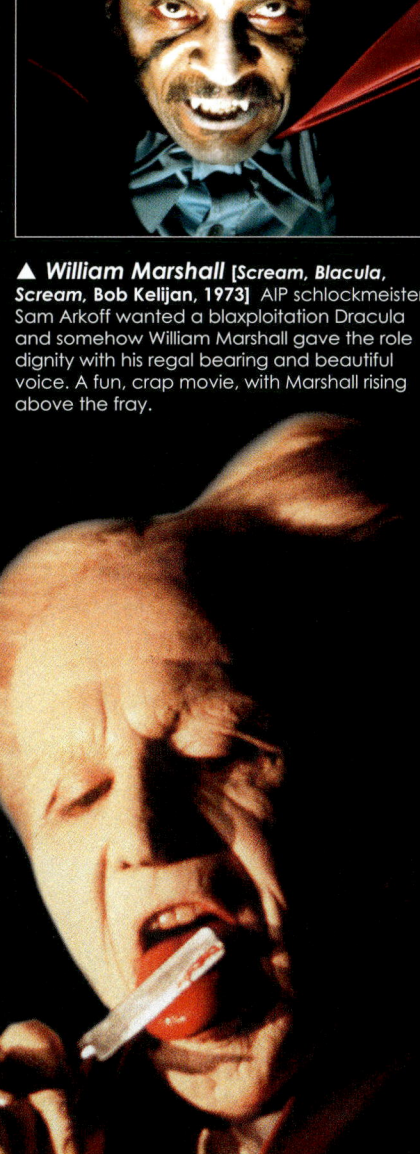

▲ **Richard Roxburgh** [*Van Helsing*, Stephen Sommers, 2004] Roxburgh tries to remain as menacing as he can under the circumstances.

VAMPIRES

A Stake Through the Heart!

Methods for killing a vampire remain fairly consistent in the movies. A wooden stake driven into the vampire's heart with a mallet is always effective, although you must make sure your aim is true. Garlic and crosses, even running fresh water, are all well and good for fending off an attack but, to make sure, keep a hammer and a wooden stake handy just in case.

▲ **House of Frankenstein** [Erle C. Kenton, 1944] Dr. Gustav Niemann (Boris Karloff) threatens Count Dracula (John Carradine) in this Universal monster rally.

▲ **Dracula** [aka *Horror of Dracula*, Terence Fisher, 1958] Jonathan Harker (John Van Eyssen) manages to stake the vampire woman (Valerie Gaunt) who has bitten him, unaware that Dracula himself (Christopher Lee) is about to show up.

▲ **I Bought a Vampire Motorcycle** [Dirk Campbell, 1990] I haven't seen this movie, nor had I even heard of it before I saw this photo of Neil Morrissey staking his vampire motorcycle. I am pretty sure it's a spoof.

◀ **Dr. Terror's House of Horrors** [Freddie Francis, 1965] An Amicus portmanteau film. In this story, a young doctor (Donald Sutherland) is convinced by a medical colleague (Max Adrian) that his new French wife (Jennifer Jayne) is a vampire. After Sutherland drives a stake through her heart, Adrian informs him that the town is too small for two vampires and two doctors and reveals his true self!

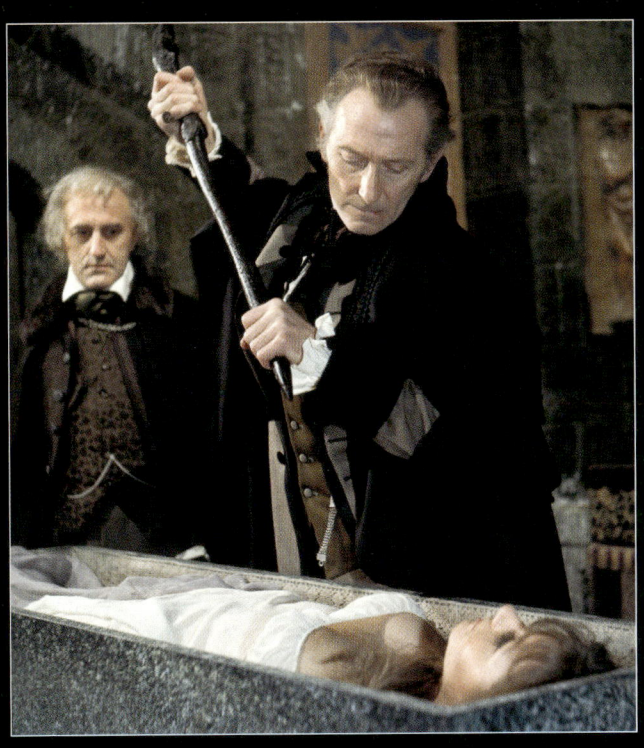

▲ **The Vampire Lovers** [Roy Ward Baker, 1970] After staking Ingrid Pitt through the heart, Peter Cushing then cuts off her head.

▲ **The Fearless Vampire Killers** [aka *Dance of the Vampires*, Roman Polanski, 1967] Alfred (Roman Polanski) is about to stake Count von Krolock (Ferdy Mayne) in this bloody comedy.

◀▼ **Dracula Has Risen From The Grave** [Freddie Francis, 1968] The priest has lost his faith and the man his nerve when they stake Count Dracula. But their aim is not true and Dracula pulls out the stake (with lots of gushing red gore, unusual at the time)!

"I am the monster that breathing men would kill. I am Dracula."

Count Dracula (Gary Oldman),
Bram Stoker's Dracula [1992]

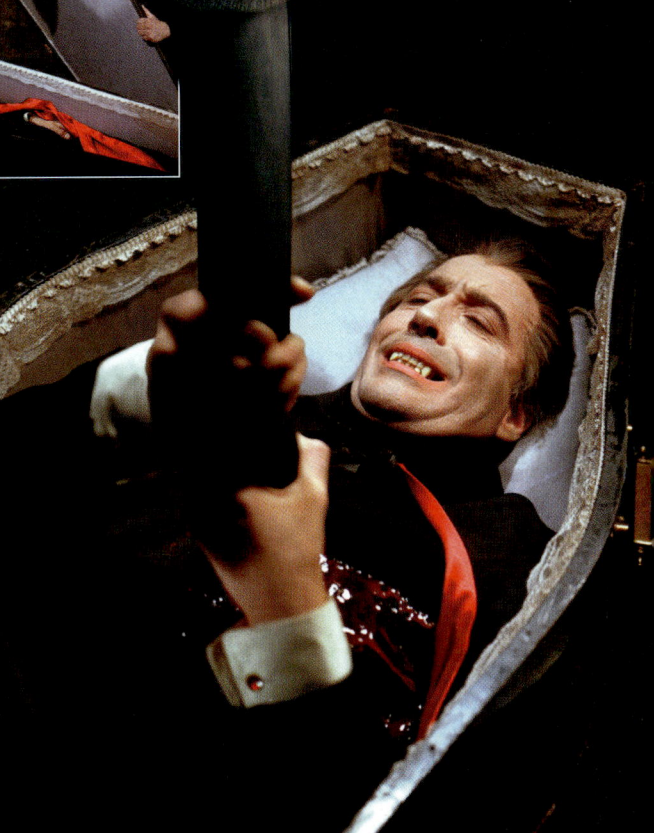

▲ **Lost Boys: The Tribe** [P. J. Pesce, 2008] In this sequel to *The Lost Boys* [1987], an older Corey Feldman prepares to stake a vampire.

IN CONVERSATION

Christopher Lee

Schlock reads *Famous Monsters of Filmland* magazine sitting next to its editor, Forrest J Ackerman. On the cover is Sir Christopher Lee as Dracula.

JL: Chris, you were just about to say why you shy away from the term "horror film."

CL: It's a very simple answer. I did films with Boris Karloff who, like myself, made his name as a monster. He was a wonderful man, a superb actor, far better than the parts he was often given to play. What he had to do, and what I had to do, was to make the unbelievable believable. And that's very difficult, especially with today's audience. The reason I don't like the word "horror," is because it conjures up something really nasty, horrific, horrendous, evil, vile. The word that Boris used to use, and indeed I use, is "fantasy." The French always refer to these films as "films of the fantastic," which I think is a very good description. I never looked upon my films as horror films. I always tried to give the impression that the characters I played were doing things they couldn't help doing. And Boris did the same.

JL: You've played some of the classic monsters. You are the definitive Dracula, and you've played the Mummy, as well as Frankenstein's Monster. Your Dracula is pretty ferocious, whereas your Frankenstein's creature is very sympathetic…

CL: This is what I've always tried to do. Even when playing, not necessarily a monster, but the bad guy, I've always tried to do something, say something, the audience doesn't expect.

JL: Your performance in *The Curse of Frankenstein* [Terence Fisher, 1957] is fabulous.

CL: The Creature is a very pitiful character. He didn't ask to be made; he's a victim. More so than the people he kills.

JL: I think the people he kills are victims, too.

CL: Well, I didn't kill many people, as I remember. And Boris didn't either. In (the Karloff *Frankenstein*), there was that famous scene when he throws the little girl into the lake thinking that she will float like the flowers. The censors cut that out, but I believe it's back in now. That scene is pitiful, pitiful. The audience has to see this other side to the Creature.

JL: What's interesting about *The Curse of Frankenstein*, is that Peter Cushing's role, Dr. Frankenstein, is the real monster.

CL: Oh, absolutely. As you say, I'm the victim.

JL: And in the sequels, Frankenstein's creature becomes less and less important.

CL: I never saw them.

JL: Well, they vary greatly in quality. But Peter's always good!

CL: He was a superb actor.

JL: Marty Scorsese said that your entrance in *Horror of Dracula* [aka *Dracula*, Terence Fisher, 1958] made a huge impression on him. You walk quietly down the stairs and say, "I am Count Dracula. And this is my house." Something elegant and simple like that.

CL: I remember our first night in New York with Peter [Cushing]. I'd never been to America. This was about '57, I think. There was a great big building near the theater that was covered with an enormous painting of me (as Dracula) carrying one of the girls.

JL: How many stories high was it?

CL: At least 10 stories. That made me reel! Then we had to go to the first performance. And I'm not good in public, few actors are. I said to Peter, "I don't think this is a very good idea." And he said, "Oh, my dear fellow, this is what we've come for! We've got to do it!" It was close to midnight, and many in the audience had had a few, to put it mildly. So I said to Peter, "I'm going to sit in the very top row, underneath the projection booth with you, near the exit, so that if anything happens I can leave." Because I didn't like seeing myself on screen, and I didn't know what the audience reaction was going to be. Finally, the lights go down, the curtains part, up come the credits, and I recall there was a coffin with my name and blood splashes onto it. There was a huge roar of applause, and then the moment comes where you see me at the top of the stairs: a silhouette. The place exploded. Everyone shouting and yelling, and laughing, and I thought, "Oh God, this really is the end." And I walk down the stairs in a perfectly normal way, and I say quite calmly, "Mr. Harker," or "Good evening, Mr. Harker" or something, and he says, "Count Dracula," and I say, "Yes, I am Dracula," or something… The audience went completely quiet! Total silence for the rest of the film!

JL: The audience must have reacted to the scares?

CL: A few shudders or squeaks, but every time I appeared on screen—silence. The biggest shock in the film, was when the girl [Valerie Gaunt credited as "Vampire Woman"] tries to seduce Jonathan Harker. And there's a shot of me in the doorway, teeth bared, wearing those contact lenses—couldn't see a thing—and I leap up onto a table, and I leap off—that's no stunt, no fake—shoot across the floor, fling her aside and go straight for him. There were no cuts. I don't think anybody had ever seen an actor playing a vampire do anything like that before.

JL: Your Dracula is terribly physical, and very, very sexual.

CL: Which I did not intend.

JL: Whether you intended it or not, it made a big impression.

CL: I know it did, but I tried to play him as a man with a kind of compulsion. I obviously gave the impression that he enjoyed it.

JL: You played it very sexual, though, Chris. You're saying it was an accident?

CL: I tried to make him attractive to women. That was in the script!

JL: Now, what about all the sequels. They got sillier and sillier.

CL: That gives rise to a true story. The first film came out, and it rocketed around the world.

JL: It was a huge hit.

CL: And it made me world famous. As Dracula, though, not necessarily as Christopher Lee.

JL: But not only was your Dracula so striking and remarkable, it was really the first color Dracula movie. And the blood was so Technicolor red.

CL: Well, that was Hammer's idea. Eight years later, they asked me…

JL: …It was 8 years until the second one? I didn't know that.

CL: Yes, 7 or 8. I did *Rasputin* [full title, *Rasputin, the Mad Monk*, Don Sharp, 1966] and *Dracula: Prince of Darkness* [Terence Fisher, 1966] back to back. Same sets. When I read the script, I said to my agent, "I'm not saying any of this dialog. It's appalling."

JL: You don't say anything in the movie!

CL: Not a word.

JL: But you have a hell of a presence!

CL: When Chekhov went to see one of his plays at a local theater, they asked him at the end what he thought of it, and he came up with this wonderful expression: "Not enough gunpowder." That's the secret. If you have the physical presence, all right: you're lucky. If you have power, well, you're lucky. But, gunpowder, that's the real secret!

JL: Well, your Dracula certainly has fire and brimstone.

CL: I refused to do the second one at first. In the end, I played Dracula five or six times…

JL: I hope they paid you well!

CL: Oh, you're joking. I think they paid me about £750.

JL: Even for the later ones?

CL: I think they paid me a little bit more later, but not much. Certainly not five figures.

JL: But you were the selling point of the movies!

CL: I bought my first car when I was 35. It was a second-hand Merc. I could just about afford it. Anyway, the process went like this: The telephone would ring and my agent would say, "Jimmy Carreras [President of Hammer Films] has been on the phone, they've got another Dracula for you." And I would say, "Forget it! I don't want to do another one."

JL: So how would Hammer get you to agree?

CL: I'd get a call from Jimmy Carreras, in a state of hysteria. "What's all this about?!" "Jim, I don't want to do it." "You've got to do it!" "Jim, I don't want to do it, and I don't have to do it." "No, you have to do it!" And I said, "Why?" He replied, "Because I've already sold it to the American distributor with you playing the part. Think of all the people you know so well, that you will put out of work!" Emotional blackmail. That's the only reason I did them.

JL: "Emotional blackmail" is a tradition in the movie business. Tell me about *The Mummy* [Terence Fisher, 1959].

CL: The Mummy was a real person at one time, a high priest, and he falls in love with a princess.

JL: It's a romantic story.

"I never looked upon my films as horror films."

CL: Oh yes! This love is forbidden, and they find out, cut out his tongue, and ball him up.

JL: Was that terribly uncomfortable?

CL: Yes! Swathed in bandages. Boris [Karloff, star of the original *The Mummy*, Karl Freund, 1932] said it was absolute hell, because he was covered in make-up and wrapped so tightly in bandages. If he took a deep breath, the bandages would crack and you would see there was a real person underneath.

JL: Luckily for him, Karloff is only the bandage-wrapped Mummy in one scene…

CL: The way I played it, I tried to make people feel sorry for me. The problem with the role was a physical one. I had to move like an automaton, but the Mummy also had a mind of its own. Because of the bandages I could only act with my body movements and my eyes. In one of the most effective scenes, I come crashing through the windows and Peter Cushing thrusts a spear into me, which goes right through, and shoots me. And then Yvonne Furneaux comes in. And Peter shouts, "Let down your hair! Let down your hair!" while I'm strangling her with one hand. And she does. And it's Ananka, the princess I fell in love with. I see her and I am riveted. And after quite a long time, I just turn around and walk away. Which I thought was very moving.

JL: And didn't you have to go into a swamp?

CL: Ah, the business in the swamp: I had to carry about three or four girls, sometimes as much as 80 yards, and they were pretending to be unconscious, so they were dead weight. It didn't help my shoulder muscles! In the swamp, Yvonne was saying to me under her breath, "Don't drop me, don't drop me," and I was using the most appalling language, because I was crashing into these pipes which were producing the bubbles in the water and the mud.

JL: Which brings us to Mr. Hyde.

CL: I'd forgotten that one. I think that was one of the best things I've ever done. But it had a ridiculous title: *I, Monster* [Stephen Weeks, 1971]. And they changed Jekyll's name.

JL: He's not called Dr. Jekyll?

CL: Jekyll and Hyde became Marlowe and Blake. But all the other people in the story have the correct names.

JL Why on earth would they do that?

CL: Don't ask me!

JL: Fredric March played Hyde as a bestial, ape-like character.

CL: Yes, and Spencer Tracy was very frightening, too.

JL: Tracy played him more like a psychopath. It was John Barrymore who first made Hyde into a physical monster.

CL: Oh yes, that was extraordinary.

JL: And he did it live on stage on Broadway!

CL: I don't know how he did that.

JL: George Folsey, the camera operator on the silent *Dr. Jekyll and Mr. Hyde* [John S. Robertson, 1920], told me that on stage Barrymore would drink from the flask, then stagger and fall down behind a desk and quickly get right up again transformed into the hideous Mr. Hyde! It happened very fast. All he did was put on a pointed, bald cap and shove crooked teeth into his mouth. He could distort his face so grotesquely.

CL: I played Hyde in stages of degeneration. I became worse and worse and worse. In the name of science. Curiosity. What would happen if I took this drug? All scientists are curious. The make-up man, Harry Frampton, did a wonderful job. There were about five or six stages of degeneration.

JL: Is there any particular monster that you were frightened of as a kid?

CL: Well, I remember after seeing Boris Karloff in *Frankenstein*, aged 11, I used to wake up in the middle of the night and think he was in the room. And I wasn't the only one!

WEREWOLVES

The belief in shape-shifting is universal. In every culture, from the ancient Greeks to the Native Americans, men and women often become animals and vice versa. In stories like the god Zeus turning himself into a swan to seduce the mortal Leda, or the magical Puck giving Bottom the head of an ass in Shakespeare's *A Midsummer Night's Dream* (see page 60), the theme of man-into-animal appears countless times in art and literature. In cinema, by far the most popular shape-shifter is the werewolf.

The shape-shifting "rules" change from film to film. Usually a man becomes a werewolf by being bitten by another werewolf, as in *Werewolf of London* [Stuart Walker, 1935], *The Wolf Man* [George Waggner, 1941 and Joe Johnston, 2010], and *An American Werewolf in London* [John Landis, 1981].

In *The Curse of the Werewolf* [Terence Fisher, 1961] Oliver Reed is born a werewolf because his mother was raped and he is born on Christmas Day! This movie claims that for an unwanted child to share his birthday with Jesus Christ is "an insult to heaven." When the poor bastard baby is to be baptized, the Holy Water in the baptismal font begins to boil. Not a good sign.

In the *Underworld* series of films, an entire race of werewolves battles a race of vampires for supremacy, and in Neil Marshall's *Dog Soldiers* [2002], a troop of British soldiers has the misfortune of running into a family of werewolves in the Scottish Highlands. In *How to Make a Monster* [Herbert L. Strock, 1958], an insane make-up artist uses Michael Landon's actual make-up and mask from the earlier film *I Was a Teenage Werewolf* [Gene Fowler, Jr., 1957] to turn an innocent actor into a homicidal wolf man! Val Lewton's production *Cat People* [Jacques Tourneur, 1942], centers on a beautiful woman (Simone Simon) descended from an ancient European race. When her passions (jealousy and lust) are aroused, she turns into a murderous black panther!

▲ *Little Red Riding Hood,* German postcard illustration [c. 1900]. Charles Perrault wrote the first account of the French folk tale in the 17th century. In Perrault's telling, Little Red Riding Hood ends up as a tasty meal for the devious Wolf.

The full moon has long been associated with violence and madness—the word "lunatic" shows the power we give the full moon. Against his will, the body of the lycanthrope changes into that of a werewolf whenever a full moon appears in the night sky.

A common term for the natural menstruation cycle of women is "the curse." This idea is explored in the clever Canadian picture *Ginger Snaps* [John Fawcett, 2000]. This film, like *I Was a Teenage Werewolf* and *The Beast Within* [Philippe Mora, 1982], uses lycanthropy as a metaphor for adolescence. In adolescence, youngsters begin to grow hair in unexpected places and parts of their anatomy swell and grow. Everyone experiences these physical transformations in their bodies and new, unfamiliar, sexual thoughts in their minds. No wonder we

Previous pages: *The Wolfman* [Joe Johnston, 2010] An atmospheric shot from the very disappointing remake.
Opposite page: (1) *An American Werewolf in London* [John Landis, 1981] Scotland Yard's Inspector Villiers (Don McKillop) attacked by the werewolf in Piccadilly Circus.
(2) **Michael Jackson** as a teenage werecat "strangling" me on the set of *Michael Jackson's Thriller* [John Landis, 1983]. Photo by Douglas Kirkland.
(3) *The Werewolf* by Lucas Cranach the Elder [1472-1553]. This woodcut by the German Renaissance painter, engraver, and printmaker shows a lycanthrope attacking a village.

readily accept the concept of a literal metamorphosis.

In Curt Siodmak's original screenplay for Universal's seminal *The Wolf Man*, he emphasized the notion of the werewolf as a victim. The Wolf Man of the title, Larry Talbot, played by Lon Chaney, Jr. in all five Universal *Wolf Man* movies), is horrified by his plight and spends most of his time trying to find a cure or contemplating suicide.

Every single werewolf film always has a major "transformation" sequence: Larry Talbot's transformation was accomplished by a series of optical dissolves. Chaney sat very still (usually with his head, hands, and feet held in place) while make-up man Jack Pierce gradually applied more and more yak hair and putty to his face. This was a tedious, time-consuming process, and the use of optical dissolves resulted in a rather gentle transformation from man into wolf man.

When I wrote the script for *An American Werewolf in London* written in 1969, produced in 1981), envisioned the metamorphosis from man to beast as a violent and painful one. The character of David Kessler (David Naughton) would transform from a two-legged human into a four-legged "hound from hell." I also specified that the sequence take place without cutaways and in bright light. The gifted make-up artist Rick Baker accomplished this with an elaborate combination of make-up, foam appliances, and what he called "change-o" body parts. These were elaborate puppet reproductions of parts of Naughton's body including his torso, hands, feet, head, and face) that could actually stretch and transform into the wolf monster in real time on camera. This sequence took five days to shoot. I ended up using one cutaway: of a toy Mickey Mouse silently watching. Rick won the first of his many Academy Awards for his groundbreaking work.

In Joe Dante's terrific *The Howling* [1981], the character of Eddie Quist (Robert Picardo) positively relishes his lycanthropy and gleefully transforms in front of a terrified Terry Fisher (Belinda Belaski). In this movie, werewolves seem to transform either at will or from sexual arousal. TV anchorwoman Karen White (Dee Wallace-Stone) has a particularly disturbing encounter with Quist in a porno booth at a sex shop while a film of a rape is being projected. Karen White eventually turns into a sort of fluffy, poodle-dog-werewolf during a live television news broadcast!

As in the *Underworld* pictures, the popular *Twilight* movies also chronicle the conflict between a race of vampires and werewolves. Also like the *Underworld* movies, the *Twilight* series uses computer-generated imagery to accomplish not only the man-into-wolf transformations, but also the monsters themselves. In *Eclipse* [David Slade, 2010] the werewolves tend to all be very buff, shirtless young men who transform into wolves by leaping into the air.

Hogwarts' unfortunate Defense Against the Dark Arts teacher Professor Lupin (David Thewlis), introduced in *Harry Potter and the Prisoner of Azkaban* [Alfonso Cuarón, 2004] is another werewolf who uses CGI to "morph," while Jack Nicholson in *Wolf* [Mike Nichols, 1994] uses a far more subtle, traditional make-up by Rick Baker.

Since the werewolf is here to stay, I suggest taking the excellent advice given by the customers of The Slaughtered Lamb pub in *An American Werewolf in London*: "Stay on the road. Beware the moon."

▲ ***The Wolf Man*** **[George Waggner, 1941]** This ad for Universal Studios' newest monster stresses the transformation "from Man to Beast" as a major marketing strategy.

***Opposite page: Cat People* [Jacques Tourneur, 1942]** French actress Simone Simon stars as Irena Dubrovna in this intelligent thriller from the Val Lewton B Picture Unit at RKO Studios. The sequence where a jealous Irena follows her husband's secretary to her apartment building's swimming pool is still eerie after all these years.

WEREWOLVES

▲ **The Wolf Man** [George Waggner, 1941] Lon Chaney, Jr. as the tragic Wolf Man of the title holding the lovely Evelyn Ankers in his arms. I've never understood why the werewolf that bit him (the Gypsy Bela, played by Béla Lugosi) was a proper, four-footed wolf and Talbot became a two-footed wolf man.

◀ **Werewolf of London** [Stuart Walker, 1935] Henry Hull refused to wear the make-up Jack Pierce designed for the werewolf, as he felt it hid too much of his face. Pierce and Hull settled on the face pictured here in a highly retouched publicity photo from the original release. Pierce ended up using his first *Werewolf of London* design on Lon Chaney, Jr. in *The Wolf Man*.

▲ **House of Frankenstein** [Erle C. Kenton, 1944] Lon Chaney, Jr. as mournful Larry Talbot again, this time with Boris Karloff as the mad Dr. Gustav Neimann and John Carradine as Count Dracula.

> "The werewolf is neither man nor wolf, but a Satanic creature with the worst qualities of both."
>
> Dr. Yogami (Warner Oland), *Werewolf of London*

TEENAGE WEREWOLVES

▲ **Abbott and Costello Meet Frankenstein** [Charles Barton, 1948] The last gasp of the classic Universal monsters: The studio threw Dracula (Béla Lugosi), the Frankenstein monster (Glenn Strange), and the Invisible Man (Vincent Price) into the pot. Here, Larry Talbot (Lon Chaney, Jr.) approaches the oblivious Lou Costello. Surprisingly, this was a handsome production that treated the monsters with respect.

▲ **The Undying Monster** [aka *The Hammond Mystery*, John Brahm, 1942] The Hammond family has been cursed with lycanthropy since the Crusades. A detective tries to discover which Hammond is the werewolf as the bodies pile up.

▲ **The Werewolf** [Fred F. Sears, 1956] Duncan Marsh (Steven Rich) is injected with serum made of wolf's blood by two scientists trying to restore his memory after he is in a car accident. Naturally this turns him into a vicious werewolf.

▶ **Werewolf in a Girls' Dormitory** [Paolo Heusch, 1962] is the title that MGM gave the Italian-Austrian co-production *Lycanthropus* for its US release. A fairy grisly early *giallo* set in an all-girls' school, the murderer this time turns out to be a werewolf.

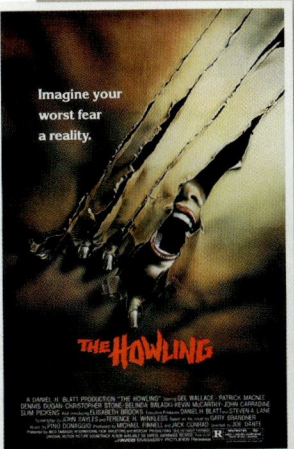

◀ **The Howling** [Joe Dante, 1981] Serial murderer Eddie Quist (Robert Picardo) is the epitome of the young punk our parents warned us to stay away from. He is also a werewolf. Note the poster design for *The Howling* is essentially the other side of the poster for *I Was a Teenage Werewolf!*

▶ **I Was a Teenage Werewolf** [Gene Fowler, Jr., 1957] A troubled teen is exploited by an evil scientist. As we were told in school, this is where masturbation can lead. Not to mention rock'n'roll!

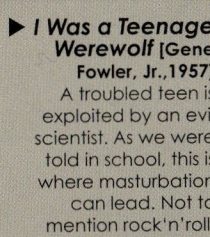

◀ **How to Make a Monster** [Herbert L. Strock, 1958] Actor Gary Clarke in Michael Landon's Teenage Werewolf make-up from the earlier film, poses with Gary Conway, the Teenage Monster from *I Was a Teenage Frankenstein* [Herbert L. Strock, 1957].

▶ **Teen Wolf** [Rod Daniel, 1985] Scott Howard (Michael J. Fox) is the quintessential high-school nerd. But when he discovers he comes from a family of lycanthropes, he uses his lycan abilities to become the big man on campus as a basketball star. A Disney movie in everything but name.

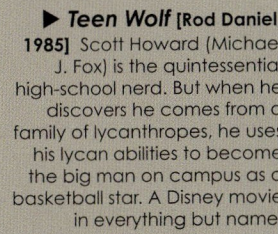

◀ **Ginger Snaps** [John Fawcett, 2000] A smart take on werewolf mythology and a clever examination of teenage angst and sexuality. Two "goth" sisters, Ginger and Brigitte Fitzgerald (Katharine Isabelle and Emily Perkins) meet the Beast of Bailey Woods and find out that it's a lycanthrope.

WEREWOLVES

AN AMERICAN WEREWOLF IN LONDON

This was my attempt to make a movie dealing with the supernatural in a completely realistic way. Because there is no such thing as men who become monstrous wolves when there is a full moon, I tried to explore how one would react when confronted with this as truth. What do you do when the unreal is real? That was my premise and *An American Werewolf in London* is the result.

▲ **David Kessler** (David Naughton) wakes up to find himself naked inside the wolf cage in The Regent's Park Zoo.

▼ **David Kessler** (David Naughton) halfway through his painful metamorphosis.

▲ **A publicity shot** of David surrounded by the victims of his "carnivorous lunar activities" at a porno theater in Piccadilly Circus. His best friend Jack (Griffin Dunne), now also one of the "Living Dead," is on his right. Jack is not a fresh kill and by now looks a little worse for wear.

> "The wolf's bloodline must be severed. The last remaining werewolf must be destroyed. It's you, David!"
>
> Jack (Griffin Dunne),
> *An American Werewolf in London*

◄ **The transformation** from a man into four-legged "hound from hell" is a painful one. Sinew, muscle, and bone stretch, bend, and crack. New, non-human flesh grows and limbs elongate, teeth become fangs, hair sprouts from all over the body, claws burst from fingers. The jaw unhinges from the skull and actually begins to grow into a snout. I recommend you do not try this at home.

▲ **Santo y Blue Demon vs. Drácula y el Hombre Lobo**
[Miguel M. Delgado, 1973] El Santo was the most popular Mexican Luchador Enmascarado (masked wrestler) and starred in many movies. This time, he teams up with another popular masked wrestler, Blue Demon, to take on both Dracula and the Wolf Man!

▲ **The Howling** [Joe Dante, 1981] Belinda Belaski watches in horror as Robert Picardo changes into a werewolf. Dante's movie is full of sly references to other werewolf films and has a truly wacky ending, as TV station manager Kevin McCarthy watches in amazement as anchorwoman Dee Wallace-Stone turns into a kind of were-poodle on live television. Joe's witty movie has spawned too many terrible sequels. Sequels in name only.

▼ **Bram Stoker's Dracula** [Francis Ford Coppola, 1992] As in the Stoker novel, Dracula can become a wolf (or whatever that thing is) at will.

▲ **The Monster Club** [Roy Ward Baker, 1981] An almost unwatchable movie from producer Milton Subotsky where you can literally see Vincent Price, John Carradine, Donald Pleasence, Britt Ekland, and Stuart Whitman take the money and run.

▲ **The Boy Who Cried Werewolf** [Nathan H. Juran, 1973] The star (Kerwin Mathews) and the director of *The 7th Voyage of Sinbad* [1958] reunited to make this ludicrous movie.

◀ **Silver Bullet** [Dan Attias, 1985] Based on the novella *Cycle of the Werewolf* by Stephen King, about a werewolf on the loose in Maine. This time the lycanthrope turns out to be a man of God!

WEREWOLVES

▲ **Dog Soldiers** [Neil Marshall, 2002] A squad of British soldiers on a training mission in the Scottish Highlands has a nasty encounter with a family of werewolves in Neil Marshall's exciting, action-packed horror movie.

▲ *The Chronicles of Narnia: Prince Caspian* [Andrew Adamson, 2008] The sequel to *The Lion, the Witch and the Wardrobe*. Pictured is a good example of Howard Berger's Academy Award-winning make-up work.

> "They were always here. I just unlocked the door."
>
> Megan (Emma Cleasby), *Dog Soldiers*

▲ **Underworld** [Len Wiseman, 2003] The first movie in the *Underworld* series, the story of the ongoing battle between the Vampires and the Lycans (short for lycanthrope, get it?), chock-full of computer-generated effects. Here Michael Corvin (Scott Speedman) turns into a werewolf as his vampire warrior lover Selene (Kate Beckinsale) looks on in anguish.

▲ *The Twilight Saga: New Moon* [Chris Weitz, 2009] The second film in the *Twilight* series. In this picture all of the werewolves have nice bodies and rarely wear shirts in their human form.

▲ *Skinwalkers* [James Isaac, 2006] A half-Skinwalker/half-human boy is protected by his family and friends from another group of Skinwalkers who believe he may end their curse.

▲ *The Wolfman* [Joe Johnston, 2010] Despite production difficulties and an inane departure from the original Curt Siodmak story, Rick Baker won his seventh Academy Award for his make-up, turning Benicio Del Toro's Lawrence Talbot and his stunt doubles into the Wolf Man.

▶ *Underworld: Evolution* [Len Wiseman, 2006] A great-looking CG Lycan from the second movie in the *Underworld* series.

IN CONVERSATION

Joe Dante

Director Joe Dante checks a shot on the set of *Gremlins* [1984].

JL: So, Joe, here on your office wall you have a poster from *Creature From the Black Lagoon* [Jack Arnold, 1954]...

JD: One of the great monsters of all time.

JL: Why?

JD: It's one of the best-designed monsters. It's a triumph, considering what was available at the time. There has to be something recognizably human about a great monster. And the greatest thing about the Creature is, of course, that he lusts after Julie Adams!

JL: But what's he going to do when he gets Julie Adams? Isn't he a fish?

JD: Well, I think he's certainly part fish.

JL: Okay, we love the Creature. And you also have a large poster of *La Belle et la Bête* [Jean Cocteau, 1946] on the wall.

JD: Yes. That monster is also a great design, by Jean Cocteau. It's kind of a Wolf Man design. The great thing about wolf men characters is that they are sort of dog-like, and so we tend to feel a kinship to them. The Jack Pierce make-up for *The Wolf Man* [George Waggner, 1941] is great, but there is something dog-pet-like about him.

JL: What about your werewolves in *The Howling* [1981]?

JD: The werewolves in *The Howling* were an attempt to get away from that dog-like look. We thought they should be more lupine, like they are in the old woodcuts.

JL: Do you really think the most effective monsters are humanoid?

JD: Well, what is a monster? A monster is something that isn't normal, that doesn't look like regular people. In the Middle Ages, anybody who had any kind of a deformity was considered to be a monster. There are a lot of superstitions about deformity. There are many fantasy creatures that are half man and half something else, like the Minotaur. But the fascination for monsters for my generation was basically that we were powerless kids and monsters were misshapen individuals who didn't fit into society, who didn't have any power, and who had to strike back. So, as a kid, you felt a kind of power watching a monster doing his stuff.

JL: Do you have a theory on why people like monster movies?

JD: It's a difficult question. It's confronting death without having to really die.

JL: What was the first monster movie that genuinely frightened you?

JD: I remember finding Christopher Lee's Frankenstein Monster very scary [*The Curse of Frankenstein*, Terence Fisher, 1957].

JL: How old were you? Five?

JD: I was eleven. I imagined that he was going to be coming upstairs from the cellar in our house! The whole thing about these movies is that you took them home with you. When I saw *Them!* [Gordon Douglas, 1954], the giant ants made a sort of cricket-like, chirping kind of noise, very much like the sounds that would come from the field behind my house. Whenever a tree branch would rap on the window pane, I would think it was a giant ant antenna!

JL: But you really enjoyed seeing these movies, even though they would haunt you when you got home.

JD: I would come home and have nightmares, and my parents would say, "If you're going to have nightmares, then why do you go to see these pictures?"

JL: And how would you answer them?

JD: "I have to." I had to go see them. I couldn't *not* go. I loved those movies. I loved all movies when I was a kid—particularly cartoons—but there was something about those pictures. They weren't like other movies. They took place in worlds that I couldn't even imagine, places that I couldn't go to.

JL: *The Exorcist*, for me, is still probably the most successful horror movie.

JD: Yeah, it's a brilliantly nasty movie. It's very cleverly put together. At the beginning of the movie there are no make-up tricks or revolving heads or green vomit. By the time you get to that stuff, the audience has been pummelled into a state of being unable to resist watching whatever they're going to do. They've got a girl peeing on the floor, they've got her masturbating with a crucifix... The movie breaks down your defenses until you're just numb and ready to take all of the classic horror tropes which, had they been at the beginning, would not have worked.

JL: What was the first monster movie you saw?

JD: *The Mad Monster* [Sam Newfield, 1942]. It's about a mad scientist (George Zucco) who turns this dim-witted handyman (Glenn Strange) into a werewolf. The reason this picture was so fascinating to me was that there was a little girl in it, whom the monster kills off-screen. We just see her ball bouncing back into frame.

JL: Were you scared by it?

JD: Sure I was scared: He killed a little girl! But it was a contained scared, because I saw it on TV. When I saw movies in the theater, that's when I had nightmares. When you're in a big theater and it's dark, it's truly scary! I was small and I didn't want to have any heads to see over, so I would always sit in the front row, looking upwards, which I'm sure is why I have to wear glasses. I really liked movies that were about things that didn't happen in real life—the fantastic. And in the early '50s, when the space movies came out—*This Island Earth* [Joseph M. Newman, 1955] was a revelation—I was in heaven.

JL: The visual effects and those vivid Technicolor colors still hold up.

JD: Plus it was written on the level of a ten year-old. It's fabulous! I saw *Invaders From Mars* [William Cameron Menzies, 1953] and then *Forbidden Planet* [Fred M. Wilcox, 1956] when they came out. If you saved up enough Quaker Oats box-tops you could get into that for free...

JL: You're only five years older than I am and it makes such a difference to the films you actually saw in a movie theater.

JD: It makes a tremendous difference, because from '53 to '58 were a kind of golden years for science fiction movies.

JL: I saw *The 7th Voyage of Sinbad* [Nathan H. Juran] at the Crest Theater on Westwood Boulevard in 1958. But those other films I saw on television in black and white.

JD: Well, that was the beginning for you, but I had already been watching sci-fi and horror films for a long time at the movies. They were marketed to kids. You'd maybe have one friend, or two, who liked monster movies, but you really didn't know how many people who liked them, so you felt a little isolated. But when you went to the supermarket and you saw *Famous Monsters of Filmland* magazine on the shelf next to *Lady's Home Journal*, you realized: "My God, there must be other people like me out there!" I spent years writing letters to *Famous Monsters*, trying to get my name in it. If you could get your name in it, you were immortal! I wrote letters about everything: all the movies I'd seen, who were my favorite monsters, whatever.

I finally got to the point where I wrote about the *worst* movies I'd ever seen. It was published in the magazine as an article titled "Dante's Inferno!" And when Forrest J Ackerman sent me the magazine, annotated with "Go, Joe! Go!" it was the greatest thing that had ever happened to me. I was 12 or 13. Then I read the article and, of course, he'd completely re-written it. He used words like "symbiotic"—things I didn't even understand. But nonetheless, I felt like, "Wow! I'm part of a community." There was this feeling of solidarity with other kids like me. Now there are online fan communities, but there wasn't anything like that then. If you wanted to find out about a movie, you had only the TV guide. If you went to the library, the movie books were very scholarly and serious and not interesting to kids. The great boon of *Famous Monsters* was that it got people interested in film history.

JL: Yeah, it had articles not just about actors, but on writers, directors, technicians... like Willis O'Brien, Ray Harryhausen, Jack Pierce, Fritz Lang, Tod Browning, Lon Chaney, Richard Matheson, James Whale, and on and on.

JD: *Famous Monsters of Filmland* put all those disparate strands together in a way comprehensible to kids.

JL: Most horror magazines and websites now are just about maiming and killing. People are really into gore!

"It's confronting death without having to really die."

JD: It's all spectacle. It's pure, transgressive spectacle. It involves the same kinds of emotions that the Romans experienced when the Christians were thrown to the lions. Except in movies, it's safe, we're not really killing anybody. Now extreme gore is an accepted part of the way films are made. If you have a gory death scene, you can build a whole film around it, like *The Final Destination* [David R. Ellis, 2009].

People are so jaded. They've seen every plot, they've seen every twist, they've seen every gore effect. They've seen it all! And there are many things competing for their attention now that didn't exist when we were growing up. Plus, they know nothing about film; they know nothing about film history. They don't know who Jimmy Stewart was! They don't know!

JL: It kind of freaks me out.

JD: And you say, "How ignorant of them," but the fact is, in order to know about something you have to see it! The Marx Brothers—who are they? Laurel and Hardy? Nobody programs them. People don't want to see them.

JL: My kids grew up with all the old movies, so I was so shocked when my daughter brought a bunch of girls home for a sleepover and she wanted to put *The Women* [George Cukor, 1939] on for them. The girls refused to watch it because it was in black and white! It was very upsetting to me.

JD: The Marx Brothers, Harold Lloyd, Buster Keaton, and all that kind of stuff is only going to be kept alive in universities. They are no longer part of popular culture. This stuff runs only on cable or satellite. It's considered niche programming.

JL: Why do you think that so many vampire, werewolf, and zombie movies are now being made?

JD: It's an astonishment to me—particularly because I was loyal to the genre when people thought it was trash, and now it has become mainstream. The fact is that the motion picture industry has become a glorified B-movie factory. Nowadays, the studios mine all the old, low-budget serials and monster titles, give them massive budgets, and cast them with big stars.

JL: Well, that's directly because of Spielberg and Lucas!

JD: Exactly! But there was a moment during the *Jaws* and *Star Wars* period in the '70s, when it seemed like movies were going to grow up. Look at what the studios made in those decades. But now it's like the suits realized: "Wait a minute! We can just make fantasy films with no content and they will all show up all over the world! So now it's all elves and *Lord of the Rings*, special effects in *Transformers*... it's non-content film. Films that aren't *about* anything.

JL: *Gremlins* [Joe Dante, 1984] was a case where there was a new fantasy film with a political subtext. And the wonderful malevolence of the Gremlins was so subversive! And *Gremlins 2: The New Batch* [Joe Dante, 1990] had some brilliant stuff in it. I saw that movie a hundred times—because my son Max adored it. But there are extraordinary moments in that. Really funny, brilliant, and dark...

Okay, enough about you. Let's talk about some specific monsters: The Mummy.

JD: The bromide about the Mummy was that you just need to walk away, and if you walked fast, you could get away from him. But when I was a kid, even though he was slow, he always got his victims. So it seemed to me that he had this magical power.

JL: And vampires?

JD: They're back. And now they're sexy and young, and they're...

JL: Mormon!

JD: Absolutely, the whole appeal of the *Twilight* thing is that they can't have sex. It's the abstinence thing—that's why parents are saying: "You should see these *Twilight* movies; they're really good!"

JL: So summing up, do you have any thoughts about why it is we like monsters?

JD: They're sources of melodrama; they're dangerous; they make people run in fear; they decimate; they kill; they do all the things that a bomb does. Maybe it's an embracing of death that starts at an early age. But basically, monsters do bad things and usually cause lots of death and heartache. Monsters are metaphors. Godzilla is a perfect example. Here is atomic war come to life, to be visited upon the people of Japan. That would be a good game: Name the monster movie and then the metaphor!

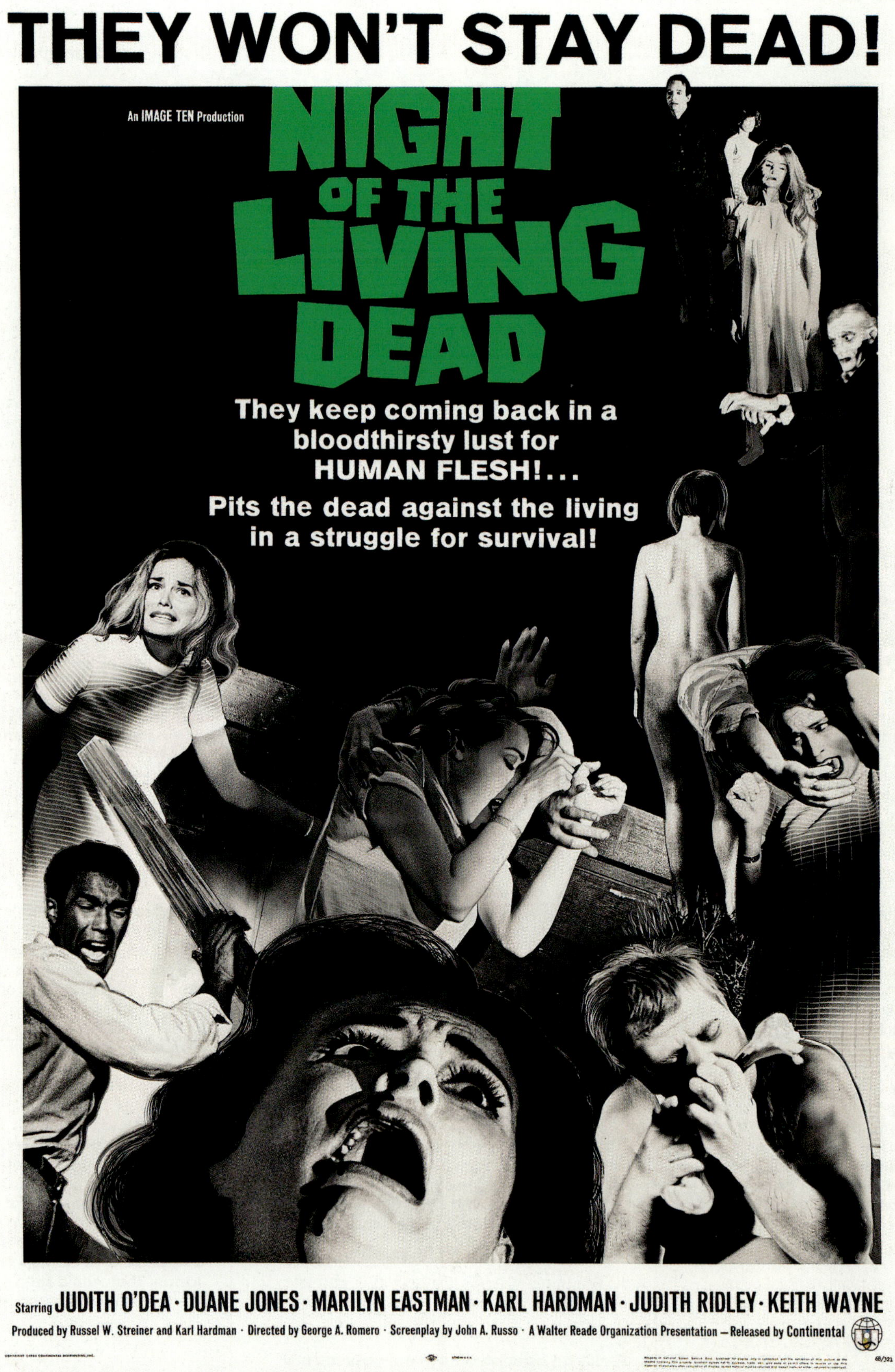
THEY WON'T STAY DEAD!
An IMAGE TEN Production
NIGHT OF THE LIVING DEAD
They keep coming back in a bloodthirsty lust for HUMAN FLESH!...
Pits the dead against the living in a struggle for survival!
Starring JUDITH O'DEA · DUANE JONES · MARILYN EASTMAN · KARL HARDMAN · JUDITH RIDLEY · KEITH WAYNE
Produced by Russel W. Streiner and Karl Hardman · Directed by George A. Romero · Screenplay by John A. Russo · A Walter Reade Organization Presentation — Released by Continental
68/321

Zombies

For decades, zombie movies drew on the traditional figures of Haitian Voodoo ritual. The clichéd image of a zombie was a tall, lean black man with glassy eyes. A prime example appears in *I Walked With A Zombie* [Jacques Tourneur, 1943], which is a much better movie than it sounds. Zombies were called the "Walking Dead" and they tended to shamble along. They may have been slow, but they just kept coming...

The mystical figure of Baron Samedi, Master of the Dead, a spirit (or Loa) that can be summoned by a Voodoo priest (or houngan), is always depicted wearing a top hat. Baron Samedi has been portrayed onscreen by Geoffrey Holder in the James Bond film *Live and Let Die* [Guy Hamilton, 1973] and by Don Pedro Colley in the blaxploitation/horror/gangster picture *Sugar Hill* [Paul Maslansky, 1974]. A Voodoo priestess is called a mambo (also the name of a popular Latin American dance).

▲ *Night of the Living Dead* [George A. Romero, 1968]
On a scene still from his film, George gives me some good advice: "John—don't ever let the bastards in!"

In Haitian Voodoo, a houngan uses poisons and ritual burials to convince victims that they are dead. The houngan then uses their new zombies to pick sugar cane and for other menial tasks. Many claim that this practice continues today. In Voodoo and in the movies, zombies are symbols of exploitation and social decay.

Previous pages: *Dawn of the Dead* [aka *Zombi*, George A. Romero, 1978] Romero's vision of the North American consumer; a fairly typical day at the mall.
Opposite page: *Night of the Living Dead* [George A. Romero, 1968] Original poster for the little black and white movie from Pittsburgh, Pennsylvania that has had enormous impact on popular culture.

Hammer Films' *The Plague of the Zombies* [John Gilling, 1966] places witchcraft (Voodoo)-created zombies at the center of a story of typically English class warfare, using the zombies as a menace and as slave labor.

Zombies are basically the Walking Dead. How the dead come to be walking varies. In Stuart Gordon's wild *Re-Animator* [1985], a concoction of glowing green liquid injected by syringe does the trick. In *An American Werewolf In London* [John Landis, 1981], the unfortunate lycanthrope David Kessler (David Naughton) is first visited by his increasingly decayed dead best friend Jack (Griffin Dunne), then surrounded by the gory victims of his "carnivorous lunar activities" who demand he kill himself. Apparently, when the "last remaining werewolf" is destroyed, his victims will cease being "undead." So are Jack and his companions zombies?

What about those poor unfortunates in all those movies who turn into flesh-eating crazies thanks to medical experimentation, atomic radiation, pollution, or some bizarre virus?

The term zombie has become a bit like pornography—even if we are unable to make a definitive description of exactly what a zombie is, we know a zombie when we see one!

The Spanish zombies in *Rec* [co-directed by Jaume Balagueró and Paco Plaza, 2007] or the British zombies in *Shaun of the Dead* [Edgar Wright, 2004], and *28 Days Later* [Danny Boyle, 2002] or the French zombies in *Paris by Night of the Living Dead* [Grégory Morin, 2009] and *La Horde* [Yannick Dahan, Benjamin Rocher, 2009], the New Zealand zombies in Peter Jackson's

Dead Alive [aka Braindead, 1992], and all those Italian zombies from Michele Soavi's *Dellamorte Dellamore* [aka *Cemetery Man*, 1994] to Lucio Fulci's *Zombi 2* [1979] to the Japanese (I swear this is a real movie) *Big Tits Zombie* [Takao Nakano, 2010] to the all-American *Zombie Strippers* [Jay Lee, 2008], I think we can safely say that zombies are an international audience favorite.

My personal favorite zombie movie is *King of the Zombies* [Jean Yarbrough, 1941], a low-budget B movie from Monogram, in which the wonderful Mantan Moreland's supporting character, Jefferson "Jeff" Jackson, steals the picture as the only one who actually sees the zombies. He is then hypnotized by the villain to believe that he is a zombie, too. Once he thinks he is a zombie, his fear of the authentic zombies is replaced by feelings of camaraderie and good fellowship. Of course, when he discovers that he is not a zombie, he runs in terror from his former "brothers."

In the 1960s, movie zombies started to eat the flesh of the living, often feasting specifically on brains. In the very funny *Return of the Living Dead* [Dan O'Bannon, 1985] the zombies even speak! A police car is surrounded by hungry zombies who viciously attack the two cops inside and then gleefully eat their brains. The patrol car's radio crackles and a voice asks if they need assistance. One of the zombies clumsily takes the microphone and croaks, "Send more cops."

The Walking Dead is now no longer an all-encompassing term for zombies. In films like *Return of the Living Dead* and *28 Days Later* [Danny Boyle, 2002], the zombies no longer shamble along, they can also run very fast. Assorted causes for their zombification have gone way beyond Voodoo to include atomic radiation, alien invasion, pollution, and weird Ebola-type viruses, sometimes natural, sometimes produced by the military. In *Dead Alive*, an outbreak of crazed, flesh-eating zombies in New Zealand is started by the bite of a "Sumatran Rat Monkey!"

In contemporary films, zombies are frequently agents of anarchy and represent the collapse of an orderly society. Films like *28 Days Later*, *Zombieland* [Ruben Fleischer, 2009], and both versions of *Dawn of the Dead* [George A. Romero, 1978 and Zack Snyder, 2004], unleash berserk, flesh-eating zombies and suddenly, it's every man for himself as hordes of rotting corpses roam the streets and chaos reigns.

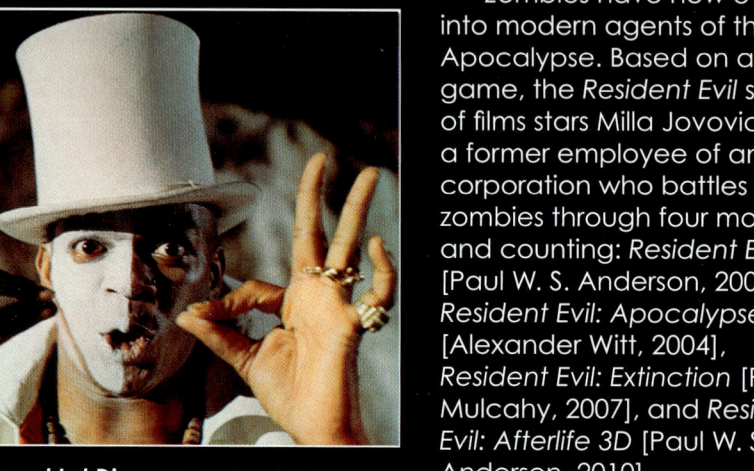

▲ *Live and Let Die* [Guy Hamilton, 1973]
Geoffrey Holder as Baron Samedi in this James Bond blaxploitation movie. The first time Roger Moore played Bond, James Bond.

Zombies have now evolved into modern agents of the Apocalypse. Based on a video game, the *Resident Evil* series of films stars Milla Jovovich as a former employee of an evil corporation who battles zombies through four movies and counting: *Resident Evil* [Paul W. S. Anderson, 2002], *Resident Evil: Apocalypse* [Alexander Witt, 2004], *Resident Evil: Extinction* [Russell Mulcahy, 2007], and *Resident Evil: Afterlife 3D* [Paul W. S. Anderson, 2010].

Maybe one of the reasons for the increasing popularity of the zombie movie is the aging population of the Western world. As the director David Cronenberg pointed out, "As we grow older, we transform into something monstrous. Our minds begin to fail us, as do our bodies themselves." Whether or not we like to admit it, we have all felt a horror of the aged and infirm. No one escapes the indignities and terrors of old age, physical decrepitude, and death. One day, the ravages of time will reduce all of us to shambling, drooling, "walking corpses" covered in lesions and clad in loose-fitting hospital robes. As Walt Kelly's brilliant comic-strip character Pogo discovered, "We have met the enemy, and he is us."

Opposite page: (1) *The Return of the Living Dead* [Dan O'Bannon, 1985] A very funny sequel to Romero's *Night of the Living Dead* [1968] that puts the blame for a zombie outbreak directly on the military. **(2)** *I Walked with a Zombie* [Jacques Tourneur, 1943] Producer Val Lewton was given this title by RKO and told to make a movie out of it. What they got was a Voodoo version of *Jane Eyre*! **(3)** *The Omega Man* [Boris Sagal, 1971] The second film version of Richard Matheson's novel *I Am Legend*. Charlton Heston battles albino zombie vampires. **(4)** *Shaun of the Dead* [Edgar Wright, 2004] Simon Pegg shines as he and a group of friends and loved ones deal with a zombie attack in contemporary London by seeking sanctuary at his favorite pub.

1

THEY'RE BACK FROM THE GRAVE AND READY TO PARTY!
THE RETURN OF THE LIVING DEAD

2

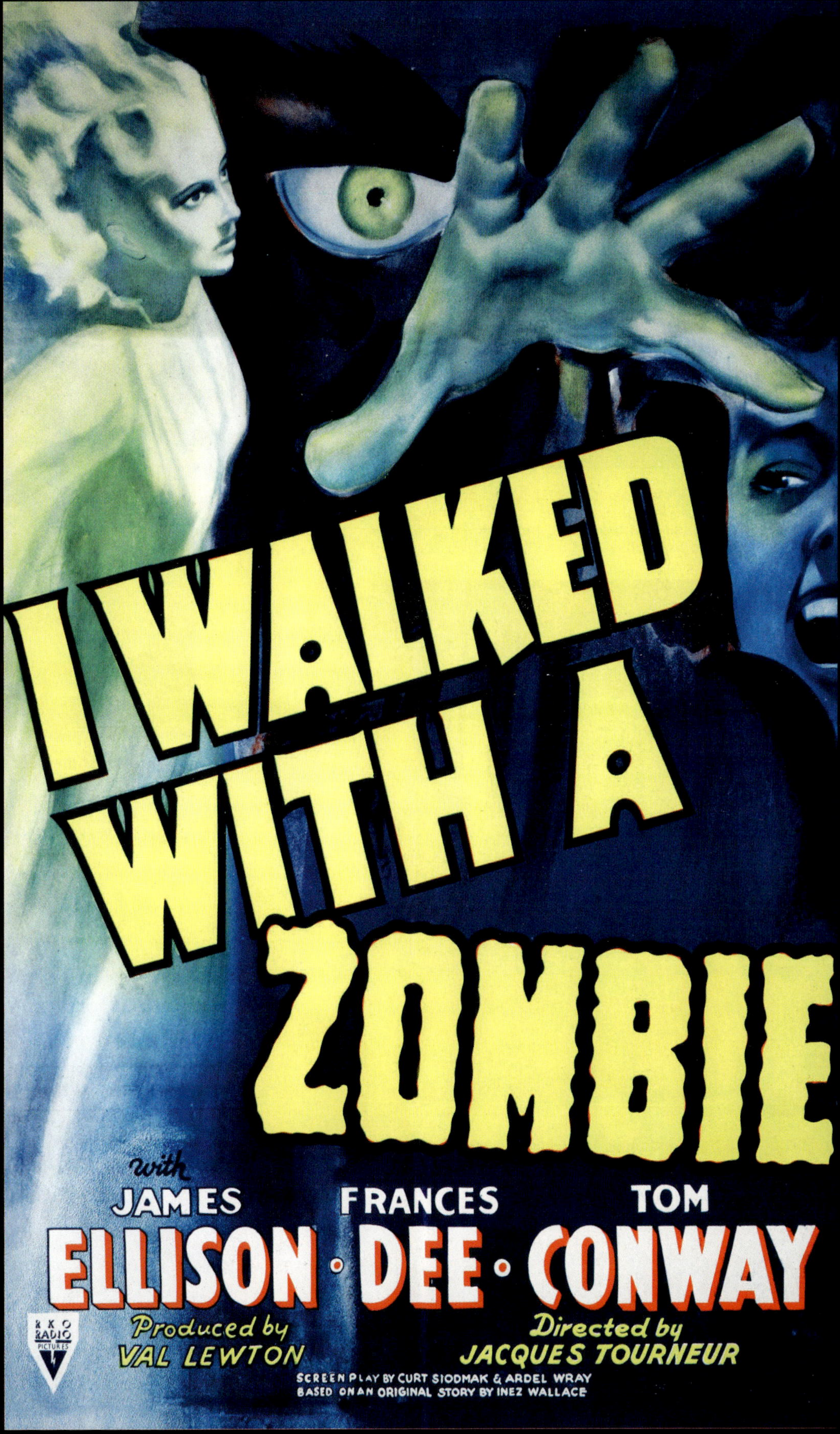
I WALKED WITH A ZOMBIE
with
JAMES ELLISON · FRANCES DEE · TOM CONWAY
RKO RADIO PICTURES
Produced by VAL LEWTON
Directed by JACQUES TOURNEUR
SCREEN PLAY BY CURT SIODMAK & ARDEL WRAY
BASED ON AN ORIGINAL STORY BY INEZ WALLACE

4

A Romantic Comedy. With Zombies.
SHAUN OF THE DEAD
This September aim for the head.

3

The last man alive... is not alone!
CHARLTON HESTON THE ΩMEGA MAN

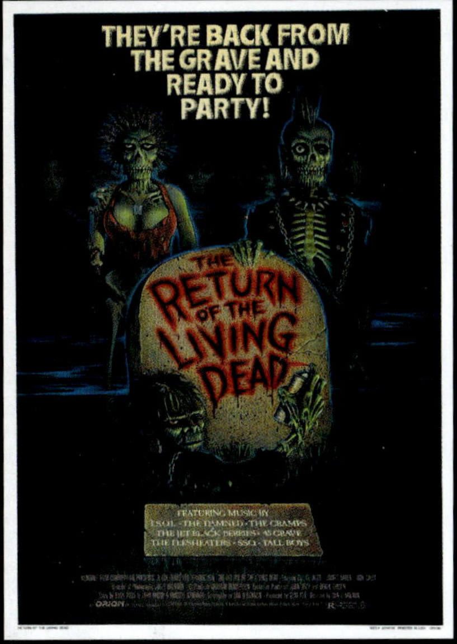

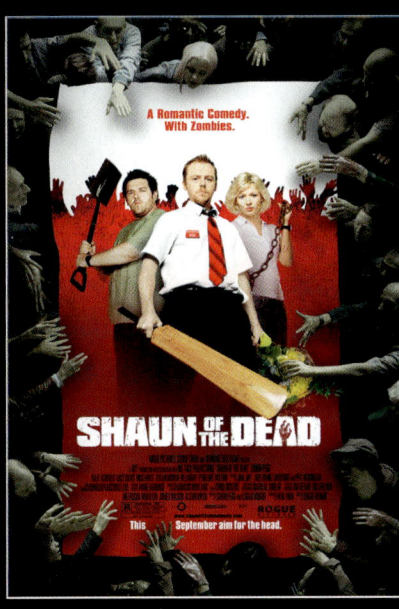

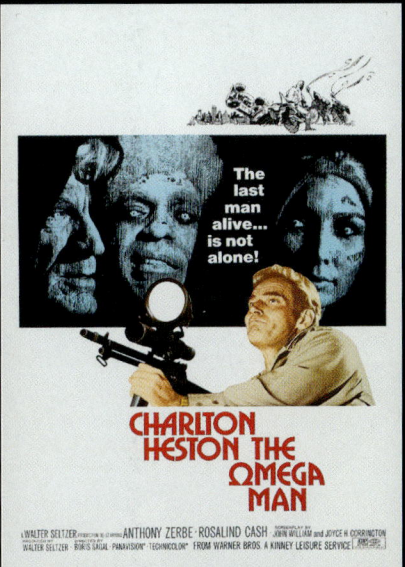

ZOMBIES

▲ **White Zombie** [Victor Halperin, 1932] Béla Lugosi as Murder Legendre, a white voodoo master on Haiti, who uses zombies as labor in his sugar cane mill. A rich plantation owner enlists Legendre's aid to help him with a sexual conquest. This is considered to be the first feature-length zombie movie.

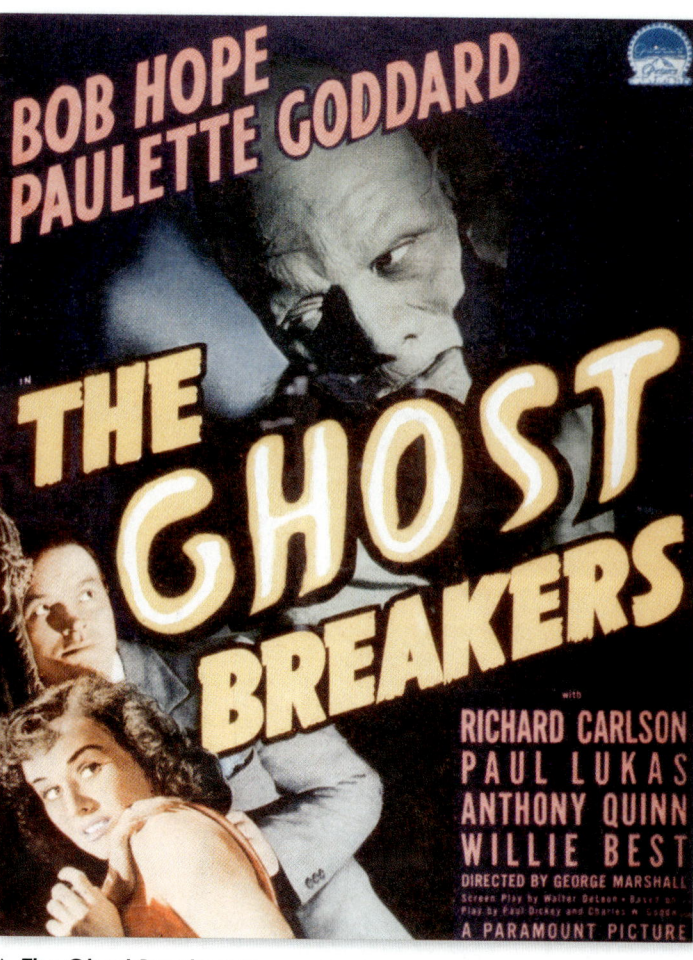

▲ **The Ghost Breakers** [George Marshall, 1940]
A Bob Hope comedy mystery with Willie Best and Bob taking turns being funny by being scared by Noble Johnson's genuinely creepy zombie. Remade by the same director as *Scared Stiff* in 1953 with Dean Martin and Jerry Lewis.

▲ **The Ghoul** [T. Hayes Hunter, 1933] Boris Karloff is the living dead in this, the first British horror film. Not really good, but an amazing cast: Karloff, Ralph Richardson, Ernest Thesiger, and Cedric Hardwicke.

▶ **I Walked With a Zombie** [Jacques Tourneur, 1943] Nurse Frances Dee with her patient and a zombie in the sugar cane field. I really don't want to tell you more, go see the movie!

▲ **Revenge of the Zombies** [Steve Sekely, 1943] A Monogram programmer; here we see John Carradine cower as the zombies (like the title says) get their revenge. An unusual group of racially integrated zombies for the time this movie was made.

▶ **Zombies on Broadway** [Gordon Dines, 1945] Béla Lugosi regards the same zombie that Frances Dee met in that sugar cane field on the Caribbean island of Saint Sebastian (see the photo below from *I Walked With a Zombie*)!

▶ **Teenage Zombies** [Jerry Warren, 1959] The poster's tagline—"A fiendish experiment performed with sadistic horror!"—could apply to any movie directed by Jerry Warren. Teenagers! Zombies! And a gorilla! What's not to like?

◀ **Zombies of Mora Tau** [Edward L. Cahn, 1957] From the prolific Edward L. Cahn, a movie about a ship's crew of zombies who protect their sunken ship's treasure.

▶ **The Dead One** [aka *Blood of the Zombie*, Barry Mahon, 1961] Set in New Orleans. To inherit the family plantation, a woman uses Voodoo to make her brother a zombie and murder her rivals.

ZOMBIES

◀▼ **The Incredibly Strange Creatures Who Stopped Living and Became Mixed-Up Zombies** [Ray Dennis Steckler, 1964] Left: a photograph of one of the incredibly strange creatures who stopped living and became a mixed-up zombie. Below: the poster for this Fairway International SCHOCK Release.

▶ **The Plague of the Zombies** [John Gilling, 1966] Gilling's period Hammer film, with zombie slave labor being used by the upper class, is a zombie movie, of course, but like many British horror films, it is really about class.

▲ **The Last Man on Earth** [Ubaldo Ragona, Sidney Salkow, 1964] Shot in Rome pretending to be the USA. Vincent Price stars in the first (and most faithful) adaptation of Richard Matheson's *I Am Legend*. George A. Romero states that the zombies in this film inspired his "blue collar zombies." Released in 1964, the action takes place in the future—1968!

▲ *Sugar Hill* [Paul Maslansky, 1974] Those white gangsters should never have fooled around with a Voodoo priestess in the first place! Another AIP blaxploitation picture.

▲ *Rabid* [David Cronenberg, 1977] Zombies or vampires? Porn star Marilyn Chambers has a disturbing, penile parasite coming from her underarm. As I write this, David just finished making a movie about Freud and Jung, but you could make the argument that he's been making that movie for many years now!

▲ *Tales From the Crypt* [Freddie Francis, 1972] Peter Cushing as Arthur Grimsdyke (1907 – 1972) remembers an appointment he intends to keep. Cushing's bone structure made for an outstanding zombie.

"If this picture doesn't make you scream and squirm, you'd better see a psychiatrist—quick!"

Trailer for *Shivers*

▲ *Shivers* [David Cronenberg, 1975] An entire apartment building's residents become sex-crazed zombies in Cronenberg's extreme situation comedy.

▲ *Zombie* [aka *Zombie Flesh Eaters*, Lucio Fulci, 1979] Fulci's gore fest had a terrific tagline: "We are going to eat you!" This film is infamous for the scene where a zombie pulls a woman by the hair, forcing a large wooden splinter into her eye.

ZOMBIES

▲ **Le Notti Del Terrore** [aka *Burial Ground*, Andrea Bianchi, 1981] Peter Bark, an adult dwarf with a bad wig, plays an adolescent boy who lusts after his mother in this grade Z Italian zombie picture. It's actually pretty funny if you're in a weird mood.

▲ **An American Werewolf in London** [John Landis, 1981] Griffin Dunne as Jack Goodman does not look his best, and it will get worse. Jack is not happy being one of "the undead."

▲ **Day of the Dead** [George A. Romero, 1985] Sherman Howard as Bub, a zombie that seems to have some intellect and emotion. A bleak film, full of angry or psychotic characters and dead people who want to eat you.

> "Have you ever talked to a corpse? It's boring."
>
> Jack Goodman (Griffin Dunne),
> *An American Werewolf in London*

▼ **Evil Dead** [Sam Raimi, 1981] Raimi's very scary thrill ride. Five college students find a cabin in the woods and inside it a book called *Necronomicon Ex-Mortis*. With vines that rape and a whirling dervish, demonic POV, achieved through Sam's patented Shaky Cam. Crazy and frightening. And, oh yeah, there's this possessed girl in the cellar!

▲ **Evil Dead II** [Sam Raimi, 1987] Bruce Campbell suffering through whatever insane torments Sam Raimi could think of next in this reimagining of the first *Evil Dead*. This time Sam decided that instead of ripping the audience's heart out, he would tickle their funny bones. A brilliantly inventive movie—the Three Stooges do Grand Guignol!

▲ **Deadly Friend** [Wes Craven, 1986]
Kristy Swanson in the title role as a part-robot, part-zombie avenger.

▶ **The Serpent and the Rainbow**
[Wes Craven, 1988]
Wes went to Haiti to shoot this adaptation of the book by Wade Davis. Here, Bill Pullman suffers from chemically-induced hallucinations. The movie deals with Voodoo and zombies at their source—African and Christian rituals mixed with drugs.

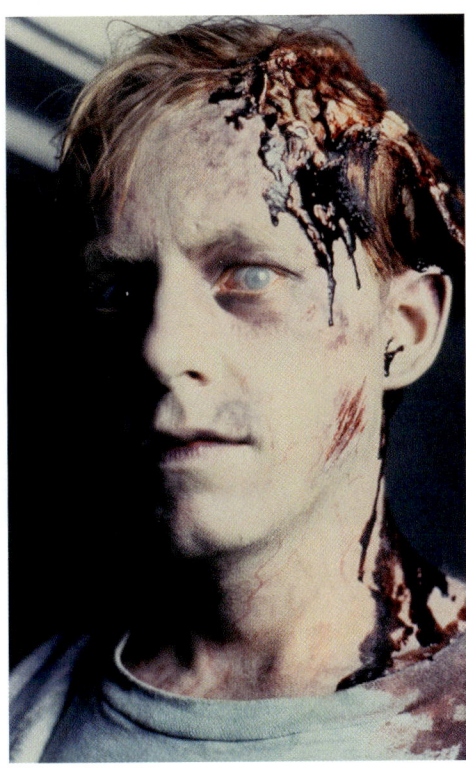

▲ **Pet Sematary** [Mary Lambert, 1989] Based on the Stephen King novel, a variation of the famous short story *The Monkey's Paw* by W. W. Jacobs [1902]. Be careful what you wish for.

▶ **Michael Jackson's Thriller**
[John Landis, 1983]
Michael surrounded by zombies, before he suddenly becomes one himself! Then they dance.

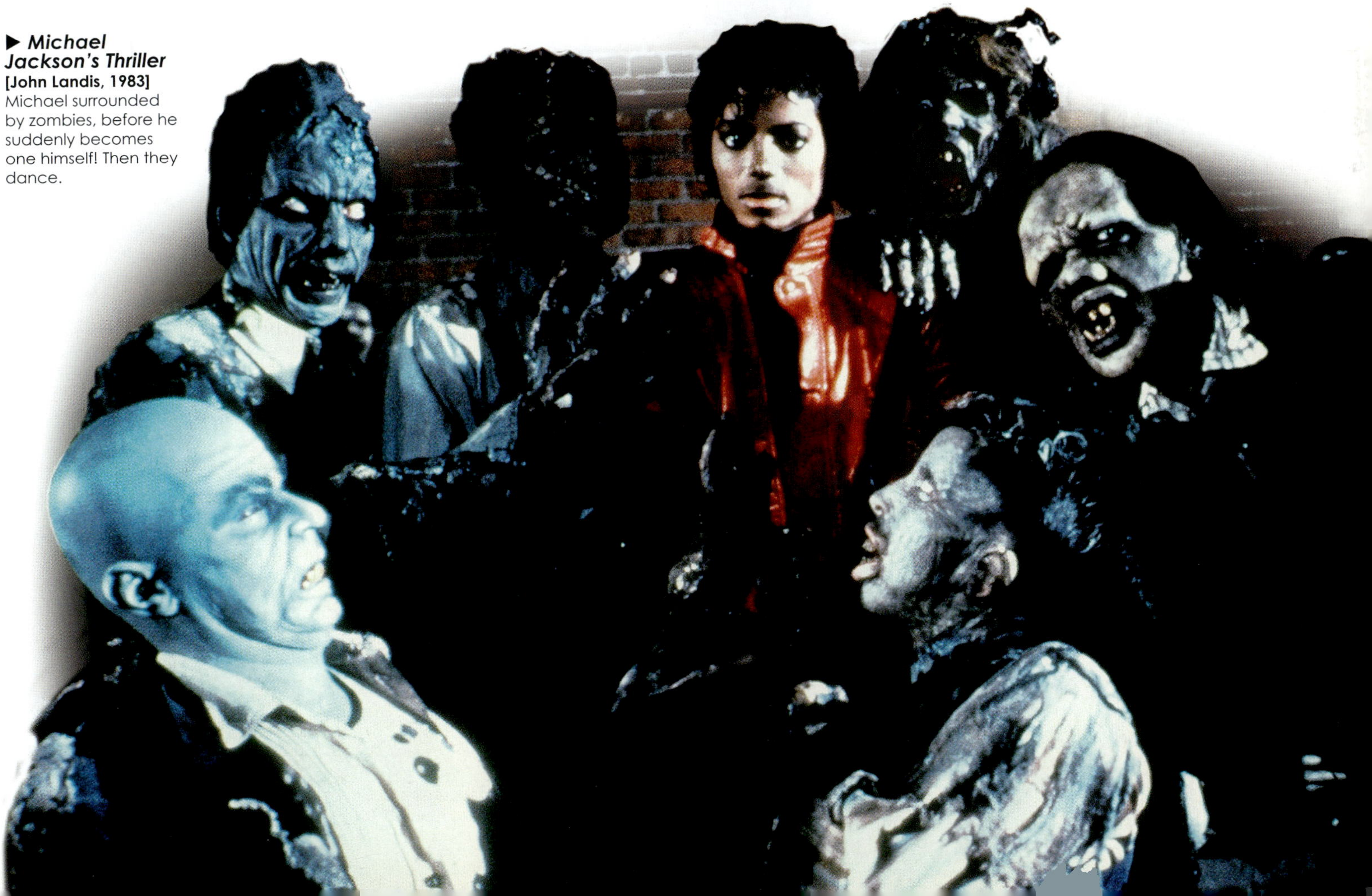

ZOMBIES

◀ **Dead Alive** [aka *Braindead*, Peter Jackson, 1992] Jackson's uproarious movie about zombies in Auckland is so gory it becomes Dada. With a cameo from Forrest J Ackerman.

▲ **Death Becomes Her** [Robert Zemeckis, 1992] A black comedy about cosmetic surgery, and our generation's fears of aging. Bruce Willis plays a doctor whose formula keeps both Meryl Streep and Goldie Hawn ambulatory long after their shelf life has expired.

"They're not dead exactly, they're just … sort of rotting!"

Lionel Cosgrove (Timothy Balme), *Dead Alive*

▼ **Army of Darkness** [Sam Raimi, 1992] A demented mash-up of Mark Twain's *A Connecticut Yankee in King Arthur's Court* with the *Necronomicon Ex-Mortis*, Ray Harryhausen, and the Three Stooges! Bruce Campbell again plays Ash and, in a singularly bananas sequence, battles hundreds of little versions of himself. A surreal, nightmarish, and funny scene. Here, in a slapstick homage to Harryhausen, two Deadites are busy digging up more soldiers for their Army of Darkness.

▲ **Cemetery Man** [aka *Dellamorte Dellamore*, Michele Soavi, 1994] Anna Falchi as Rupert Everett's great love, only now she's dead and returned from the grave. An interesting story about the caretaker of a small cemetery in a small Italian town and his mentally handicapped friend who try to deal with the dead who refuse to stay in the ground.

◀ *Susan's Plan* [aka *Dying to Get Rich*, John Landis, 1998] Lara Flynn Boyle has a nightmare while taking a bath.

▲ *House on Haunted Hill* [William Malone, 1999] Some former residents of the House on Haunted Hill in Malone's stylish remake.

◀ *Mortuary* [Tobe Hooper, 2005] After their father dies, the Doyle family moves into a mortuary to begin a new business and a new life. This turns out to be an extremely bad idea. From the director of *The Texas Chainsaw Massacre* [1974].

▲ *Undead* [Michael & Peter Spierig, 2005] An Australian zombie comedy. This time the zombie plague is caused by aliens.

▶ *Dawn of the Dead* [Zack Snyder, 2004] A remake of the Romero classic [1978]. The living dead overwhelms an escape vehicle.

ZOMBIES

▶ **Flight of the Living Dead: Outbreak on a Plane** [Scott Thomas, 2007] Okay, I have to admit I've never seen this movie, but the title is funny. Maybe the pitch was: "Like *Snakes on a Plane*, but with zombies!"

◀ **Fido** [Andrew Currie, 2006] Billy Connolly is a zombie who becomes more than just a house pet in this Canadian comedy, set in the 1950s.

▶ **Gay Zombie** [Michael Simon, 2007] Okay, I haven't seen this one, either. Maybe the pitch was: "Like *Harry Met Sally*, only they're gay men and one of them is a zombie!"

◀ **I Am Legend** [Francis Lawrence, 2007] The third movie made based on Richard Matheson's outstanding novel *I Am Legend*. There is some terrific stuff in this film and Will Smith gives a strong performance. The realization of a Manhattan empty of people is very well done. But it all goes wrong in the third act with too many computer-animated zombies.

▲ **Resident Evil: Extinction** [Russell Mulcahy, 2007] An ugly lady zombie from the third movie in the *Resident Evil* franchise. Every *Resident Evil* movie is basically Milla Jovovich kicking zombie ass. You could take random scenes from each of these films and cut them together and I don't think anyone would notice.

▲ **28 Weeks Later** [Juan Carlos Fresnadillo, 2007] Zombification by virus… Rose Byrne is hoping that the zombie guy doesn't notice her in this sequel to Danny Boyle's *28 Days Later* [2002], which had a great opening sequence with plague-carrying monkeys.

▶ **Grindhouse** [Robert Rodriguez, Quentin Tarantino, 2007] I think this is Quentin Tarantino as Lewis but I'm not sure. It definitely is someone infected with whatever it is that makes you melt! Rodriguez's wacky movie reminded me of watching those triple features on Hollywood Boulevard in the 1970s and, I believe, that was exactly his intention.

"Have you come in contact with… the infected?"

Scarlet (Rose Byrne), *28 Weeks Later*

▶ **The Walking Dead** [Frank Darabont, 2011] One of special-effects company KNB's zombies from this popular and surprisingly graphic television series.

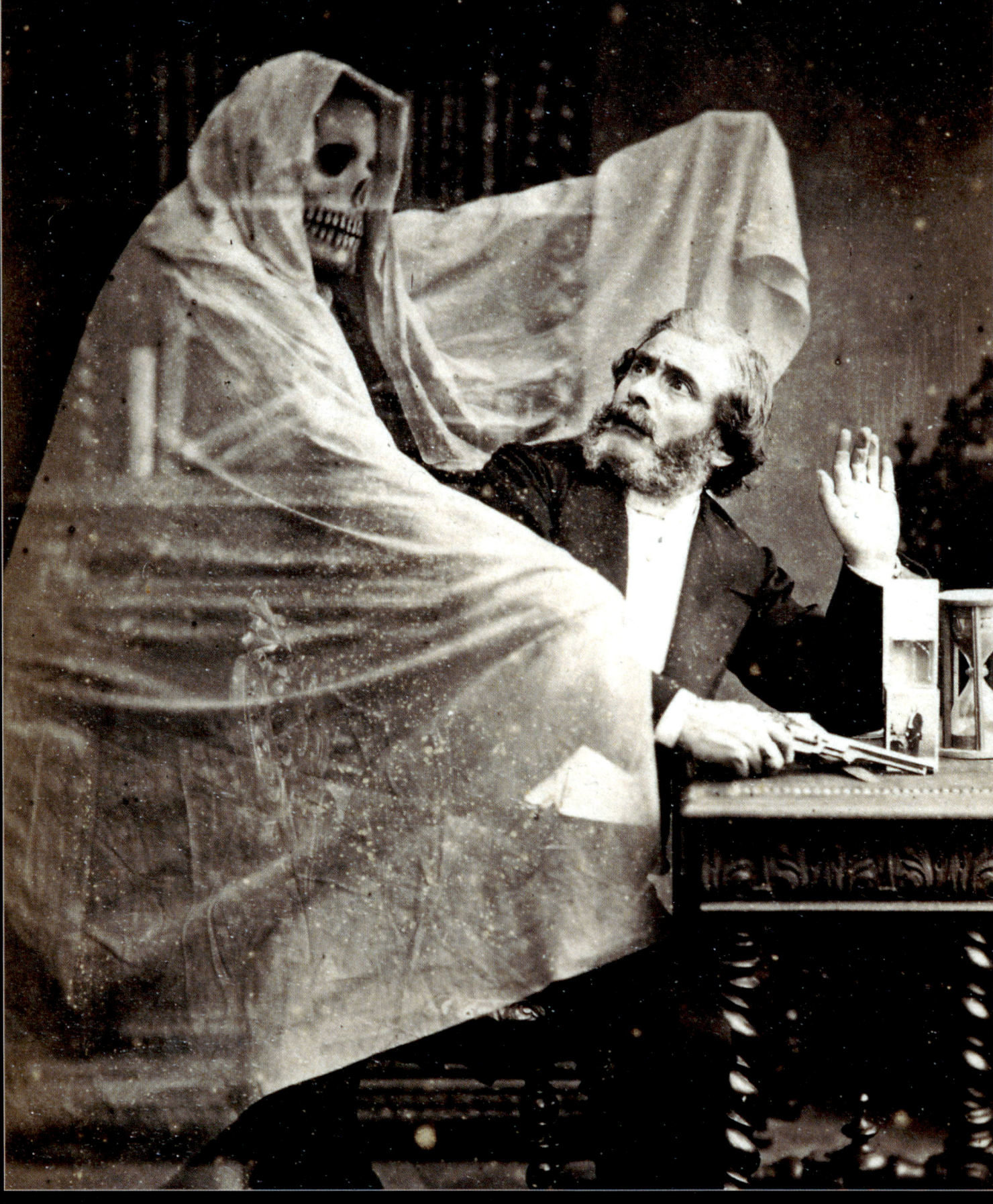

Ghosts

The easiest Halloween costume to make is that of a ghost—all you need is a white bed sheet over your head. I suppose this comes from the custom of wrapping a corpse in a winding sheet. Certainly, pulling a sheet over a patient's face is a clear signal that the doctors have given up!

People who have lost loved ones are easy prey for "mediums" that claim they can communicate with those who, as Hamlet said, "shuffle off this mortal coil." The great magician Harry Houdini, devastated by the death of his mother, attended enough séances to be appalled by the blatant tricks and scams mediums used to convince people of their special skills in contacting the "dear departed."

The outrageous medium, Madame Arcati (Margaret Rutherford) in David Lean's movie of Noel Coward's comedy *Blithe Spirit* [1945] is not so far away from the medium depicted in Sam Raimi's *Drag Me To Hell* [2009]. Both summon up the spirits of the deceased and both are unable to control the spirits they summon.

Ghosts are literally the spirits of the dead. They can manifest themselves in many ways. And every way you can imagine a ghost to manifest itself has been exploited in the movies. *The Uninvited* [Lewis Allen, 1944] begins with Ray Milland's narration, "They call them the haunted shores, these stretches of Devonshire and Cornwall and Ireland which rear up against the westward ocean. Mists gather here, and sea fog, and eerie stories. That's not because there are more ghosts here than in other places, mind you. It's just that people who live hereabouts are strangely aware of them." Disregarding his own voice-over, Ray and his sister, played by Ruth Hussey, buy an empty house on a cliff overlooking the sea. While they wander around looking into the rooms, their terrier Bobby refuses to go up the stairs to the second floor. One room smells "like mimosa" and Ruth casually puts down the bunch of flowers she has just picked. Ray and Ruth do not notice, but we are shown the flowers quickly wilt and die. Suffice to say, the house is haunted. *The Uninvited* is romantic and frightening. It's also one of the few pictures to clearly show the ghost that still manages to keep us in suspense. I recommend that you see it.

▲ **The Ghost of Banquo** by Théodore Chassériau [1819-1856] depicts the scene in William Shakespeare's *Macbeth* at the banquet when only Macbeth can see the ghost of the murdered Banquo.

Poltergeists are spirits that cause a physical disturbance, either by making loud noises, tossing objects around, or actually attacking people. In *Poltergeist* [Tobe Hooper, 1982], the spirits of long-dead Native Americans, whose burial ground has been built over by a housing development, make it very clear that they are unhappy with the situation. In *The Entity* [Sidney J. Furie, 1982] Barbara Hershey is repeatedly raped by an unseen force.

In *The Shining* [Stanley Kubrick, 1980], an isolated hotel with a murderous past slowly drives its winter caretaker, a writer named Jack Torrance, mad. Jack Nicholson's intense performance as Torrance is scarier than the

Previous pages: *The Devil's Backbone* [Guillermo Del Toro, 2001] An orphanage during the time of the Spanish Civil War is haunted in Del Toro's wonderful ghost story.
Opposite page: *Henry Robin and a Specter* [1863] A man about to shoot himself is confronted by his own ghost in this photomontage by Thiébault.

49

ghosts Kubrick shows us. The most frightening moment in the film is when Jack's wife Wendy, played by Shelley Duvall, looks at the pages he has been working on in the typewriter. All she sees are the words "All work and no play makes Jack a dull boy," neatly typed, over and over and over again.

Many films center around a team of researchers investigating a supposed haunted house, with unpredictable, but always spooky, results. *The Haunting* [1963], Robert Wise's movie version of Shirley Jackson's classic ghost story "The Haunting of Hill House" creates unbelievable tension by showing us nothing. Jan de Bont's terrible remake [*The Haunting*, 1999] does not scare us because it shows us way too much. Another team of paranormal investigators attempt to unravel *The Legend of Hell House* [John Hough, 1973], which Richard Matheson adapted from his own novel. Matheson and Hough craft a rip-roaring shocker with an unexpected ending.

Perhaps the best known haunted house franchise in movie history began with *The Amityville Horror* [Stuart Rosenberg, 1979], a supposedly true story about a house on Long Island. The poster declared, "FOR GOD'S SAKE, GET OUT!" So far the movie has spawned eight sequels and a remake, so clearly no one has taken this warning seriously.

Movie ghosts aren't always out to terrify or destroy. Phantoms of a far gentler disposition feature in *Casper* [Brad Silberling, 1995], a live-action movie (albeit with computer-animated ghosts) based on the *Casper the Friendly Ghost* comic books and cartoons. In the comedy *Topper* [Norman Z. McLeod, 1937] the ghosts are not only friendly but, as played by Constance Bennett and Cary Grant, handsome, glamorous, and fun.

The Innocents [1961], Jack Clayton's elegant adaptation of Henry James' novella *The Turn of the Screw*, features a very fine performance from Deborah Kerr as the governess who fears for her sanity, and superb use of deep focus in gleaming black and white CinemaScope by director of photography Freddie Francis. When Deborah Kerr is kissed on the lips by Miles (Martin Stephens), the little boy she is supposed to be looking after, I defy you not to get the creeps.

Set during the Spanish Civil War in the 1930s, *The Devil's Backbone* [Guillermo Del Toro, 2001] is the tale of a haunted orphanage. This is the first in Del Toro's trilogy of fantastic tales set during that period (the second is *Pan's Labyrinth*, 2006; the third is yet to come). *The Devil's Backbone* is a straightforward ghost story. The surprise discovery at the end of the film is who is telling the tale!

We have had sad ghosts, vengeful ghosts, mischievous ghosts, evil ghosts, and loving ghosts, but my favorite ghosts appear in the beautiful Japanese film *Kwaidan* [Masaki Kobayashi, 1964]. The title translates literally as "Ghost Story." Based on Japanese folk tales collected by Lafcadio Hearn, the film comprises four, unrelated stories. With magnificent production and costume design, the film is a visual delight with moments of real terror. My two favorite stories are "Hoichi, the Earless" and "In a Cup of Tea." A magnificent and (I've got to say it), *haunting* film.

▲ **The Shining** [Stanley Kubrick, 1980]
Jack Nicholson as Jack Torrance, driven insane by the ghosts of Overlook Hotel, breaks down the door in an attempt to kill his wife and child. Based on the novel by Stephen King.

Opposite Page: (1) *The Innocents* **[Jack Clayton, 1961]** Deborah Kerr as Miss Giddings, the governess. Beautifully photographed by Freddie Francis, this is one

(2) *The Orphanage* **[Juan Antonio Bayona, 2007]** Another disturbing ghost story, set in an orphanage in Spain. Produced by Guillermo Del Toro.

(3) *The Uninvited* **[Lewis Allen, 1944]** After watching this film, you will never smell mimosa again without looking anxiously over your shoulder.

1

2

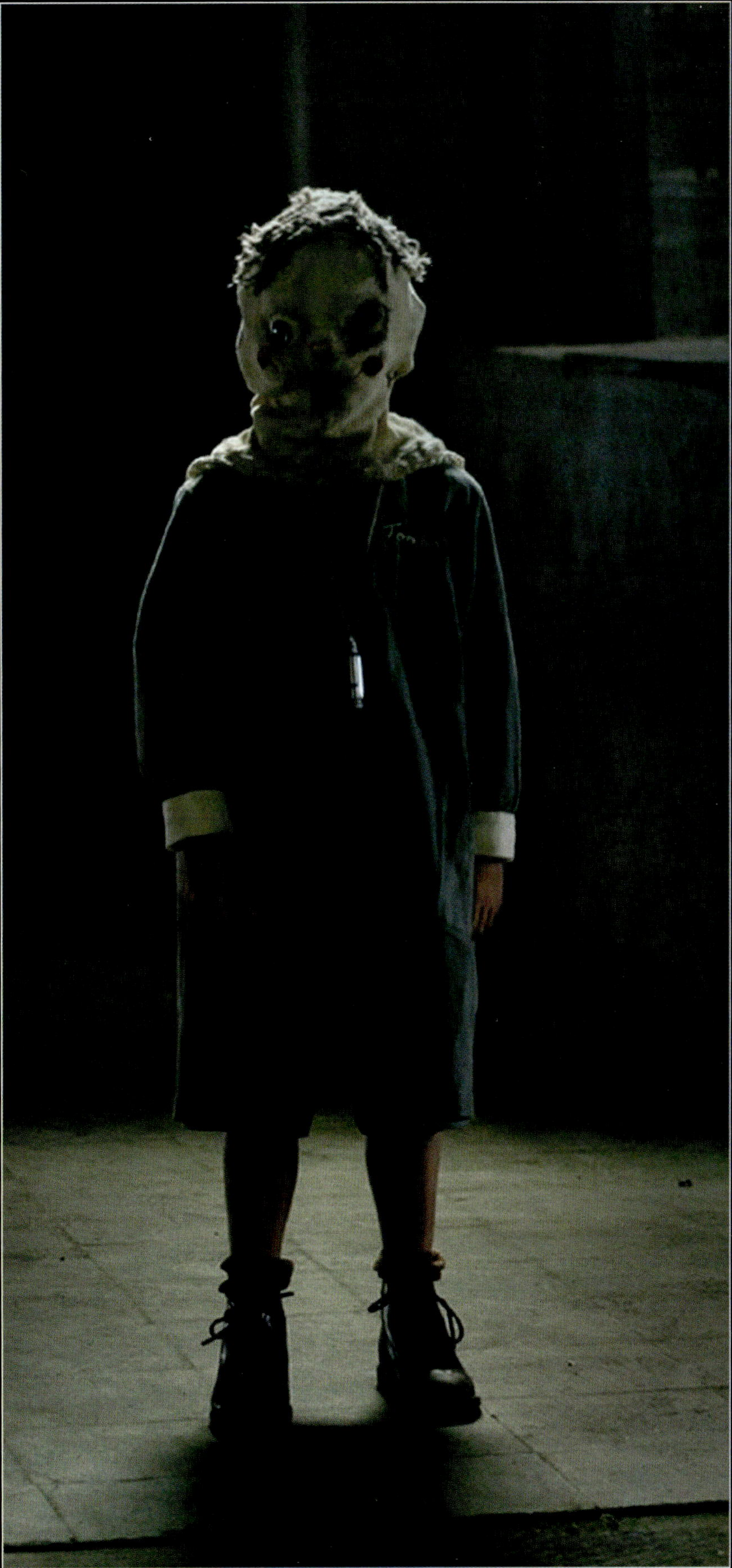

3

From the Most Popular Mystery Romance since "Rebecca"!
The Uninvited
The Story of a Love That is Out of This World!
Introducing the Exciting Beauty of Paramount's New Star Gail Russell!
starring
RAY MILLAND
RUTH HUSSEY
DONALD CRISP
with
CORNELIA OTIS SKINNER
and introducing GAIL RUSSELL
Directed by LEWIS ALLEN · Screen Play by Dodie Smith and Frank Partos · A PARAMOUNT PICTURE

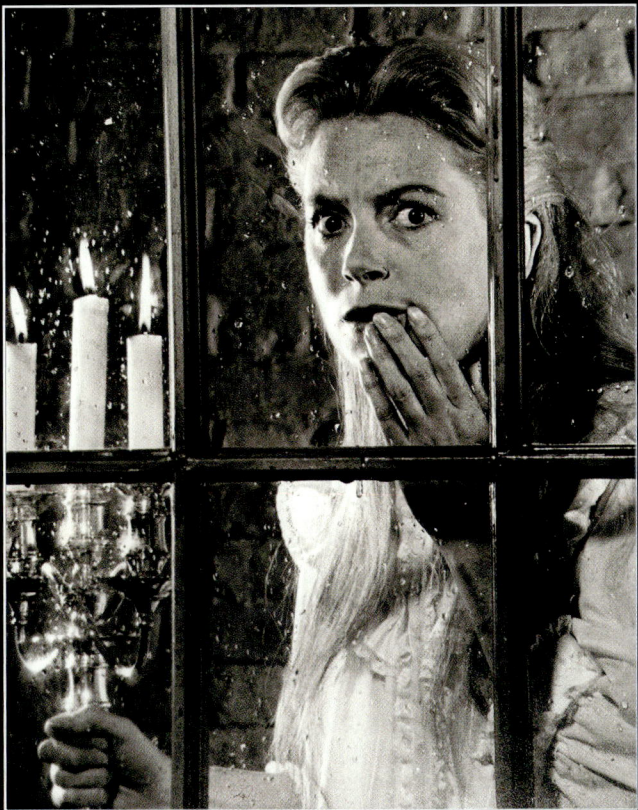

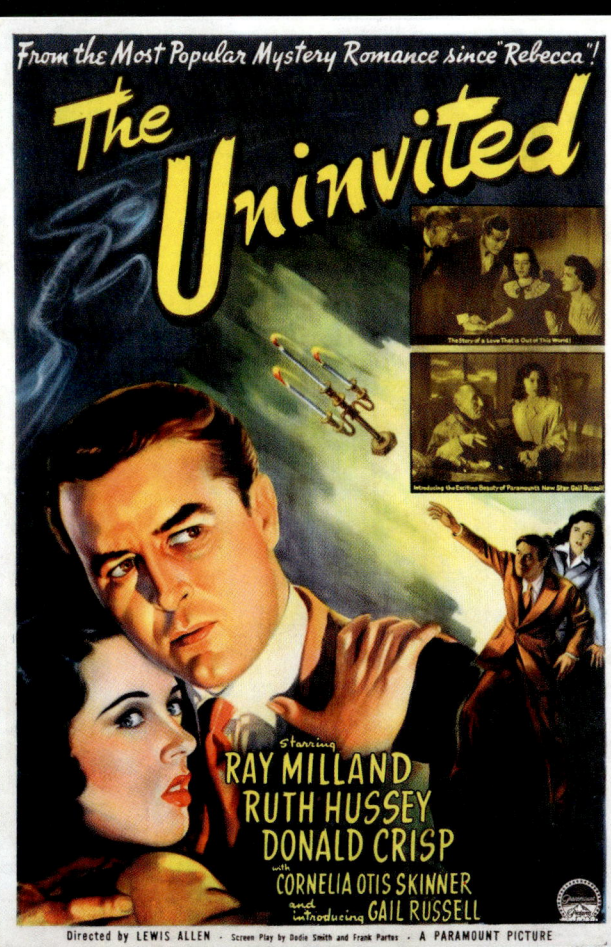

GHOSTS

◀ **Topper**
[Norman Z. McLeod, 1937] Cary Grant and Constance Bennett as the ghosts of George and Marion Kerby, killed in a car accident. This delightful comedy also stars Roland Young as Cosmo Topper, the only person who can see or hear them. Based on the novel by Thorne Smith.

> "You know something George? I think we're dead."
>
> Marion Kerby (Constance Bennett), *Topper*

▶ **Liliom**
[Fritz Lang, 1933] "God's Police" come to take Charles Boyer to heaven to face judgment in Lang's only French film. Based on the play by Ferenc Molnár.

▶ **House on Haunted Hill**
[William Castle, 1959] Millionaire Vincent Price and his fourth wife invite five people to spend the night; those alive in the morning will receive $10,000 each. The entertaining 1999 remake, directed by William Malone is great fun and features a witty performance by Geoffrey Rush doing his best Vincent Price.

◀ **The Ghost and Mrs. Muir**
[Joseph L. Mankiewicz, 1947] This romantic comedy has a very strange happy ending. When Gene Tierney grows old and dies, she can finally be united with the ghost of Rex Harrison's dashing sea captain!

Christmas Carols

A Christmas Carol by Charles Dickens was published on December 17th, 1843 and television has broadcast some version of his story about miser Ebenezer Scrooge and his visitations by the Ghosts of Christmas Past, Present, and Yet to Come every December since 1949. "And God bless Tiny Tim!"

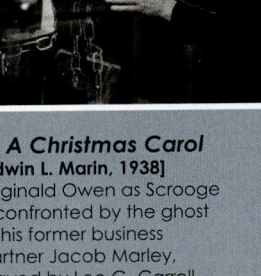

▲ **A Christmas Carol** [Edwin L. Marin, 1938] Reginald Owen as Scrooge is confronted by the ghost of his former business partner Jacob Marley, played by Leo G. Carroll.

▲ **The Canterville Ghost** [Jules Dassin, 1944] Based on a short story by Oscar Wilde. Charles Laughton hams it up in the title role.

▲ **A Christmas Carol** [aka Scrooge, Brian Desmond Hurst, 1951] Alastair Sim as Scrooge is shown his own grave by the Ghost of Christmases Yet to Come.

▲ **Scrooge** [Ronald Neame, 1970] Albert Finney's Scrooge is confronted by Death in this musical version. A great cast cannot overcome the terrible songs (with the exception of "Thank You Very Much," sung by a fellow dancing on Scrooge's coffin).

▶ **The Muppet Christmas Carol** [Brian Henson, 1992] A surprisingly faithful adaptation with Michael Caine as a first-rate Scrooge.

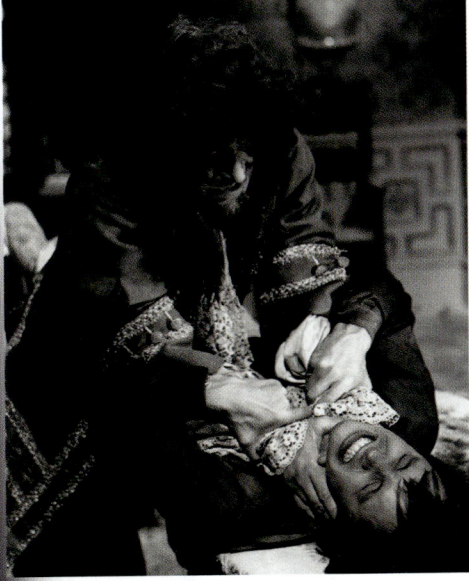

▲ **From Beyond the Grave** [Kevin Connor, 1973] An anthology horror film from Amicus and producer Milton Subotsky. Peter Cushing runs an antique shop called Temptations Ltd., and woe to those who enter. Here, Ian Ogilvy already regrets his purchase.

◀ **Scrooged** [Richard Donner, 1988] A modern comedy take on Dickens' story. Pictured here are Bill Murray as selfish TV exec Frank Cross with David Johansen of the New York Dolls as a New York Cab Driver Ghost of Christmas Past.

GHOSTS

◀ **The Haunting**
[Robert Wise, 1963]
Claire Bloom and Julie Harris react to the very loud sounds made by "something" in the hallway outside their bedroom door in this Robert Wise classic.

▶ **Halloween**
[John Carpenter, 1978]
Michael Myers disguised as a ghost in John Carpenter's influential slasher film. Carpenter also wrote *Halloween*'s much-imitated score. Is Michael Myers, in fact, a ghost himself?

"It was an evil house from the beginning —a house that was born bad."

Dr. John Markway (Richard Johnson), *The Haunting*

▲ **Kwaidan** [Masaki Kobayashi, 1964] Kwaidan means "ghost story" in Japanese, and this beautiful anthology film is comprised of four Japanese folk tales compiled by Lafcadio Hearn. Pictured is "Hoichi the Earless," a blind musician who has an intense and agonizing encounter with the ghostly subjects of his songs.

▶ **Ghostbusters II**
[Ivan Reitman, 1989] The sequel to Reitman's blockbuster comedy *Ghostbusters* [1984]. Co-scripter Dan Aykroyd (with Harold Ramis) originally conceived the premise as a vehicle for himself and close friend John Belushi. Both movies have rousing scores by Elmer Bernstein [*Ghostbusters*] and Randy Edelman [*Ghostbusters II*].

◀ **Beetlejuice** [Tim Burton, 1988] Michael Keaton in the title role is hilarious in Tim Burton's imaginative supernatural comedy.

◀ *The Fog*
[John Carpenter, 1980]
In this good-old-fashioned spook story, the ghosts of a ship's crew, deliberately shipwrecked off the coast of a small town 100 years ago, return to exact their revenge. The phantoms emerge from a supernatural fogbank.

▲ *The Amityville Horror* [Stuart Rosenberg, 1979]
Based on the best selling "true story" about a haunted house in Long Island, New York, *The Amityville Horror* was sold with the wonderful tagline, "FOR GOD'S SAKE, GET OUT!"

▼▶ *The Shining*
[Stanley Kubrick, 1980]
The creepy, twin little-girl ghosts and a vision of the grisly way they died. Stephen King was dissatisfied with Kubrick's film of his book and wrote the teleplay for the TV mini-series version, directed by Mick Garris in 1997.

▲ *Poltergeist* [Tobe Hooper, 1982] Steven Spielberg produced this all-American suburban ghost story. JoBeth Williams' initial delight at invisibly moving kitchen chairs turns to terror when her daughter stares into a television showing nothing but static and announces, "They're here."

GHOSTS

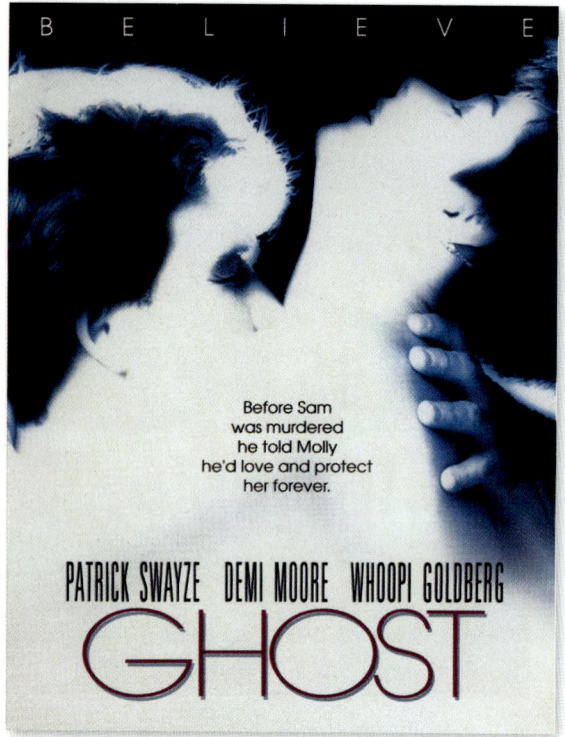

▲ **Ghost** [Jerry Zucker, 1990] The ghost of Patrick Swayze uses fake medium Whoopi Goldberg to warn his widow Demi Moore of danger. This silly romantic movie was a tremendous box-office success.

▲ **The Sixth Sense** [M. Night Shyamalan, 1999] Moving performances from Haley Joel Osment, Bruce Willis, and Toni Collette help make this clever tale of a little boy who can communicate with the dead so powerful.

▶ **The Changeling** [Peter Medak, 1980] George C. Scott, Melvyn Douglas, and Trish Van Devere are terrific in Medak's shivery ghost story set in Seattle. Supposedly based on screenwriter Russell Hunter's true experiences living in an old mansion in Denver, Colorado.

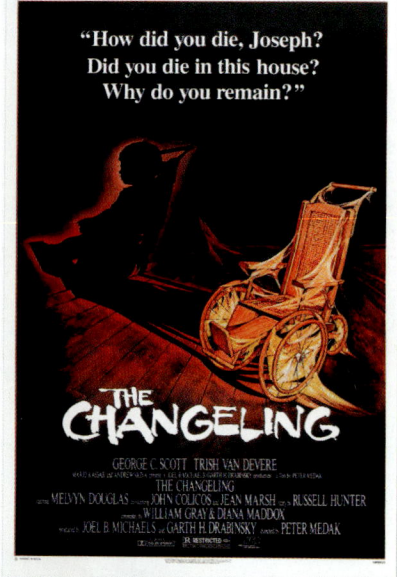

◀ **The Ring** [Gore Verbinski, 2002] The American remake of a 1998 Japanese movie based on Kôji Suzuki's novel *Ring*. Naomi Watts stars in the story of a cursed video tape that dooms all who watch it.

◀ **Sleepy Hollow** [Tim Burton, 1999] Johnny Depp stars in Burton's take on the famous short story "The Legend of Sleepy Hollow" by Washington Irving.

▲ **Paranormal Activity** [Oren Peli, 2007] Shot in seven days for very little money in his own home by writer/director Oren Peli; this film clearly demonstrates that sometimes less is more. An intensely scary experience, *Paranormal Activity* is a real crowd-pleaser.

▲ **Pirates of the Caribbean: The Curse of the Black Pearl** [Gore Verbinski, 2003] The first of the hugely successful franchise based on the ride at Disneyland. Pictured is Geoffrey Rush as Hector Barbossa, the captain of a crew of ghostly pirates.

▲ **Ju-on** [aka *The Grudge*, Takashi Shimizu, 2003] Shimizu also directed the American remake of his own film which, for me, was not as scary or ethereal as his original. The *Ju-on* series began with two direct-to-video films that evolved into both Japanese and American theatrical movies.

▶ **The Grudge 2** [Takashi Shimizu, 2006] Shimizu's American remake of his own Japanese film stars Sarah Michelle Geller. She brings the curse from the first movie, created by a murdered housewife in Nerima, Japan, to Chicago, Illinois.

Myths, Legends, & Fairy Tales

The world's myths, legends, and fairy tales have provided the movies with a plethora of monsters. Walt Disney introduced many of us to folk and fairy tales in his beautifully animated movies. In fact, the first ever feature-length, animated film is Disney's *Snow White and the Seven Dwarfs* [1937].

As captivating as Snow White is, it is the jealous and wicked Queen we all remember. The elegant and sensual Queen who turns herself into an Old Crone to give Snow White the poisoned apple was unforgettably voiced by an uncredited Lucille La Verne. Disney's films were often genuinely scary, as in *Sleeping Beauty* [1959], when actress Eleanor Audley gave voice to the evil fairy Maleficent's splendid line: "Now you must deal with me and all the powers of Hell!" as she magically transforms into a gigantic fire-breathing dragon to do battle with the dashing Prince.

▲*Cinderella* [Georges Méliès, 1899] An early Méliès "trick film."

The delightful Disney version of Carlo Collodi's classic book *The Adventures of Pinocchio* [1881], released as *Pinocchio* [1940], was also not without its dark side. The sequence when Pinocchio and his friend Lampwick's bad behavior causes them to "make asses of themselves" and they turn into donkeys, is as startling and sinister as any transformation scene in a werewolf movie.

The traditional French fairy tale "Beauty and the Beast" has been made into a number of movies. The best one is Jean Cocteau's magical *La Belle et la Bête* [1946]. The Beast, played by Jean Marais, is so glorious, that at the "happy ending," his metamorphosis into the handsome human prince is a bit of a let-down. The Disney *Beauty and the Beast* [1991] is a full-on operetta, with witty songs by Howard Ashman and Alan Menken and outstanding voice work by Paige O'Hara as Beauty and Robby Benson as the Beast.

The Irish fairies known as leprechauns have starring roles in movies in which they are good, like the charming *Darby O'Gill and the Little People* [Robert Stevenson, 1959] and movies where they are evil, like the series of films that started with *Leprechaun* [Mark Jones, 1993]. Warwick Davis has played the malicious little magical bastard in six Leprechaun films so far, with no end in sight! Davis has also written an entertaining autobiography called *Size Matters Not* [Arum Press, 2010], in which he talks about his little person roles in countless fantasy films, including *Willow*, *Star Wars*, *Harry Potter*, and more.

Elves and dwarfs feature in all of *The Lord of the Rings* trilogy of films [Peter Jackson, 2001, 2002, 2003]. Based on the books by J. R. R. Tolkien, the trilogy contains thousands of fantasy beings including giants, trolls, fairies, wizards, ambulatory

---

Previous pages: Belle (Josette Day) soothes the savage Beast (Jean Marais) in Jean Cocteau's classic fairy tale adaptation *La Belle et la Bête*.
Opposite page: **(1)** *Jason and the Argonauts* [Don Chaffey, 1963] Talos, the gigantic Man of Bronze that comes to life when Hercules takes a javelin-sized pin from the treasure he guards. Ray Harryhausen's animation is extraordinary as Talos somehow moves as a Man of Bronze would move. Here, Talos, like the ancient Colossus of Rhodes, waits to grab Jason's ship, *Argo*.
(2) *Jason and the Argonauts* [Don Chaffey, 1963] Jason (Todd Armstrong) fighting the Hydra, the seven-headed dragon that guards the Golden Fleece. Another scene lit up by Harryhausen's breathtaking stop-motion animation. **(3)** *Legend* [Ridley Scott, 1985] Princess Lily (Mia Sara) reaches out to a unicorn in Scott's beautiful-looking fairy tale.

talking trees, demons, goblins, and an army of Orcs. Through a powerful motion-capture performance by Andy Serkis, the emotionally tortured creature Gollum stands out from the rest of the extraordinary array of mythical characters on display.

The one-eyed giants called Cyclops show up occasionally in films based on both Greco-Roman and Arabian Nights mythology. My favorites are the incredible Cyclops that live on the Island of Colossa in Ray Harryhausen's first feature film shot in color, *The 7th Voyage of Sinbad* [Nathan H. Juran, 1958]. I saw this movie at the age of eight and it changed my life in the same way that the original *King Kong* [Merian C. Cooper, Ernest B. Schoedsack, 1933] changed Harryhausen's (see my conversation with Ray on pages 72-73). I was enchanted, not only by the impressive Cyclops, but also by the fabulous dragon, and especially the skeleton brought to life by the wicked magician Sokurah (played in a wonderfully hammy turn by Torin Thatcher). Towards the beginning of the film, Sokurah turns the Princess' handmaiden into a dancing Snake Woman, Ray's favorite monster from this particular voyage of Sinbad's.

▲ ***A Midsummer Night's Dream*** **[Max Reinhardt, William Dieterle, 1935]** Anita Louise as Titania, Queen of the Fairies and James Cagney as Bottom the Weaver, who has been given the head of a jackass by Puck (Mickey Rooney), in this lavish, Warner Brothers production of the play by William Shakespeare.

Harryhausen took Sinbad on two more voyages, *The Golden Voyage of Sinbad* [Gordon Hessler, 1973] and *Sinbad and the Eye of the Tiger* [Sam Wanamaker, 1977], both movies adding even more mythological monsters to the Harryhausen menagerie, including ghouls, a one-eyed centaur, a griffin, and a multi-armed statue of Kali that comes to life to sword-fight Sinbad and his crew.

The poet Homer gave us the Cyclops in the *Odyssey*, and *Ulysses* [Mario Camerini, 1955] starring Kirk Douglas in the title role, is a good retelling of the hero's epic voyage to his homeland of Ithaca following the fall of Troy. An Italian wrestler named Oscar Andriani plays the Cyclops, who is tricked by wily Ulysses into getting drunk so that once more we can watch a poor Cyclops have something sharp jammed into his only eye. Also based on Greek mythology is *Jason and the Argonauts* [Don Chaffey, 1963], which allowed Harryhausen to create more of his remarkable creatures to illustrate the story of Jason and his quest for the Golden Fleece. On Jason's adventure, we meet the colossal bronze statue Talos, brought to life by the hubris of Hercules, the flying Harpies sent to torment the blind Phineas for misusing his gift of prophecy, the many-headed Hydra who guards the Golden Fleece, and the "Children of the Hydra's teeth"—screaming skeleton warriors. The Gods themselves watch Jason's adventures from Mount Olympus and occasionally intercede on his behalf (as Hera does by sending the sea god Triton to hold back the Clashing Rocks, enabling Jason's ship Argo to pass through unharmed).

Harryhausen's final foray into Greek myth was the story of Perseus, told in *Clash of the Titans* [Desmond Davis, 1981]. Here, Pegasus the flying horse, giant scorpions, the snake-haired Medusa, and the Kraken compete for our attention.
The movie was remade in 2010 [Louis Leterrier] with CG effects and mediocre 3D. But at least we got to hear once more those delicious words: "Release the Kraken!"

Opposite page: (1) *Peter Pan* **[Clyde Geronimi, Wilfred Jackson, Hamilton Luske, 1953]** The fairy Tinker Bell in the Disney version of J. M. Barrie's play, here with Captain Hook. Hook was splendidly voiced by Hans Conried. **(2)** *Hook* **[Steven Spielberg, 1991]** Julia Roberts as the fairy Tinker Bell in this misguided sequel to *Peter Pan*. However, Dustin Hoffman made a fine Captain Hook. **(3)** *Peter Pan* **[P. J. Hogan, 2003]** Ludivine Sagnier as Tinker Bell (here just called Tink) in this straightforward adaptation of Barrie's story. With Jason Isaacs as an excellent Captain Hook.

(4) *The Thief of Bagdad* **[Ludwig Berger, Michael Powell, Tim Whelan, 1940]** The magnificent Rex Ingram as the Djinn (genie), finally free of his bottle prison, grants Abu (Sabu) three wishes in Alexander Korda's Technicolor production. With the great Conrad Veidt as Jaffar, the evil Grand Vizier.

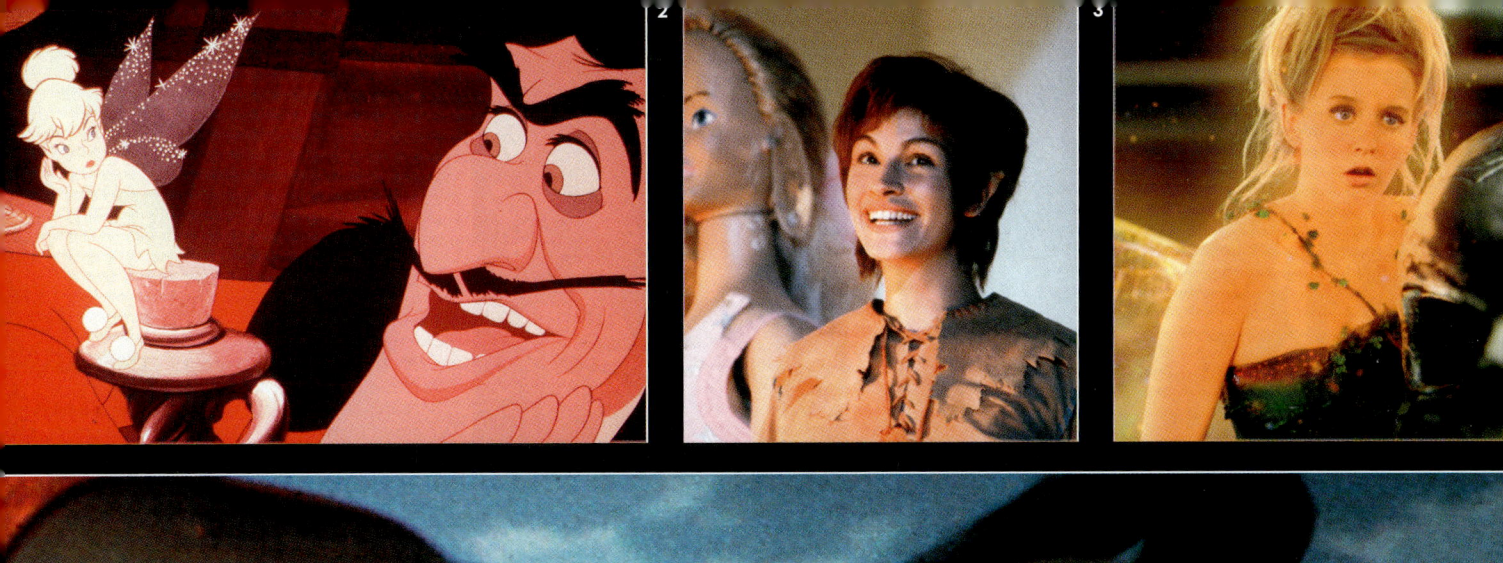

MYTHICAL MONSTERS

◀ **The Thief of Bagdad** [Ludwig Berger, Michael Powell, Tim Whelan, 1940]
Mary Morris as the Silver Maid, an exotic—and deadly—mechanical toy made by the evil Jaffar to assassinate the Sultan of Basra. This lavish fantasy began shooting in London but moved to Hollywood to finish when the war broke out.

▼ **The Golden Voyage of Sinbad** [Gordon Hessler, 1973] The second in Harryhausen's Sinbad trilogy. Here, a living stone statue of Kali, the Hindu Goddess of death, sword fights Sinbad (John Phillip Law, in the white turban) and his crew.

▲ **Alice in Wonderland** [Norman Z. McLeod, 1933]
There have been at least 22 feature films based on Lewis Carroll's classic children's story. This Paramount Pictures version is suitably bizarre. Here is Charlotte Henry as Alice, with Polly Moran as the Dodo Bird. W. C. Fields played Humpty Dumpty, Gary Cooper the White Knight, and Cary Grant was the Mock Turtle!

"Where is Belle? Where is Belle?"

The Beast (Jean Marais), searching for Belle in his magic mirror, *La Belle et la Bête*

▼ **Beauty and the Beast** [Gary Trousdale, 1991]
Disney's delightful musical, with witty songs by Howard Ashman and Alan Menken. Robby Benson and Paige O'Hara gave the Beast and Beauty their voices. Based on Jeanne-Marie Leprince de Beaumont's story, first published in 1757.

▲ **La Belle et la Bête** [Jean Cocteau, 1946]
Cocteau's magical film combines Jeanne-Marie Leprince de Beaumont's story with *La Chatte Blanche* by Catherine d'Aulnoy, published in 1697! Surreal and gorgeous, Cocteau's movie is truly romantic in the best sense of the word. Josette Day is Belle and Jean Marais is the fabulous Beast.

GORGONS

◀ **The Gorgon** [Terence Fisher, 1964] Hammer Films ignores Greek mythology and sets this in a rural German village in 1910. Prudence Hyman is Megaera the Gorgon who, at the time of the full moon, turns victims to stone with a single glance. With Peter Cushing as Dr. Namaroff and Christopher Lee as Prof. Karl Meister.

▶ **7 Faces of Dr. Lao** [George Pal, 1964] Tony Randall as Medusa (one of seven parts Randall plays in the film), a deadly exhibit in the Circus of Dr. Lao.

◀ **Clash of the Titans** [Desmond Davis, 1981] Ray Harryhausen's Medusa, Ray Bradbury's favorite Harryhausen creature. In a tense, torch-lit sequence, Perseus (Harry Hamlin) stalks Medusa, hoping to use her severed head to turn the Kraken to stone.

◀ **Perseus and the Gorgon** [Jim Henson, 1998] A good retelling of the Greek myth on Jim Henson's *The Storyteller*, an excellent, but short-lived, television series.

▶ **Percy Jackson & The Lightning Thief** [aka *Percy Jackson & the Olympians: The Lightning Thief*, Chris Columbus, 2010] Uma Thurman as Medusa in Chris Columbus's attempt to create another franchise like he did with the *Harry Potter* books by J. K. Rowling. This one is based on *The Lightning Thief*, the first novel in the *Percy Jackson & The Olympians* series by Rick Riordan.

▲ **Clash of the Titans** [Louis Leterrier, 2010] The remake, based on Harryhausen's design for his Medusa. This film suffered from being made 3D in an imperfect post-production process.

MYTHICAL MONSTERS

cyclops

▲ **The Three Stooges Meet Hercules** [Edward Bernds, 1962] The Three Stooges encountered this unusual, giant, two-headed Cyclops in this slapstick adventure.

▲ **Ulysses** [Mario Camerini, 1955] Kirk Douglas stars as Ulysses in this Italian movie that is fairly faithful to Homer's *Odyssey*. Italian wrestler Oscar Andriani made an impressive Cyclops.

▲ **Krull** [Peter Yates, 1983] Bernard Bresslaw as Rell the Cyclops in this odd fantasy film. Bresslaw is unrecognizable in his make-up; otherwise you would remember him as a regular in the *Carry On* movies! Peter Yates was a wonderful director, but this is not one of his best.

▶ **The 7th Voyage of Sinbad** [Nathan H. Juran, 1958] One of the awe-inspiring Cyclops that live on the Island of Colossa in the first of Harryhausen's *Sinbad* trilogy. When roasting one of Sinbad's crew on a spit, he licks his lips in anticipation of his meal! One of the screen's greatest fantasy creations.

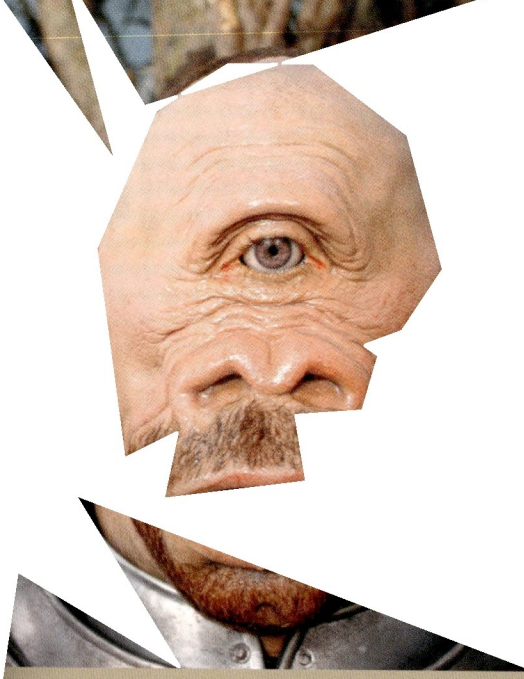

▲ **The Chronicles of Narnia: The Lion, the Witch and the Wardrobe** [Andrew Adamson, 2005] Howard Berger, Gregory Nicotero, and Nikki Gooley won an Academy Award for Best Make-up for their work on this film.

▲ **The Wonderful World of the Brothers Grimm** [Henry Levin, George Pal, 1962] Laurence Harvey and Karlheinz Böhm as Wilhelm and Jacob, the Brothers Grimm in this Cinerama spectacular. Henry Levin directed the framing story of them writing their famous tales, and George Pal directed the fairy tales. With delightful stop-motion animation by Wah Chang and Gene Warren in the George Pal tradition. Years later, I was shocked to discover that the deranged killer in *Peeping Tom* [Michael Powell, 1960] was one of the Brothers Grimm!

▲ **The Brothers Grimm** [Terry Gilliam, 2005] Mackenzie Crook not looking well in Terry Gilliam's very different vision from George Pal's. Matt Damon and Heath Ledger played the Brothers Grimm.

"The gods of Greece are cruel! In time all men will learn to live without them!"

Jason (Todd Armstrong), *Jason and the Argonauts*

▲◀◀ **Jason and the Argonauts** [Don Chaffey, 1963] Here are just three of Jason's encounters with the marvels of Greek myth in Harryhausen's wondrous movie. Above: The Argonauts fight the winged Harpies sent by Zeus to punish blind Phineas for misusing his gift of prophecy. Left: The grateful Phineas gives Jason an amulet, which summons the god Triton, shown here holding back the Clashing Rocks so that the *Argo* may pass unharmed. Above left: The teeth from the slain Hydra (see page 58) are sown by wicked King Aeetes and, up from the ground, sprout skeleton warriors that attack Jason and his men. This four-minute sequence took Ray more than four months to animate!

MYTHICAL MONSTERS

Trolls

▲ **Time Bandits** [Terry Gilliam, 1981] Peter Vaughan as Winston the Ogre in Gilliam's wonderful and very witty fantasy. This one is a must see.

▲ **Bridge to Terabithia** [Gábor Csupó, 2007] Based on Katherine Paterson's novel about kids who invent their own fantasy world called Terabithia.

▶ **Troll** [John Carl Buechler, 1986] A wicked troll king shows up in San Francisco. An interesting piece of trivia about this film, is that Michael Moriarty plays a character named Harry Potter!

◀ **Labyrinth** [Jim Henson, 1986] Rob Mills (Ron Mueck, voice) as Ludo, one of the many terrific fantasy creatures that populate Jim Henson's fairy tale. David Bowie played Jareth, the Goblin King.

▲ **The Troll Hunter** [aka *Trolljegeren*, André Øvredal, 2010] Told through the first-person camera of a "documentary" crew, this is an exciting and funny story about the existence of monstrous Trolls in Norway and the secret government agency keeping them under control.

▲▶ **Gremlins** [Joe Dante, 1984] Dante's wonderful, dark, fairy tale comedy. When cute little Mogwai Gizmo (above) gets wet, eggs sprout from his back and produce many more Mogwai. However, these Mogwai, like Stripe (right), are downright dangerous. The enormous success of *Gremlins* allowed Dante to make the even more adventurous *Gremlins 2: The New Batch* in 1990. *Gremlins* is a marvelous mix of the sweet and the sinister.

> "How come a cute little guy like this can turn into a thousand ugly monsters?"
>
> Sheriff Frank (Scott Brady), *Gremlins*

▲ **The NeverEnding Story** [Wolfgang Petersen, 1984] The first of three films based on Michael Ende's book. All three films are chock-a-block with monsters suitable for children. Above is a living mountain.

▲ **The Golden Voyage of Sinbad** [Gordon Hessler, 1973]
A one-eyed centaur fights a griffin near the Fountain of Destiny on the lost continent of Lemuria, in the second of Ray Harryhausen's *Sinbad* trilogy.

▲ **Harry Potter and the Prisoner of Azkaban** [Alfonso Cuaron, 2004] Harry Potter encounters a griffin, one of the many fantastic creatures that populate the Harry Potter movies.

MYTHICAL MONSTERS

"Release the Kraken!"

Calibos (Neil McCarthy), *Clash of the Titans* [1981]

▲ ***Clash of the Titans*** [Desmond Davis, 1981] The Kraken comes for Princess Andromeda in a staging reminiscent of many classic paintings of the Greek myth. Will Perseus and Pegasus get there in time to save her?

▲ ***Clash of the Titans*** [Louis Leterrier, 2010]
The oddly designed Kraken in the remake. Notice how tiny Pegasus appears next to the gigantic monster.

▲ ***Pirates of the Caribbean: Dead Man's Chest*** [Gore Verbinski, 2006]
Disney's Kraken destroys a merchant ship in the second of the *Pirates of the Caribbean* franchise.

▲ **Leprechaun in the Hood** [Rob Spera, 2000] Warwick Davis stars as the evil little bastard in this, the fifth in the six Leprechaun movies in the franchise so far. This one is the blaxploitation edition.

▶ **Darby O'Gill and the Little People** [Robert Stevenson, 1959] Jimmy O'Dea as King Brian of the Leprechauns stands on a sleeping Sean Connery as Michael McBride in this delightful Disney movie based on the *Darby O'Gill* books by Herminie Templeton Kavanagh. The great Albert Sharpe played Darby O'Gill. Using the Schufftan Process (forced perspective creating the illusion of size differential) the movie has amazing scenes of Darby among the "little people."

▲ **Erik the Viking** [Terry Jones, 1989] The size of this sea monster can be seen by comparison with Erik's ship in front of it. Loosely based on Jones' own book, *The Saga of Erik the Viking*.

AFTERNOONS OF A FAUN

▶ **7 Faces of Dr. Lao** [George Pal, 1964] Tony Randall as Pan himself, here on display in Dr. Lao's circus tent. Pan plays his pipes and arouses the dormant sexuality of a young widow (Barbara Eden) in an unusually erotic scene for a "family" movie.

◀ **The Chronicles of Narnia: The Lion, the Witch and the Wardrobe** [Andrew Adamson, 2005] James McAvoy as Mr. Tumnus, a faun who switches sides and becomes an ally to the Pevensie children. Based on the book by C. S. Lewis.

▶ **Exquisite Sinner** [Josef von Sternberg, Phil Rosen, 1926] An intriguing shot of Conrad Nagel as a faun playing his pipes, which was probably in a dream sequence in this lost silent film. The cast list has the equally intriguing credit, "Myrna Loy..... Living Statue."

MYTHICAL MONSTERS

▲ **Time Bandits** [Terry Gilliam, 1981] Sean Connery as King Agamemnon fighting the Minotaur in Gilliam's wonderful fantasy adventure.

◀ **Minotaur, the Wild Beast of Crete** [Silvio Amadio, 1960] Rosanna Schiaffino in the Minotaur's clutches in this Italian sword and sandal movie.

▲ **The Chronicles of Narnia: The Lion, the Witch and the Wardrobe** [Andrew Adamson, 2005] A Minotaur, one of the many mythical creatures created by Howard Berger for this epic fantasy film.

◀▼ **The Lord of the Rings** [Peter Jackson, 2001-2003] Peter Jackson's Tolkien trilogy is jam-packed with fantastic beasts of all sizes and shapes. From left to right: Gollum, a brilliant motion-capture performance from Andy Serkis as the pathetic creature consumed with desire for the Ring; the fearsome Cave Troll in the Mines of Moria; one of the Orcs, the evil soldiers of the wizard Saruman (Christopher Lee).

"We wants it! We needs it! Must have the precious!"

Gollum (Andy Serkis),
The Lord of the Rings: The Return of the King

▲ **Pirates of the Caribbean: At World's End**
[Gore Verbinski, 2007] Bill Nighy as Davy Jones. His amazing tentacled face is a completely computer-generated animation. A fabulous-looking character.

▼▲ **Beowulf** [Robert Zemeckis, 2007] Crispin Glover in a motion-capture performance as Grendel (above) and Angelina Jolie as Grendel's mother (below) in this CG version of the tale. There is a lengthy battle between Beowulf (Ray Winstone) and Grendel in which Beowulf is naked. The lengths to which the director has to go to make sure his genitals are not seen are truly hilarious.

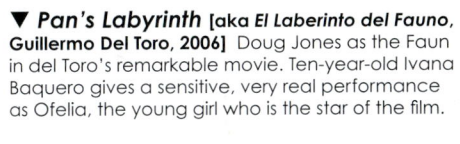

> "Do you fear death?"
> "You have no idea."
>
> Davy Jones (Bill Nighy) to Jack Sparrow (Johnny Depp),
> *Pirates of the Caribbean: At World's End*

▼ **Pan's Labyrinth** [aka *El Laberinto del Fauno*, Guillermo Del Toro, 2006] Doug Jones as the Faun in del Toro's remarkable movie. Ten-year-old Ivana Baquero gives a sensitive, very real performance as Ofelia, the young girl who is the star of the film.

▲ **How the Grinch Stole Christmas** [Ron Howard, 2000]
Jim Carrey gives a terrific performance in Rick Baker's Academy Award-winning make-up for the Grinch. From the classic children's book by Dr. Seuss. I personally prefer Chuck Jones' 1966 animated television version, which was marvelously narrated by Boris Karloff.

IN CONVERSATION

Ray Harryhausen

Ray Harryhausen, the author, and the skeleton from *The 7th Voyage of Sinbad* [1958], used again in *Jason and the Argonauts* [1963]; London, 2010.

Photo by Mark Mawston

JL: Ray, I know you don't like the term "monster."

RH: I don't like the term "monster," because that's not what we do. All our creatures are misunderstood creatures, because they usually come from another world.

JL: So what does the word "monster" mean to you?

RH: I associate the word "monster" with some sort of insane creature that growls and is physically distorted. I don't like to use the word. It has to do with things like Frankenstein and Dracula and horrible people who do horrible things.

JL: Well, some of your creatures do horrible things.

RH: They don't do horrible things. They're just out of their element!

JL: Hmm.

RH: (Laughs.)

JL: Doesn't Medusa do horrible things?

RH: Well, that's her nature! She's a snake woman! (Laughs.)

JL: All right, let me think about it…

RH: She was cursed by Hera (queen of the Greek gods).

JL: What about the Cyclops?

RH: I don't know about the Cyclops…

JL: The Cyclops in *The 7th Voyage of Sinbad* [Nathan H. Juran, 1958]. The Cyclops tries to eat people!

RH: (Laughs) But that's his nature! He's not a monster!

JL: Are there creatures in other people's movies that you are particularly fond of?

RH: Not that I'm *fond* of…

JL: I know what you're fond of: King Kong!

RH: Oh yes, but he was neither man, nor beast, as they said in the script. He was a throwback of some sort. Most gorillas have straight eyebrows, so I slanted Mighty Joe Young's eyebrows so that he would look a little different than a normal gorilla.

JL: I had a problem with Peter Jackson's *King Kong* [2005]. Peter just made him a big gorilla, not at all a mythical beast, just a very big gorilla. Do you like fantasy films in general?

RH: Oh, I love them. They stretch the imagination.

JL: What are some of your favorites… that you didn't make?

RH: (Laughs) Well I thought *Jurassic Park* [Steven Spielberg, 1993] was fascinating.

JL: And you wouldn't call them monsters, just dinosaurs.

RH: Dinosaurs are not monsters; they're just a product of their time!

JL: It's just that when they're out of their time, they are forced to behave badly.

RH: They behave badly because they don't know what they're doing. They don't normally live in this world.

JL: That's a good answer. What about something like in *One Million Years B.C.* [Don Chaffey, 1966], where you have dinosaurs living with humans?

RH: Well, we don't make these pictures for paleontologists. If you just have a bunch of dinosaurs running around barking at each other, there's no drama. You have to include humans!

JL: What about the movie *Creation*? The Willis O'Brien project that was never realized. Wasn't that just dinosaurs?

RH: Well, I think they had more than dinosaurs. They had people in it, too.

JL: What was the Irwin Allen movie you worked on?

RH: That was *The Animal World* [1956].

JL: That had drama in it, and no people.

RH: Well, it was a brief sequence. (The BBC-TV series) *Walking With Dinosaurs* doesn't have any people in it. It's more realistic, but they tried to make dinosaurs that would be acceptable for paleontologists, and we're making movies just to entertain! You can't entertain with a dinosaur just chewing on another dinosaur!

JL: Do you think you're more interested in fantastic beings, or in beings that have a basis in reality?

RH: I think the whole point of any fantasy film is to stretch the imagination, because when one lives in a dream world like me, it's always "what if this could happen?"

JL: Do you think that creatures can be manifestations of people's fantasies or fears?

RH: Sometimes, but *Dr. Jekyll and Mr. Hyde* was more about the dual personalities that we all have.

JL: What about Dr. Moreau, with his genetic experiments? Would you call him a monster?

RH: Dr. Moreau was an early one in genetic experiments and now they are coming to pass. Lord knows what they will create—I don't know!

JL: I know *King Kong* [Merian C. Cooper, Ernest B. Schoedsack, 1933] is the movie that inspired you.

RH: Oh it did. It was an inspiration because it was so different than any other movie.

JL: Do you remember when you saw it?

RH: I was 13. A few marbles have lost their way… maybe they rolled under the davenport…

JL: No, seriously, I know you know. Tell me when you saw it.

RH: I saw it back in 1933, when it first came out. At Grauman's Chinese Theater on Hollywood Boulevard. In Los Angeles, where I grew up.

JL: Was there a live show before the movie?

RH: There was a stage show. Sid Grauman was a great showman at that time. Sid had this great prolog with live actors, and then Kong came on.

JL: Kong himself came on?!

RH: No John. The movie! Although they did have a big bust in the lobby. The prolog got you in the mood to accept the fantasy, which was, at the time, very extreme.

JL: Really? There had been *The Lost World* [Harry O. Hoyt, 1925], the silent picture, and that had been a tremendous hit.

RH: There was, but most people didn't remember it. And Max Steiner's great music made *King Kong* much more impressive than *The Lost World*, which probably had only a piano accompaniment.

JL: How important is music to movies?

RH: I think music is very important to fantasy films, particularly movies that don't rely on very profound dialog. Our fantasies are mostly action pictures, and music enhances them. It makes everything bigger than life, which is the function of good film music.

JL: When you were planning scenes, did you think of the music? When you worked with Bernard Herrmann, did you talk about the score beforehand?

RH: No, no, no, no. You have to leave it to somebody like Bernard Herrmann. Different people write different kinds of music. Herrmann specialized in rousing action music while a composer like Miklos Rozsa wrote romantic music.

JL: You've done movies based on books by Jules Verne and H. G. Wells. Who is your favorite fantasy author?

RH: I couldn't choose a favorite. I like Wells; he was very profound. I liked his book, *The Island of Dr. Moreau*. Did you ever see the picture that Charles Laughton starred in?

JL: Yes, *Island of Lost Souls* [Erle C. Kenton, 1932] is great. That movie had wonderful make-up.

RH: Oh, very good make-up. I don't know who did the score, but it wasn't a complete score.

JL: I don't remember the music. I just remember the monsters! Béla Lugosi was one of them, "The Sayer of the Law!" Do you have a particular favorite of your creatures?

RH: I can't have, because the others get jealous (laughs). I like the complicated ones. They're much more interesting to animate. Like the Hydra in *Jason and the Argonauts* [Don Chaffey, 1963], and Medusa in *Clash of the Titans* [Desmond Davis, 1981]. The sword fight with the Seven Skeletons in *Jason and the Argonauts* as well.

JL: How long did the Seven Skeletons sword fight take you to animate?

RH: It took about four and a half months to put it together. I was the only animator on it. I had to time all the swords, so that when an actor brought his sword down and stopped, a skeleton's blade would be there to meet it.

JL: What are some of the fantasy films, other than *King Kong* and *Island of Lost Souls*, that had a big impact on you?

RH: *Jurassic Park* [Steven Spielberg, 1993] was very impressive. Phil Tippett and Dennis Muren did wonderful work on that. And I liked *Close Encounters of the Third Kind*, too [Steven Spielberg, 1977]. There's a space monster I particularly love in *Forbidden Planet* [Fred M. Wilcox, 1956]. A great movie!

> "The whole point of any fantasy film is to stretch the imagination."

JL: I love the creature in that: "The Monster from the Id."

RH: Yeah. It was a fascinating concept and very well done.

JL: You've already said it, but I would like you to tell me again. You never call your creatures monsters because…?

RH: Well monsters, I think, in most people's minds, are these bad men who go around scaring everybody.

JL: Doing bad things.

RH: Doing insane things! (Laughs.)

JL: Whereas, a creature…

RH: A creature, like the one in *20 Million Miles to Earth* [Nathan H. Juran, 1957] comes from a different planet, and he is not aggressive until somebody is aggressive to him—the farmer jabs him with a pitchfork! That, of course, upsets his ego. (Laughs.)

JL: What do you think of actors who are famous for their fantasy roles, like Boris Karloff, or Christopher Lee?

RH: Well, Boris Karloff was perfect for *Frankenstein*. And he's still the most profound Frankenstein's Monster, I think. He wasn't just frightening.

JL: But in your films, there are moments where you want people to be frightened.

RH: Well, yes. But that's the way you stage a film. As a director, you have to think about how you're going to stage it so you get the most effective appearance, visually.

JL: You know, I was thinking about it, and in your films, even more than a sense of fear, you often impart with a sense of wonder.

RH: Well, we try to do that. I hope that the strangeness of the subject matter also helps create a feeling of wonder.

Ray animating the dragon from *The 7th Voyage of Sinbad* [1958] on a miniature set.

Dragons & Dinosaurs

What's the difference between a dragon and a dinosaur? "Dragons" are legendary creatures with reptilian traits. The term "Dinosaurs" refers to a diverse group of animals that were on Earth from the beginning of the Triassic period to the end of the Cretaceous. That was a long time ago. So for the purposes of this book, which is about monsters in the movies, I think I can safely lump them together in one chapter. Especially since humans and dinosaurs did not coexist and most movies featuring dinosaurs have people running for their lives away from them.

Winsor McCay, the brilliant newspaper cartoonist (creator of the amazing comic strip *Little Nemo in Slumberland*), wanted an animated film to use in his vaudeville act. With thousands of drawings, McCay created *Gertie the Dinosaur* [1914], in which the dinosaur Gertie would respond onscreen to McCay's live commands from the stage. Gertie is probably cinema's first dinosaur.

The first major movie to feature dinosaurs was an adaptation of Sir Arthur Conan Doyle's novel *The Lost World* [Harry O. Hoyt, 1925]. This starred Wallace Beery as Professor Challenger and showcased the groundbreaking stop-motion animation of Willis O'Brien. *The Lost World*'s climatic scenes, in which a brontosaurus brought back by Challenger escapes and wreaks havoc on the streets of London, would inspire literally hundreds of movies in the future.

The rampaging dinosaur in *The Lost World*

▲ **Evil defeated:** St. George and the Dragon, a tinsel picture from the 19th century.

ends up swimming in London's River Thames; 36 years later, *Gorgo* [Eugène Lourié, 1961] and son wade down the Thames, making their way back home to the sea. Gorgo is one of those movie dinosaurs that relies more on the imagination of the filmmakers than on any science or research into the fossil record.

In 1924, Fritz Lang directed *Die Nibelungen: Siegfried* and *Die Nibelungen: Kriemhild's Revenge* [also 1924]. Based on the same 12th-century epic poem, *The Song of the Nibelungs*, that Richard Wagner based his Ring Cycle operas on, the first film has a marvelous dragon for Siegfried to slay. As I am sure you all remember, Siegfried bathes himself in the dragon's blood, and if you're curious about the proper way to bathe in dragon's blood, Lang shows us how.

The Russian film *Ilya Muromets* [aka *The Sword and the Dragon*, Aleksandr Ptushko, 1956] features a ferocious dragon created, like the one in *Siegfried*, as a full-size mechanical puppet for the lead actor to fight.

Since both dinosaurs and dragons are hard to come by for motion-picture work, filmmakers have used a number of methods to bring them to the screen, including full-size puppets, like those in *Siegfried* and *Ilya Muromets* and, later, sophisticated animatronics in *Jurassic Park* [Steven Spielberg, 1993] and its sequels. Traditional, hand-painted cell animation was used in the *Rite of Spring* sequence in Walt Disney's *Fantasia* [Bill Roberts, Paul Satterfield, 1940], while CG animation featured in *How to Train Your Dragon* [Chris Sanders, Dean DeBlois, 2010]. *Jurassic Park* and its sequels also makes extensive use of CG.

To save money, live lizards, iguanas, and alligators with fins attached to them were shot in slow motion in an attempt to convey great size

Previous pages: *One Million Years B.C.* [Don Chaffey, 1966] Raquel Welch as Loana in the claws of a pterodactyl! A Hammer color remake of the black and white Hal Roach original [1940], with special effects by Ray Harryhausen.
Opposite page: *The Beast From 20,000 Fathoms* [Eugène Lourié, 1953] Harryhausen's influential dinosaur-on-the-loose movie. Tagline: "They couldn't escape the terror! And neither will you!"

and weight in movies like *One Million B.C.* [Hal Roach, Hal Roach Jr., 1940], the remake of *The Lost World* [Irwin Allen, 1960], and *Journey to the Center of the Earth* [Henry Levin, 1959].

My preference in dinosaurs and dragons is for ones made with stop-motion animation, as in the silent *Lost World*, *King Kong* [Merian C. Cooper, Ernest B. Schoedsack, 1933], *The Beast of Hollow Mountain* [Edward Nassour, Ismael Rodríguez, 1956], *The Wonderful World of the Brothers Grimm* [Henry Lavin, George Pal, 1962], *Dinosaurus!* [Irvin Yeaworth, 1960], *Jack The Giant Killer* [Nathan H. Juran, 1962], and the wonderful Loch Ness Monster in *7 Faces of Dr. Lao* [George Pal, 1964]. Another, simpler technique to bring these enormous creatures to life is just to use men in dinosaur costumes stomping around miniature sets. This was done in *Gorgo* [1961], and Japanese movies like the original *Godzilla* [Ishirô Honda, 1954] and all of its sequels and imitations.

Stop-motion animator Ray Harryhausen has created some of my favorite dragons and dinosaurs. There is the majestic dragon of *The 7th Voyage of Sinbad* [Nathan H. Juran, 1958] and the unforgettable Hydra that guards the Golden Fleece in *Jason and the Argonauts*. [Don Chaffey, 1963].

Ray's *The Beast From 20,000 Fathoms* [Eugène Lourié, 1953] was the first of the many monsters unleashed by the atomic bomb. Based on a Ray Bradbury short story, "The Fog Horn," in which a lonely, prehistoric beast rises from the sea mistaking a lighthouse foghorn for a mating call, the enormous success of *The Beast From 20,000 Fathoms* provided the incentive for Toho Studios in Tokyo to produce their own gigantic-beast-rising-from-the-sea movie, *Godzilla*, in 1954. *Godzilla*'s sequel, *Godzilla Raids Again* was retitled *Gigantis, the Fire Monster* for its US release in 1955.

Harryhausen made more realistic dinosaurs in Hammer's remake of *One Million Years B.C.* [Don Chaffey, 1966]. Ray also gave us the indelible image of Raquel Welch in a fur bikini carried off by a mama pterodactyl to feed to her hungry chicks. In Harryhausen's *The Valley of Gwangi* [Jim O'Connolly, 1969], cowboys discover dinosaurs in a hidden valley and capture an allosaurus, which they put on display in a bullring. It breaks free, and dies trapped in a burning cathedral.

▲ *The Lost World* [Harry O. Hoyt, 1925] The first film version of Sir Arthur Conan Doyle's classic book. Wallace Beery played Professor Challenger in this silent movie, with stop-motion animation by the great Willis O'Brien.

Ishirô Honda's Japanese dragon (or is he a dinosaur?) *Godzilla* [1954] was an international sensation and has been followed by countless sequels and one ill-conceived, big-budget Hollywood remake [Roland Emmerich, 1998]. Godzilla himself has had a fascinating relationship with Japan. Originally a symbol of the destruction caused by the two atomic bombs dropped on Japan during World War II, Godzilla has gone from being Japan's ultimate villain, to the country's friend and protector. Godzilla has been joined by *Rodan! The Flying Monster!* [Ishirô Honda, 1956], a sort of jumbo pterodactyl, and a golden, three-headed flying dragon from outer space named *Ghidorah, the Three-Headed Monster* [Ishirô Honda, 1964] among others. The great Eiji Tsuburaya supervised almost all of Toho Studios' giant monster films, his special effects distinguished by his trademark miniatures: entire cities built to scale to be knocked down, stomped on, and blown up.

Paleontologists keep discovering new dinosaurs and I am sure that moviemakers will, too. And I for one, look forward to meeting them.

Opposite page: (1) *Gertie* [aka *Gertie the Dinosaur*, Winsor McCay, 1914] Pioneering cartoonist Winsor McCay toured in vaudeville with his hand-drawn animation, giving the onscreen dinosaur verbal commands from the stage.

(2) *The Ghost of Slumber Mountain* [Willis O'Brien, 1918] The poster for the 19-minute-long, stop-motion animation that got O'Brien the job of animating the dinosaurs for *The Lost World* [Harry O. Hoyt, 1925], which led to his masterpiece, *King Kong* [1933].

(3) *Goliath and the Dragon* [aka *La Vendetta di Ercole*, Vittorio Cottafavi, 1960] This Italian sword and sandal epic not only features a good dragon, it also has an unexpected Broderick Crawford as King Eurystheus!

WINSOR McCAY'S "GERTIE"
WONDERFULLY TRAINED DINOSAURUS
A Prehistoric Animal that Lived Thirteen Million Years Ago, Brought Back to Life. A Most Marvellous Work of Art, Science and Humor.
She's a Scream
WINSOR McCAY AMERICA'S GREATEST CARTOONIST.
GERTIE JUST LOVES AN AUTO.
BOX OFFICE FEATURE FILM
Released through BOX OFFICE ATTRACTION CO.
WILLIAM FOX, PRESIDENT
EXCHANGES IN ALL PRINCIPAL CITIES.

2

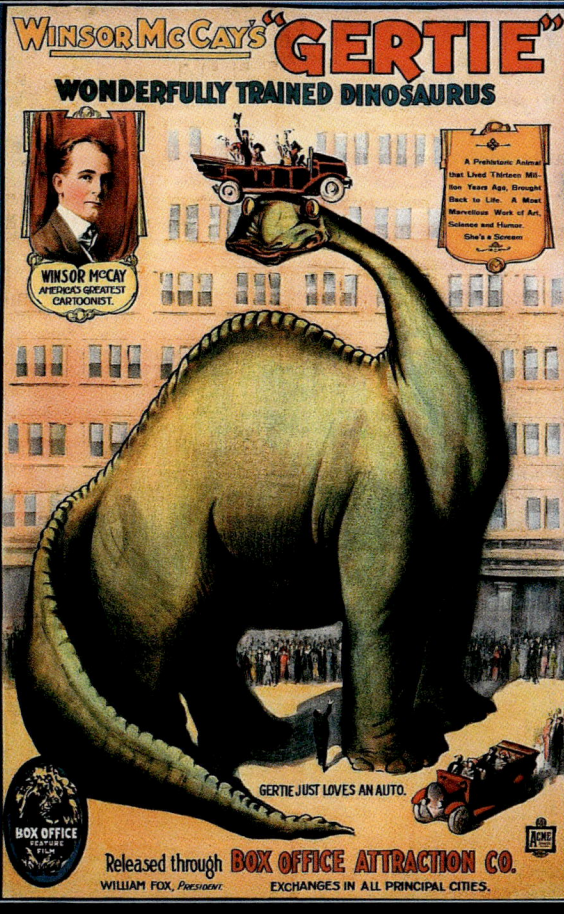

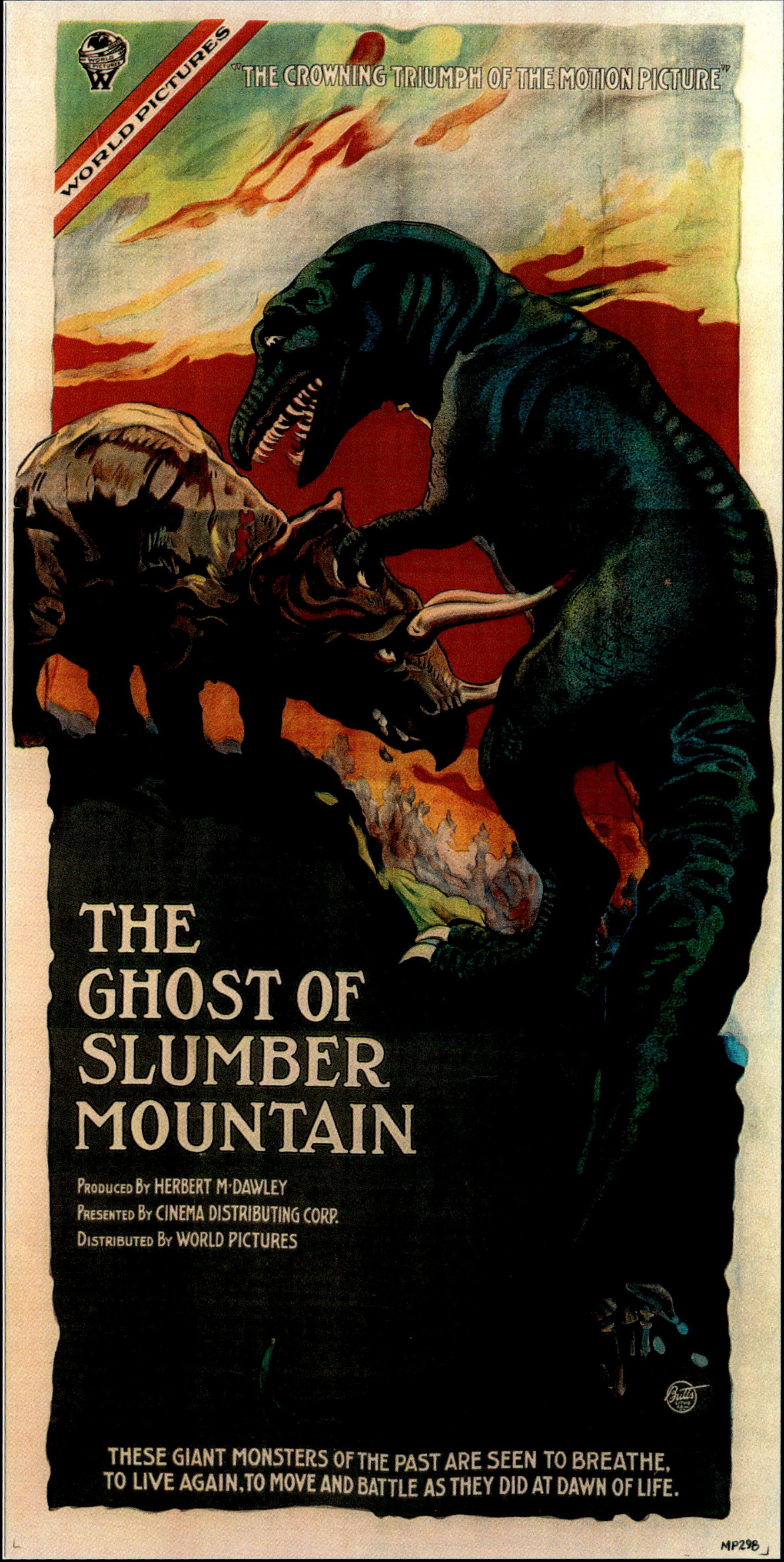
WORLD PICTURES
"THE CROWNING TRIUMPH OF THE MOTION PICTURE"
THE GHOST OF SLUMBER MOUNTAIN
PRODUCED BY HERBERT M. DAWLEY
PRESENTED BY CINEMA DISTRIBUTING CORP.
DISTRIBUTED BY WORLD PICTURES
THESE GIANT MONSTERS OF THE PAST ARE SEEN TO BREATHE, TO LIVE AGAIN, TO MOVE AND BATTLE AS THEY DID AT DAWN OF LIFE.
MP298

AMAZING! FANTASTIC! OVERWHELMING!
The mightiest adventure of them all!
JAMES H. NICHOLSON & SAMUEL Z. ARKOFF present
GOLIATH AND THE DRAGON
IN COLORSCOPE
Starring MARK FOREST · BRODERICK CRAWFORD · ELEONORA RUFFO
AND A CAST OF THOUSANDS · AN AMERICAN-INTERNATIONAL PICTURE

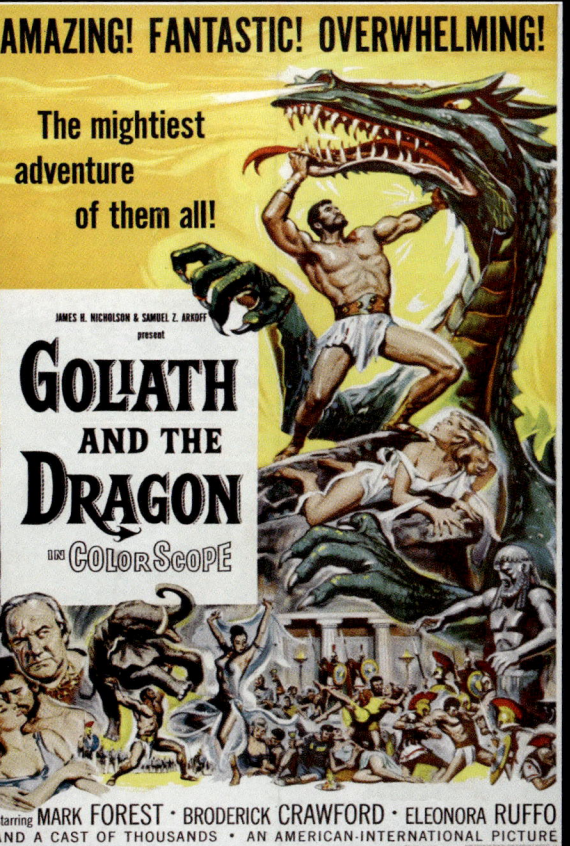

DRAGONS & DINOSAURS

◀ *Die Nibelungen: Siegfried* [Fritz Lang, 1924] Paul Richter as Siegfried bathes in the blood of the dragon he has just slain to make himself invincible. However, a falling leaf lands on his shoulder, leaving one vulnerable spot. The first of the two films Lang made based on the medieval epic poem *The Song of the Nibelungs*.

▼ *Fantasia* [Bill Roberts, Paul Satterfield; *Rite of Spring* Sequence directors, 1940] Walt Disney and conductor Leopold Stokowski's ambitious attempt to bring classical music to the masses, and the first motion picture to ever be released in Stereophonic Sound. To illustrate Igor Stravinsky's *Rite of Spring*, they created a beautifully animated history of the evolution of life on Earth, from amoebas to the extinction of the dinosaurs. A daring and still fascinating work.

◀ *King Kong* [Merian C. Cooper, Ernest B. Schoedsack, 1933] Ann Darrow (Fay Wray), high up in the tree where Kong has put her for safety, looks on as he battles a *T. Rex*. Brilliantly staged, with innovative use of sound effects (by Murray Spivack). A classic sequence from Willis O'Brien's stop-motion tour de force.

▲ **The Land That Time Forgot** [Kevin Connor, 1975] A workmanlike adaptation of Edgar Rice Burroughs' book about a World War I German U-Boat and its captives discovering an island where dinosaurs still roam. This Amicus production used big, clumsy dinosaur suits and full-size props, like this one attacking Doug McClure, for the primeval beasts.

▲ **Unknown Island** [Jack Bernhard, 1948]
Photographed in Cinecolor, this movie used men in ridiculous dinosaur suits. Pictured is a prehistoric giant ape (probably Ray "Crash" Corrigan) who seems to be tickling a *Tyrannosaurus Rex*.

▲ **Ilya Muromets** [aka *The Sword and the Dragon* and *The Epic Hero and the Beast*, Aleksandr Ptushko ,1956] Boris Andreyev as Ilya Muromets about to slay a dragon. Roger Corman recut and dubbed this Russian film and I saw it on television many times as a kid, not knowing exactly what to make of the words not matching the actors' mouth movements. The first Soviet movie shot in CinemaScope.

▶ **The Beast of Hollow Mountain** [Edward Nassour, Ismael Rodríguez, 1956] From a story by Willis O'Brien, who used the name "El Toro Estrella" for his writing credit! This particular shot is too close and clearly shows the cowboy is a puppet. O'Brien did not do the stop-motion animation for this film, which is very similar to his original screenplay *The Valley of the Mist*, later made by O'Brien's protégé Ray Harryhausen as *The Valley of Gwangi* [Jim O'Connolly, 1969].

DRAGONS & DINOSAURS

◀ **Dinosaurus!** [Irvin Yeaworth, 1960] The puppet double for the little boy Julio rides the puppet *apatosaurus* in this dumb movie. Surprisingly, *Dinosaurus!* was photographed by the great Stanley Cortez. Scenes from the film show up in *Schlock* [me, 1973].

▶ **Rodan! The Flying Monster!** [Ishirô Honda, 1956] Ishirô Honda is at it again! Tagline: "The Super-Sonic Hell-Creature No Weapon Could Destroy!" Rodan looks much less like a European dragon than the poster portrays him.

"It's disgraceful to think of putting this fabulous creature on display in a cheap circus."

Professor Bromley (Laurence Naismith) in *The Valley of Gwangi* [1969]

▲ **Jack the Giant Killer** [Nathan H. Juran, 1962] The Kerwin Mathews puppet astride the flying dragon animated by Jim Danforth in this *The 7th Voyage of Sinbad* imitation.

◀ **The Wonderful World of the Brothers Grimm** [Henry Levin, George Pal, 1962] The lovely dragon that terrorizes Buddy Hackett and Terry-Thomas in the "Singing Bone" sequence of this Cinerama movie.

▲ **The Valley of Gwangi** [Jim O'Connolly, 1969] Based on an original, unproduced script by Willis O'Brien, Harryhausen finally realized his mentor's vision and put cowboys and dinosaurs together in the Old West. Here, the captive Gwangi is being transported to be put on public display.

▲ *The Magic Sword* [Bert I. Gordon, 1962] Gordon's best film. But any movie with Basil Rathbone as an evil wizard and Estelle Winwood as a sorceress can't help but be watchable. Gary Lockwood (murdered by HAL in *2001: A Space Odyssey*) as Sir George faces the fire-breathing, two-headed dragon to save Princess Helene (Anne Helm).

▲ *Sleeping Beauty* [Les Clark, Eric Larson, Wolfgang Reitherman, 1959] Prince Phillip faces the fire-breathing dragon that the wicked fairy Maleficent has become. If you visit Disneyland Paris, below the Castle there is a full-size audioanimatronic dragon lurking. Both the Castle and the Dragon are based on the ones in this movie.

▲▶ *Gorgo* [Eugène Lourié, 1961] Lourié seemed to specialize in giant dinosaur pictures, this time it's British. Gorgo's mom is pictured here, trashing London's Tower Bridge.

▲ *Atragon* [aka *Undersea Warship*, Ishirô Honda, 1963] The lost continent of Mu threatens the world, but a Japanese World War II captain has secretly built Atragon, the greatest submarine ever (to rebuild the Japanese Empire) and uses it to fight back against the Empress of Mu. Oh yeah, the submarine is also attacked by a sea serpent. An entertaining and jingoistic Japanese fantasy film with an amazing militaristic score by Akira Ifukube.

◀ *Gamera vs. Barugon* [aka *War of the Monsters*, Shigeo Tanaka, 1966] Gamera is one of the wackier giant Japanese monsters, a gigantic flying turtle! Gamera fights Barugon, a giant lizard who can shoot a "freeze ray" out of his mouth. I love this wild publicity photo.

▲ *The 7th Voyage of Sinbad* [Nathan H. Juran, 1958] The superlative dragon the evil Sokurah (Torin Thatcher) keeps chained to protect his cave. Sinbad (Kerwin Mathews) releases the dragon to fight the Cyclops, but then orders his crew to fire a giant crossbow they've constructed and this beautiful dragon dies on the beach.

DRAGONS & DINOSAURS

▲ *Reptilicus* [Poul Bang, Sidney W. Pink, 1961] Made in Denmark. How they thought the audience would accept the incompetent marionette flailing around an awful miniature Copenhagen I do not know.

> "You swore to all of us that we were not going to harm the dinosaur!"
>
> Wade (Steven Keats), *The Last Dinosaur*

▶ *The Land That Time Forgot* [Kevin Connor, 1975] Not even Doug McClure can save Bobby Parr from being carried off by a rather stiff, full-size, prop pterodactyl in the "lost world" of Caprona.

◀ *The Last Dinosaur* [Alexander Grasshoff, Tsugunobu Kotani, 1977] A Japanese/US coproduction with appalling men-in-dinosaur-suits special effects. Richard Boone plays a big game hunter who… Oh, never mind.

◀ *One Million Years B.C.* [Don Chaffey, 1966] A Mama pterodactyl is about to feed Raquel Welch to her hungry chicks. Ray Harryhausen did the effects in an unusual "work for hire" at this stage of his career.

▶ *Amazon Women on the Moon* [Joe Dante, 1987] Jack the Ripper was really the Loch Ness Monster! A "re-enactment" from the *Bullshit or Not?* segment, starring Henry Silva.

▲ *The Private Life of Sherlock Holmes* [Billy Wilder, 1970] Wilder's bittersweet love letter to Sherlock Holmes. Here, Holmes (Robert Stephens) and Gabrielle Valadon (Geneviève Page) encounter the Loch Ness Monster—actually a disguise for a secret British submersible being tested in the loch. Holmes' brother Mycroft (Christopher Lee) informs Sherlock that the beautiful Gabrielle is notorious German spy Ilse von Hoffmanstal!

▶ *The Water Horse: Legend of the Deep* [Jay Russell, 2007] Based on Dick King-Smith's novel *The Water Horse*. A family film about a boy and his Loch Ness Monster.

▶ **Dragonslayer** [Matthew Robbins, 1981]
Phil Tippett at ILM invented a stop-motion animation technique called "go motion" for the dragon in this fantasy film. With the wonderful Ralph Richardson as Ulrich of Craggenmoor. Ken Ralston designed the flying sequences for the Vermithrax Pejorative, still the most awesome dragon in the movies.

▶ **Q, the Winged Serpent** [Larry Cohen, 1982]
The Aztec god Quetzalcoatl is living at the top of Manhattan's Chrysler Building and grabbing people off of rooftops to eat! Michael Moriarty (an extraordinary performance), plays a petty crook who discovers the monster's lair and wants the city to pay him for the information. Stop-motion animation by David W. Allen and Randy Cook. Another bizzarro movie from Larry that really works.

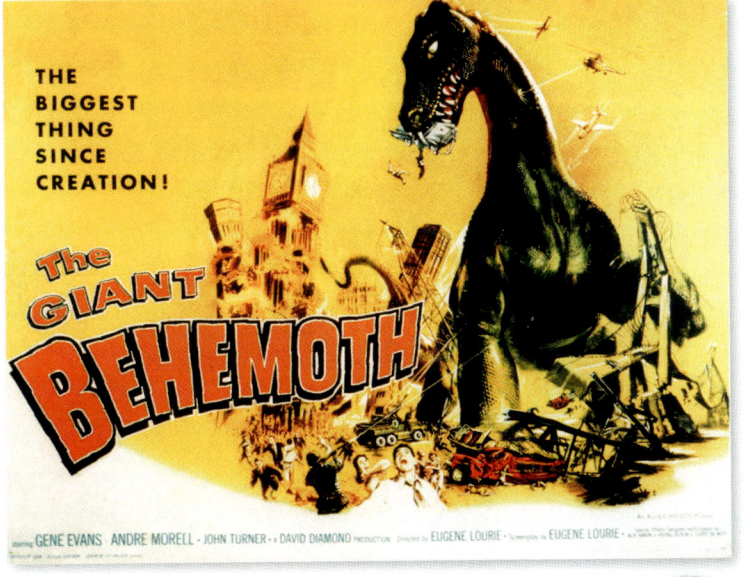

▲ **The Giant Behemoth** [Douglas Hickox, Eugène Lourié, 1959] Willis O'Brien and Pete Peterson did the stop-motion monster in LA, while the production itself was filmed in London. A prehistoric monster swims up the Thames and… Hey, wait a minute… hasn't this been done before?

▶ **The NeverEnding Story** [Wolfgang Petersen, 1984]
Noah Hathaway as Atreyu with Falkor, his flying "luckdragon" (voiced by Alan Oppenheimer). An epic fantasy from the director of *Das Boot* [1981].

> "All major theme parks have had delays. When they opened Disneyland in 1956, nothing worked!"
> "But, John. If the Pirates of the Caribbean breaks down, the pirates don't eat the tourists!"
>
> John Hammond (Richard Attenborough) to
> Dr. Ian Malcom (Jeff Goldblum), *Jurassic Park*

◀ **Jurassic Park** [Steven Spielberg, 1993] One of Stan Winston's dinosaurs up to no good.

◀ **Evolution** [Ivan Reitman, 2001] David Duchovny eyes a dinosaur in the mall in this sci-fi comedy from Ivan Reitman.

▶ **Eragon** [Stefen Fangmeier, 2006] Another talking dragon movie. This one is based on the novel by Christopher Paolini. Rachel Weisz is the voice of Saphiria the dragon.

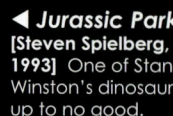

▲ **The Lost World: Jurassic Park** [Steven Spielberg, 1997] The incredible, life-size audioanimatronic *Tyrannosaurus Rex* in the second of the three *Jurassic Park* movies.

▶ **Dragonheart** [Rob Cohen, 1996] Fairy tale foolishness; although Sean Connery's voice is ideal for the voice of Draco, the dragon pictured here, in conversation with knight Dennis Quaid.

▲ **Godzilla** [Roland Emmerich, 1998] Godzilla sniffs Matthew Broderick in this misguided remake.

▲ **Dragon Wars** [aka *D-War*, Shim Hyung-rae, 2007] Korean fantasy, in which a dragon attacks Los Angeles. You could be fooled by the poster into thinking this could be fun. I was.

▶ **Avatar** [James Cameron, 2009] Jake Sully (Sam Worthington) in his Na'vi avatar body riding a Toruk, one of the many fantastic examples of the flora and fauna of Pandora.

▶ **Land of the Lost** [Brad Silberling, 2009] A Will Ferrell comedy vehicle based on the Sid and Marty Krofft children's television series. This action shot makes it look more exciting than it is.

▶ **Alice in Wonderland** [Tim Burton, 2010] The Jabberwocky! "The jaws that bite, the claws that catch!"

▲ **The Mummy: The Tomb of the Dragon Emperor** [Rob Cohen, 2008] One of the sequels to *The Mummy* [1999]. This is the one with the cool-looking, three-headed dragon.

Nature's Revenge

Whether it is rats, spiders, snakes, bees, sharks, or just big old mean dogs, we are all afraid of some animal out there. Movie makers, constantly searching for something to scare us with, have shamelessly taken advantage of our reasonable fears of bee stings, spider bites, and being devoured by sharks, by featuring these and other beasties in horror films.

Producers and directors can take a real creature and make it gigantic, like the crab in *Mysterious Island* [Cy Endfield, 1961] or the spider—"Crawling Terror, 100 Feet High"—in *Tarantula!* [Jack Arnold, 1955], or they can just unleash vast numbers of the critters we dread: bees in *The Swarm* [Irwin Allen, 1978]; or snakes in *Snakes on a Plane* [David R. Ellis, 2006]. If a vast, unstoppable army of ants in *The Naked Jungle* [Byron Haskin, 1954] isn't enough to scare you, then how about the REALLY HUGE ants of *Them!* [Gordon Douglas, 1954] or *Empire of the Ants* [Bert I. Gordon, 1977]? If the rats made you uneasy in *Willard* [Daniel Mann, 1971], schlock producer's logic says that the giant rats in *The Food of the Gods* [Bert I. Gordon, 1976] should *really* make you jump out of your seat.

I can imagine the writer's pitch now: "The great white shark that terrorized the beaches in *Jaws* [Steven Spielberg, 1975] was puny! He just wasn't really that big! How about a Mega Shark?" "Yes! Yes!" shouts the producer. "And he could battle a Giant Octopus!" And that is how *Mega Shark vs. Giant Octopus* [Jack Perez as Ace Hannah, 2009] was born. In that film, the absurdly big Mega Shark destroys San Francisco's famed Golden Gate Bridge, which had obviously been repaired since 1955 when it was heavily damaged by the giant octopus in Ray Harryhausen's *It Came From Beneath the Sea* [Robert Gordon, 1955].

If worms give you the creeps, then the millions of flesh-eating bloodworms in *Squirm* [Jeff Lieberman, 1976] will make you do just what the title says. In *The African Queen* [John Huston, 1951] the audience shared Humphrey Bogart's character's revulsion when he came out of the water covered in leeches. If a few normal-size leeches generated such disgust, then an *Attack of the Giant Leeches* [Bernard L. Kowalski, 1959] is the only way to go.

It isn't always necessary to make something we naturally avoid, like a scorpion, into a colossal version of itself to frighten us. (*The Black Scorpion* [Edward Ludwig, 1957] did that with stop-motion animation by the great Willis O'Brien.) Sometimes a rabid dog [*Cujo*, Lewis Teague, 1983] or just an angry grizzly bear [*Grizzly*, William Girdler, 1976] is enough to terrify us without the use of special effects.

Usually, the giant animal monster is explained by some pseudo-scientific theory: it's a prehistoric beast frozen in ice, or a mutant, created by atomic radiation. The monster is sometimes

▲ *It Came From Beneath the Sea* [Robert Gordon, 1955] To save time animating his stop-motion puppet, Ray Harryhausen gave it only six tentacles—so it was really a giant *hextapus* that pulled down the Golden Gate Bridge.

Previous pages: The Fabulous World of Jules Verne [aka *A Deadly Invention*, Karel Zeman, 1958] Czech filmmaker Karel Zeman's unique blend of live action, stop motion, and drawn animation reproduces the look of 19th-century etchings, which works wonderfully well in this fusion of two Jules Verne novels.
Opposite page: Creature From the Black Lagoon [Jack Arnold, 1954] Julie Adams and the Gill-Man (Ben Chapman) in an unusual color publicity still (the film is black and white).

created by toxic waste or by some covert corporate or government experiment gone terribly wrong. The man-eating piranha in Joe Dante's *Piranha* [1978] are the results of a misguided military experiment, while in the 2010 remake, *Piranha 3D* [Alexandre Aja], the vicious piranha are prehistoric fish freed from an underwater cavern by an earthquake. The change reflects the politics of the era in which each film was made.

Sometimes the reason for nature turning on us is unexplained. When Alfred Hitchcock's *The Birds* [1963] attack and kill, no reason is given for their behavior. The characters speculate on what could be making the birds turn suddenly homicidal, but the movie deliberately offers no solution to the mystery and ends on an uneasy, unresolved note.

Creature From the Black Lagoon [Jack Arnold, 1954] is a classic story of an ancient species destroyed by contact with modern civilization, essentially the plot of the first half of *King Kong* [1933]. The Gill-Man was designed by Millicent Patrick and is considered to be one of the greatest monsters in film history. The celebrated sequence where Julie Adams is swimming on the surface of the lagoon, unaware of the Creature as it swims beneath her, remains one of the most poetic in the genre. A B movie made almost entirely on the back lot of Universal Studios (except for the underwater sequences, shot in the crystal-clear waters of Wakulla Springs, Florida) *Creature From the Black Lagoon* was a great success and is still one of the best 3D movies ever made. Two sequels followed, in which the Gill-Man continued to be abused by the human leads.

▲ *Moby Dick* [John Huston, 1956] Captain Ahab (Gregory Peck) with harpoon in the jaws of the Great White Whale.

Other humanoid, water-based creatures include *The Monster of Piedras Blancas* [Irvin Berwick, 1959], the very silly fish-men of *Horror of Party Beach* [Del Tenney, 1964], and the infamous *Humanoids From the Deep* [Barbara Peeters, 1980]. Infamous because the producer, Roger Corman, had additional scenes shot in which the monsters were shown actually raping the nubile young girls hired to be topless and scream as the slimy fish-men, created by make-up maestro Rob Bottin, had their way with them. And to increase the sleaze factor, the movie ends with one of the rape victims giving birth to a baby fish monster by having it burst through her stomach in a geyser of blood, in blatant imitation of the "chest burster" scene in Ridley Scott's *Alien* [1979].

Underwater is not the only place we will find humanoid monsters—they also come from underground. The scary, carnivorous cave dwellers a group of women encounter in Neil Marshall's *The Descent* [2005] are very nasty indeed. Be warned, this is definitely not a movie for the claustrophobic. Deep in the bowels of the Earth can also be found *The Mole People* [Virgil W. Vogel, 1956], who are used as slave labor by a race of "Sumerian Albinos!"

Another movie that features an insatiable underground threat is Ron Underwood's *Tremors* [1990]. Kevin Bacon and Fred Ward play two contemporary cowboys trying to deal with the huge subterranean monsters they discover in a small town in the Nevada desert. *Tremors* is a textbook example of a well made and entertaining monster movie.

Opposite page: (1) *Mega Shark vs. Giant Octopus* [Ace Hannah, 2009] Mega Shark attacks the Golden Gate Bridge. Followed by *Mega Shark vs. Crocosaurus* [2010] and *Sharktopus* [2010]. What can I say?

(2) *Night of the Lepus* [William F. Claxton, 1972] Giant rabbits attack a small town in Arizona. Harebrained.

(3) *Jaws* [Steven Spielberg, 1975] Chief Brody (Roy Scheider) in his final confrontation with the monstrous great white shark in Spielberg's summer blockbuster.

1

2

There was no limit to the Horror...
NO END TO THE
NIGHT OF THE LEPUS
MGM PRESENTS "NIGHT OF THE LEPUS" STARRING STUART WHITMAN · JANET LEIGH · RORY CALHOUN
SCREENPLAY BY DON HOLLIDAY AND GENE R. KEARNEY · BASED UPON THE NOVEL "THE YEAR OF THE ANGRY RABBIT"
BY RUSSELL BRADDON · PRODUCED BY A. C. LYLES · DIRECTED BY WILLIAM F. CLAXTON · METROCOLOR

3

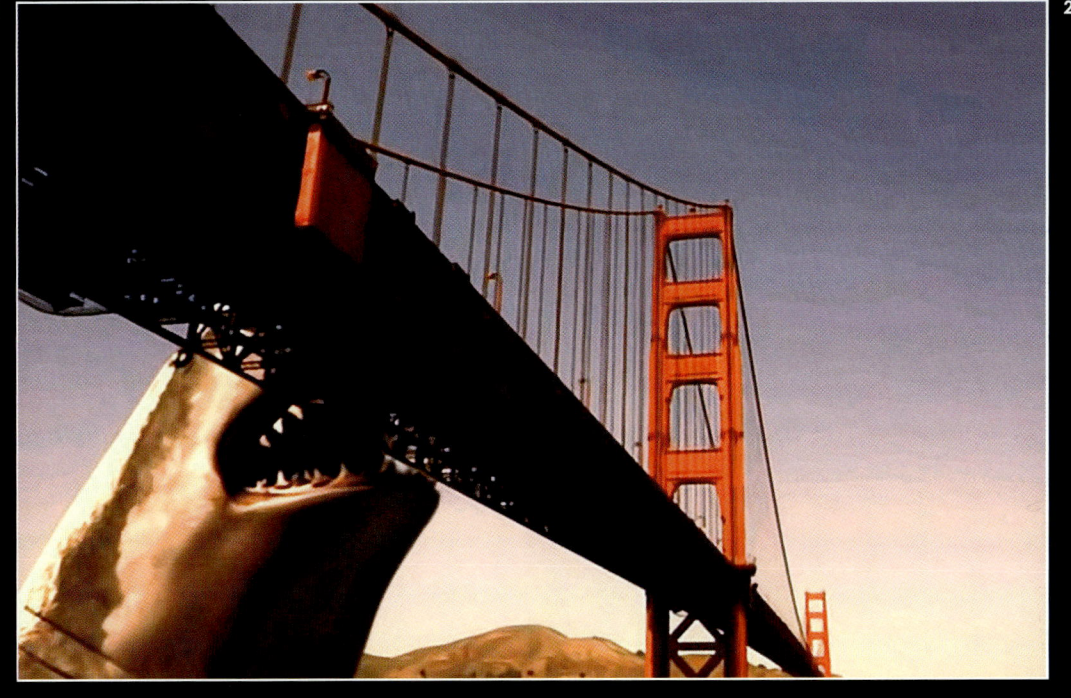

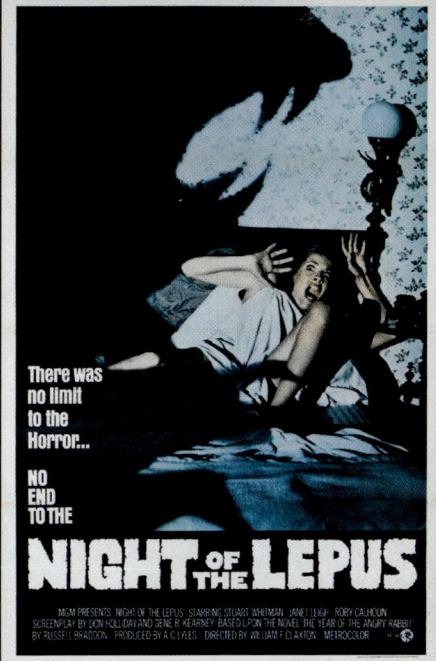

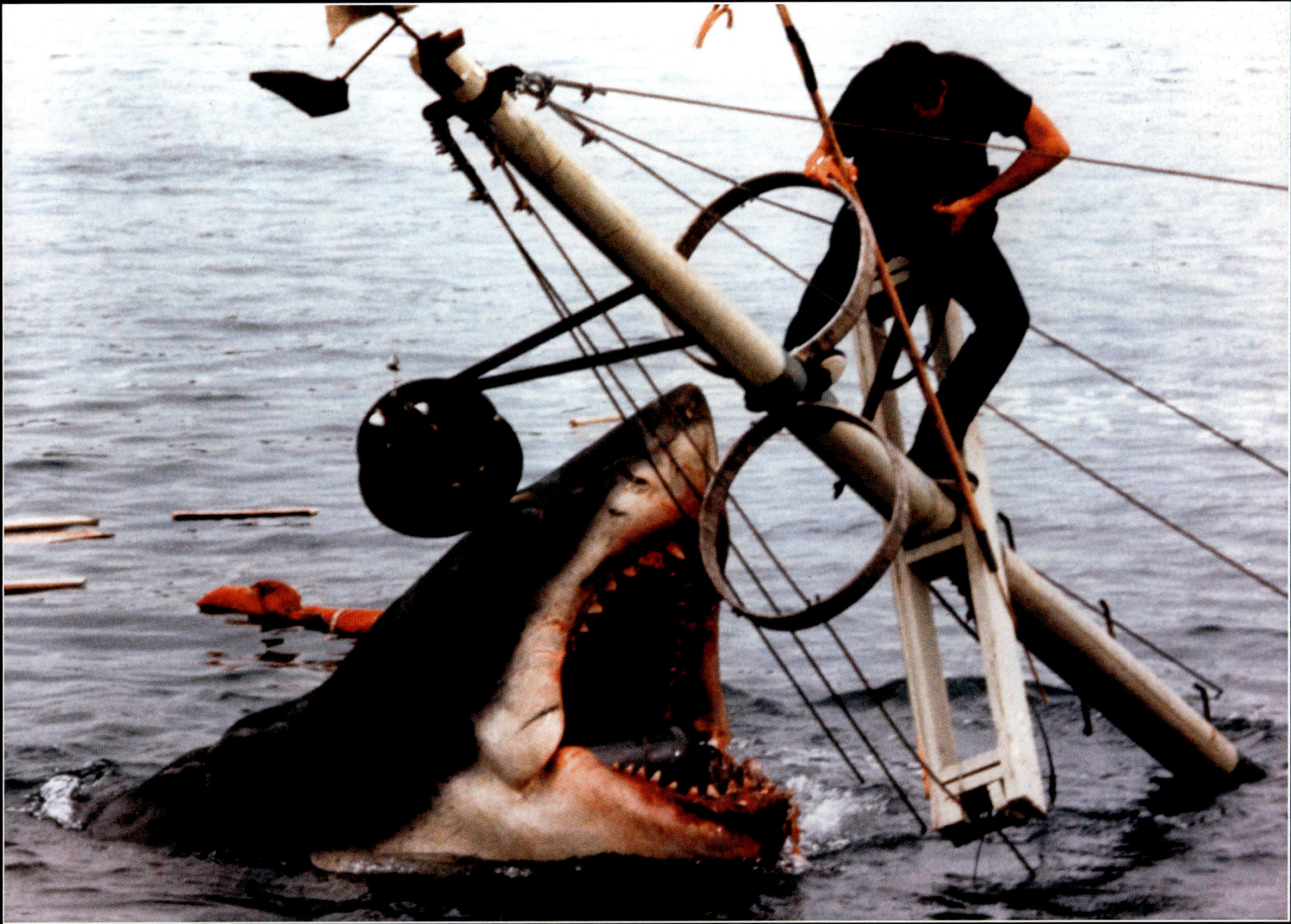

NATURE'S REVENGE

HUMANOIDS

"There are many strange legends in the Amazon. Even I, Lucas, have heard the legend of a man-fish."

Lucas (Nestor Paiva),
Creature from the Black Lagoon

▲ **Creature From the Black Lagoon** [Jack Arnold, 1954] Ben Chapman as the Gill-man on stage at Universal Studios. Ricou Browning played the Gill-man in all of the underwater sequences.

◀ **Humanoids From the Deep** [Barbara Peeters, 1980] A New World Pictures exploitation creature-feature.

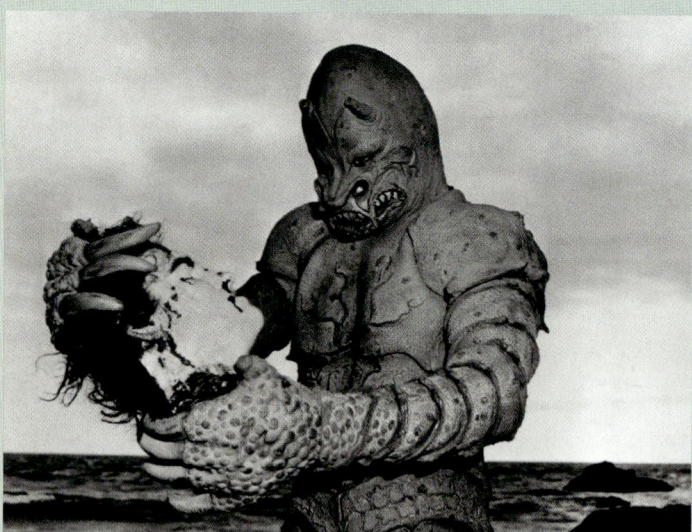

▲ **The Monster of Piedras Blancas** [Irvin Berwick, 1959] A lighthouse keeper leaves food for a sea creature. This turns out to be a mistake.

▶ **The Beach Girls and the Monster** [aka *Monster from the Surf*, Jon Hall, 1965] A mutated South American "Fantigua Fish" monster starts killing surfers and their girlfriends.

▲ **The Mole People** [Virgil W. Vogel, 1956] Archaeologists discover a race of Sumerian albinos that live underground and use humanoid Mole Men as slaves to harvest their primary food source—mushrooms!

▲ **Octaman** [Harry Essex, 1976] This photograph tells you everything you need to know about *Octaman*. Early Rick Baker.

▲ **SSSSSSS** [Bernard L. Kowalski, 1973] Mad ophiologist Dr. Stoner (Strother Martin) injects snake venom into his daughter's boyfriend, which transforms him into a malformed, half-man, half-snake.

◀ **The Bat People** [Jerry Jameson, 1974] A doctor on vacation with his wife visits Carlsbad Caverns and is bitten by a bat. He soon finds himself transforming into a vampire bat man!

▲ **The Descent** [Neil Marshall, 2005] Six women go spelunking and encounter terrifying, subterranean, flesh-eating humanoids in this claustrophobic, scary movie.

NATURE'S REVENGE

▲ **Mysterious Island** [Cy Endfield, 1961] The castaways fight a giant crab on Captain Nemo's island. Ray Harryhausen animated an actual crab shell purchased at Harrods Food Hall in London.

▶ **Attack of the Giant Leeches** [Bernard L. Kowalski, 1959] Deep in the swamps of the Florida Everglades, a giant leech attacks another victim.

▲ **The Naked Jungle** [Byron Haskin, 1954] Charlton Heston struggles to save a Peruvian cocoa plantation from the "Marabunta"—millions of voracious army ants.

▶ **The Birds** [Alfred Hitchcock, 1963] Melanie Daniels (Tippi Hedren) runs from another unexplained bird attack. Based on the novella by Daphne du Maurier.

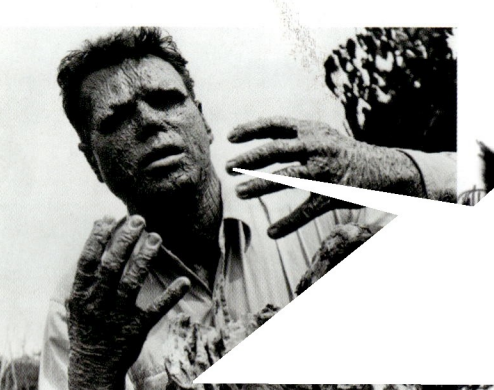

▲ **The Alligator People** [Roy Del Ruth, 1959] Strange goings-on in the bayou, as Beverly Garland locates her missing husband and discovers that he is metamorphosing into half-man, half-alligator!

Eight-Legged Terrors

▲ **The Incredible Shrinking Man** [Jack Arnold, 1957]
Growing ever smaller, Scott Carey (Grant Williams) uses a nail as a spear to defend himself from a common household spider.

"In my hunt for food, I had become the hunted."

Scott Carey (Grant Williams),
The Incredible Shrinking Man

▲ **Tarantula!** [Jack Arnold, 1955] The tremendous tarantula in the movie never holds a woman as illustrated here in the ad art. It was not unusual for exploitation picture promotional art to exaggerate.

▶ **Kingdom of the Spiders** [John Cardos, 1977]
Pesticides have killed off their normal insect diet, so the tarantulas of Verde Valley begin to attack in large numbers to bring down bigger prey.

▲ **Arachnid** [Jack Sholder, 2001]
Bad enough their plane crashed, now they're being attacked by giant spiders!

▶ **Eight Legged Freaks**
[Ellory Elkayem, 2002]
Toxic waste creates giant spiders, yet again. The CG spiders look creepy, but the movie is not.

NATURE'S REVENGE

◀ **Day of the Animals** [William Girdler, 1977] Depletion of the ozone layer causes every animal above 5,000 feet to go crazy. Bad news for hikers in a forest in Northern California.

▶ **Grizzly** [aka *Killer Grizzly*, William Girdler, 1976] Identical in plot to *Jaws*, but with an 18-foot-tall grizzly bear instead of a great white shark.

"My God, look at the rats!"

Mr. Martin (Ernest Borgnine), *Willard* [1971]

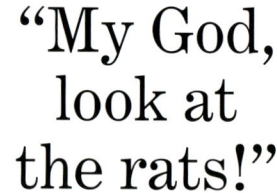

◀ **Willard** [Daniel Mann, 1971] A lonely young man is unable to kill the rats in the basement. Soon, they do his bidding. Based on the novel *The Ratman's Notebooks* by Stephen Gilbert.

▲ **Willard** [Glen Morgan, 2003] A remake of the 1971 film with Crispin Glover in the Bruce Davison role. This has none of the pathos of the original and suffers from the lack of Elsa Lanchester and Ernest Borgnine.

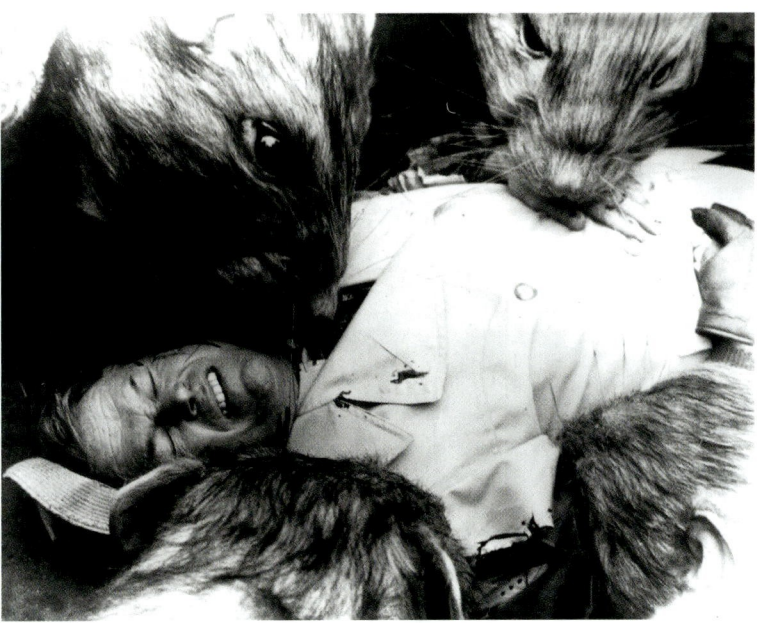

▲ **The Food of the Gods** [Bert I. Gordon, 1976] Ralph Meeker is eaten by giant rats in this low-rent and very loose adaptation of H. G. Wells' novel *The Food of the Gods and How It Came to Earth* [1904].

▲ **The Savage Bees** [Bruce Geller, 1976] A swarm of African killer bees comes ashore off a ship in New Orleans and just about ruins Mardi Gras!

Bee Stings

◀ **Empire of the Ants** [Bert I. Gordon, 1977] A toxic spill turns ordinary ants into intelligent, rampaging monsters, bent on conquering mankind. Another Bert I. Gordon trashing of an H. G. Wells story.

◀ **The Deadly Bees** [Freddie Francis, 1967] A British pop star takes a vacation on Seagull Island, where a beekeeper has specially bred bees to attack and kill.

▶ **Mysterious Island** [Cy Endfield, 1961] Michael Callan and Beth Rogan are about to be sealed up in a honeycomb by a giant bee.

"This is more than a movie. It's a prediction!"

Publicity tagline for *The Swarm*

▲ **The Bees** [Alfredo Zacharias, 1978] Gigantic swarms of South American killer bees attack North America. Not only that, "They prey on HUMAN FLESH!"

◀ **The Swarm** [Irwin Allen, 1978] Olivia de Havilland wonders how her career ever came to this. Henry Fonda and Michael Caine are also in this ridiculous Irwin Allen movie.

NATURE'S REVENGE

▲ **Piranha** [Joe Dante, 1978] "Operation Razorteeth," a covert Vietnam War research project, ends up creating the menace for New World Pictures' jump onto the *Jaws* bandwagon.

◄ **Mysterious Island** [Lucien Hubbard, 1929] Undersea creatures crowd around the unconscious Lionel Barrymore, in the first movie version of Jules Verne's sequel to *20,000 Leagues Under the Sea*.

▲ **Deep Blue Sea** [Renny Harlin, 1999] Searching for a cure for Alzheimer's disease, scientists increase the brain capacity of three mako sharks, making them—in the words of the movie's tagline—"Bigger. Smarter. Faster. Meaner." Things go awry for the scientists.

▲ **Leviathan** [George Cosmatos, 1988] Deep water miners deal with an undersea monster that is determined to eat them.

▲ **Lake Placid** [Steve Miner, 1999] A huge crocodile causes trouble in a lake in Maine. This movie got a decidedly mixed reaction but still spawned two sequels.

Calamari!

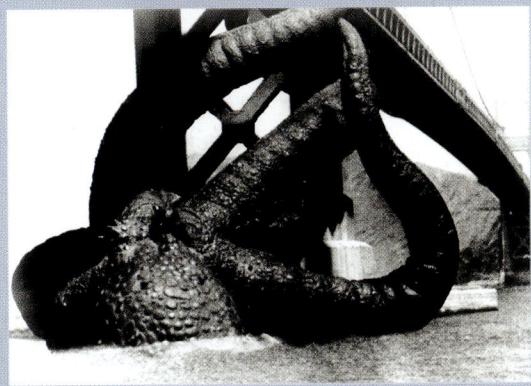

▲ **It Came From Beneath the Sea**
[Robert Gordon, 1955] A gigantic octopus destroys the Golden Gate Bridge in this Ray Harryhausen thriller.

▲ **20,000 Leagues Under the Sea** [Richard Fleischer, 1954] Ned Land (Kirk Douglas) and Captain Nemo (James Mason, in white sweater) battle a giant squid in Walt Disney's first major live-action picture.

▶ **Monster From the Ocean Floor** [Wyott Ordung, 1954] A one-eyed sea monster terrorizes Mexico. "Up from the forbidden depths comes a Tidal Wave of Terror!"

▶ **Tentacles** [Ovidio G. Assonitis, 1997] A giant octopus starts eating tourists in Ocean Beach, much to John Huston, Shelley Winters, and Henry Fonda's chagrin.

▶ **Octopus** [John Eyres, 2000] A Soviet nuclear submarine sinks off of the coast of Cuba during the Cuban Missile Crisis. The subsequent radiation leak creates a gigantic, mutant octopus, which promptly sinks passing ships.

NATURE'S REVENGE

Snakes!

◀ **Raiders of the Lost Ark** [Steven Spielberg, 1981] Indiana Jones (Harrison Ford) has only one phobia—he hates snakes!

▲ **Stanley** [William Grefe, 1972] A young Seminole Indian uses rattlesnakes to get revenge on those who have wronged him.

▲ **Jaws of Satan** [aka *King Cobra*, Bob Claver, 1981] Satan takes the form of a giant snake in this silly movie.

▲ **Snakes on a Plane** [David R. Ellis, 2006] The passengers and crew are not happy about snakes on the plane.

▲ **Anaconda** [Luis Llosa, 1997] An insane hunter enlists a film crew to help him find and trap the biggest snake in the Amazon.

▶ **Piranha 3D** [Alexandre Aja, 2010] Spring Break brings lots of college co-eds in bikinis—and out of bikinis—to be eaten by prehistoric piranhas in 3D!

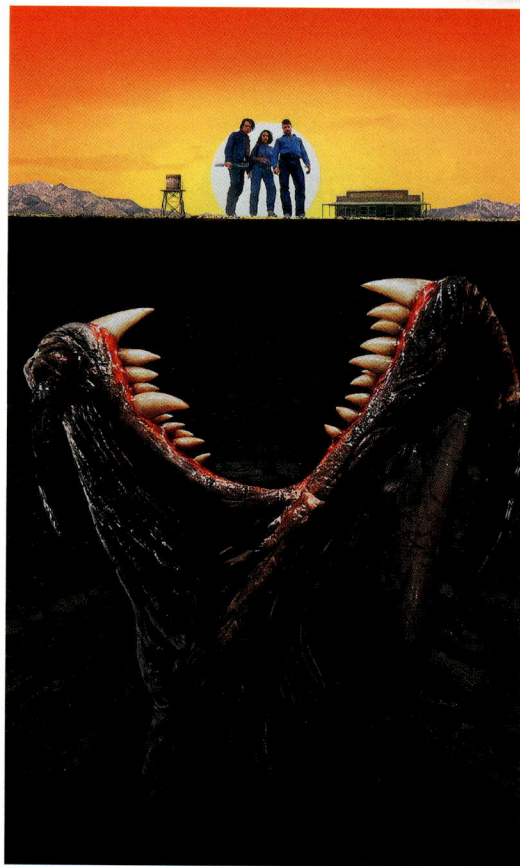

▲ **Tremors** [Ron Underwood, 1990] A very entertaining movie about two modern cowboys (Kevin Bacon and Fred Ward) coping with big underground monsters in the Nevada desert.

◄ *Squirm* [Jeff Lieberman, 1976]
A storm knocks down high power lines, sending electricity into the ground. For some reason, this causes thousands of bloodworms to attack humans. This actor is actually covered in thousands of real bloodworms, which is not dangerous, but is pretty gross.

► *Cujo* [Lewis Teague, 1983]
A rabid St. Bernard is enough to generate real chills in this suspenseful adaptation of the book by the prolific Stephen King.

▲ *Frankenfish* [Mark Dippé, 2004] "Genetic engineering" turns normal snakehead fish into enormous monsters, killing people in the bayou.

Space Monsters

There are monsters *from* outer space who come to the planet Earth to be in our movies [*Invaders From Mars*, William Cameron Menzies, 1953] and then there are monsters *in* outer space whom we send rocket ships to encounter [*The Green Slime*, Kinji Fukasaku, 1968]. There are aliens who come to Earth to *befriend* us [*Close Encounters of the Third Kind*, Steven Spielberg, 1977], there are aliens who come to Earth to *warn* us [*The Day the Earth Stood Still*, Robert Wise, 1951—I refuse to mention the remake!], and there are aliens who come to Earth to *destroy* us [*Mars Attacks!*, Tim Burton, 1996].

Most movie aliens want to destroy us. Howard Hawks produced one of the best scary alien-who-wants-us-dead movies, *The Thing from Another World* [Christian Nyby, 1951], a taut thriller based on the disturbing short story by John W. Campbell, Jr. *Who Goes There?*. When remade in 1982 as *John Carpenter's The Thing*, Bill Lancaster's screenplay stayed much closer to the Campbell story and Carpenter, with the aid of the extraordinary make-up effects of Rob Bottin, created a truly horrific and suspenseful classic. *The Thing* has one of my favorite lines in a monster movie: When one of the characters sees another character's decapitated head grow crab-like legs and skitter across the floor, he says, "You've got to be fucking kidding me!" Which, in context, is an extremely realistic reaction. Two years later *John Carpenter's Starman* [1984] landed on our planet with a sensitive performance by Jeff Bridges in the title role. Almost as if to make up for the ferocity of *The Thing*, *Starman*'s alien is so handsome, sweet, and charming, lovely Karen Allen falls in love with him.

Pioneering French special-effects filmmaker Georges Méliès probably made the first outer space movie with his silent version of Jules Verne's *A Trip to the Moon* in 1902. Méliès combined Verne's novel with H. G. Wells' novel *The First Men in the Moon* and brought us cinema's first aliens—the insectoid Selenites. This film is most famous for its iconic image of the Man in the Moon with a rocket ship stuck in his eye! Sixty-two years later, Ray Harryhausen gave us another version of H. G. Wells' *First Men in the Moon* [Nathan H. Juran, 1964] with remarkably similar-looking Selenites. The charming screenplay by Nigel Kneale adds an opening sequence in which modern-day astronauts discover a tattered Union Jack, left behind by the intrepid explorers who had set foot on the moon when Queen Victoria was still on the throne!

▲ *Le Voyage dans la lune* [aka *A Trip to the Moon*, Georges Méliès, 1902] One of the first, if not *the* first, sci-fi movies, this image of the rocket ship stuck in the Moon's eye is unforgettable.

For every benign alien visitor, there are 50 hostile ones. And we Earthlings almost always greet our guests from space with suspicion and gunfire—like the Ymir in Ray Harryhausen's *20 Million Miles to Earth* [Nathan H. Juran, 1957], which is brought back from Venus as an egg. The rocket ship splashes down off the coast of Sicily, the egg hatches, and the alien creature is eventually gunned down atop Rome's Coliseum.

One of the greatest of all space monsters appears in *Forbidden Planet* [Fred M. Wilcox, 1956]. A lavish MGM production, with glorious Technicolor cinematography by George Folsey, and the first all-electronic score by avant-garde musicians Louis and Bebe Barron, this is one of the

Previous pages: *This Island Earth* [Joseph M. Newman, 1955] A Metaluna Mutant checks out his looks on a sound stage mirror before being filmed. Based on the novel by Raymond F. Jones, this is an exciting science-fiction film in glorious Technicolor.
Opposite page: *The Green Slime* [aka *Gamma 3: Operation Outer Space*, Kinji Fukasaku, 1968] Shot at Tokyo's Toei Studios with an entirely Caucasian cast. Luciana Paluzzi is pictured being harassed by one of the Green Slime. With a great title song!

most influential science-fiction films ever made. William Shakespeare's *The Tempest* inspired the screenplay by Cyril Hume and, although some of the costumes and dialog are dated, the ideas expressed are startlingly modern. Dr. Morbius (Walter Pidgeon) with his beautiful daughter Alta (Anne Francis) are the only survivors of a colony of settlers on the planet Altair. A rescue mission led by Commander John J. Adams (Leslie Nielsen) discovers that the two survivors are doing well, Dr. Morbius having learned much about the planet's former inhabitants the Krell and their amazing technology. But Alta's innocent sexual curiosity about the handsome men who have come to rescue them disturbs her father. A terrible, invisible monster kills several of the crew. It is an awesome sight, revealed only in outline by the crew's neutron-beam weaponry. Eventually, Dr. Morbius reveals the terrible secret of the Krell's disappearance... This splendid movie is clearly the template for the television series *Star Trek* and all of its sequels and prequels.

Two years after the release of *Forbidden Planet*, a meteor crashes down near the small town of Phoenixville, Pennsylvania. A red substance attacks an old man named Doc. Steve McQueen, in his first starring role, tries to convince the police of what he witnessed: "Something" was killing the Doc! The "something" turns out to be *The Blob* [Irvin Yeaworth, 1958], a gelatinous goo that grows larger as it consumes more and more victims. This quintessential 1950s sci-fi movie features a wonderfully loony cha-cha-cha title song by Burt Bacharach and Mack David.

Ridley Scott's seminal *Alien* [1979] revitalized the genre by placing a monster in an Old Dark House in outer space. Swiss artist H. R. Giger designed the creature, combining organic and mechanical elements in a truly original way. Dan O'Bannon's screenplay is rife with cliché, but Scott's stylish direction and a fine cast overcome the silliness and create a handsome, truly scary film. The wreckage of an alien spacecraft they find on another planet comes directly from Mario Bava's excellent *Planet of the Vampires* [1965], and once the alien is loose aboard the space ship *Nostromo*, *Alien* basically follows the storyline of *It! The Terror From Beyond Space* [Edward L. Cahn, 1958] a low-budget picture featuring Ray "Crash" Corrigan in a rubber monster suit.

Alien was a worldwide sensation and it was followed by James Cameron's *Aliens* in 1986, which brilliantly swapped horror for full-on action and made Sigourney Weaver's character Ripley into a feminist icon.

▲ **Le Voyage dans la lune** [aka *A Trip to the Moon*, Georges Méliès, 1902] One of the Selenites (the Moon's insectoid inhabitants) tries to prevent the humans' rocket ship from escaping.

John McTiernan's *Predator* [1987] was a vehicle for Arnold Schwarzenegger, then at the height of his stardom. But the wonderfully designed Predator, an alien big-game hunter on Earth for sport, was far too interesting to disappear after just one movie. Sequels followed until, in 2004, *Alien vs. Predator* [Paul W. S. Anderson] attempted to become a contemporary *Frankenstein Meets the Wolf Man* [Roy William Neill, 1943]. I'm sure that if Abbott and Costello were still alive, they too would have eventually met the Predator and the Alien!

Roland Emmerich's *Independence Day* [1996] and 2011's *Battle: Los Angeles* [Jonathan Liebesman] clearly demonstrate that our planet is still not safe from alien invasion; however 2011 also brought us another gentle (if foulmouthed) alien in *Paul* [Greg Mottola]. So I think it's wise to remember the last words broadcast from that Arctic station at the end of *The Thing From Another World* [1951]: "Watch the Skies!"

Opposite page: (1) *The Blob* [Irvin Yeaworth, 1958] The quintessential 1950s teenage creature feature. The jelly-like goo from a meteorite is growing larger with each human it consumes! Can nothing stop it? **(2)** *The Blob* [Chuck Russell, 1988] A remake of the 1958 classic, with the addition of villainous government operatives and better special effects. **(3)** *Paul* [Greg Mottola, 2011] Two English sci-fi geeks (Simon Pegg and Nick Frost) embark on a road trip across the US and have a close encounter of the third kind with an alien slacker (voiced by Seth Rogan) who is being pursued by mysterious government agents. **(4)** *20 Million Miles to Earth* [Nathan H. Juran, 1957] A spaceship returning from Venus crashes into the sea off the coast of Sicily bringing with it the Ymir, one of Ray Harryhausen's most unique creations.

1

INDESCRIBABLE...
INDESTRUCTIBLE!
NOTHING CAN STOP IT!
THE BLOB
STEVEN McQUEEN ANETA CORSEAUT · EARL ROWE
PRODUCED BY JACK H. HARRIS · DIRECTED BY IRVIN S. YEAWORTH, JR. · SCREENPLAY BY THEODORE SIMONSON AND KATE PHILLIPS

2

3

4

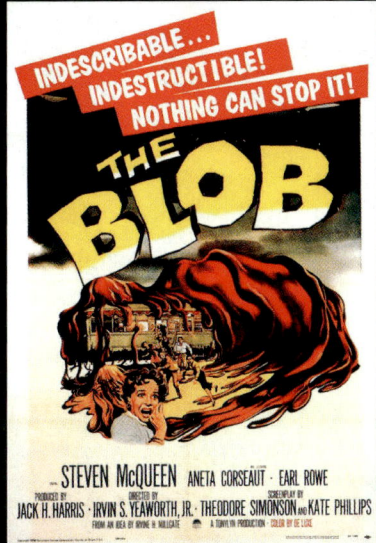

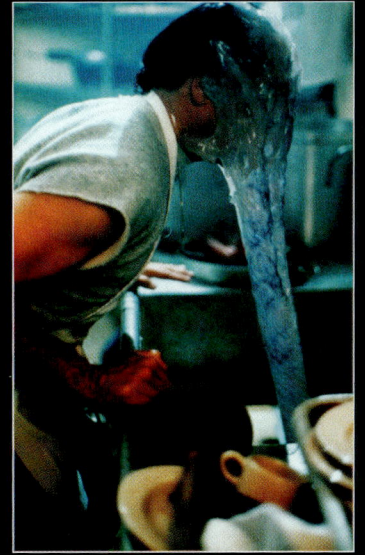

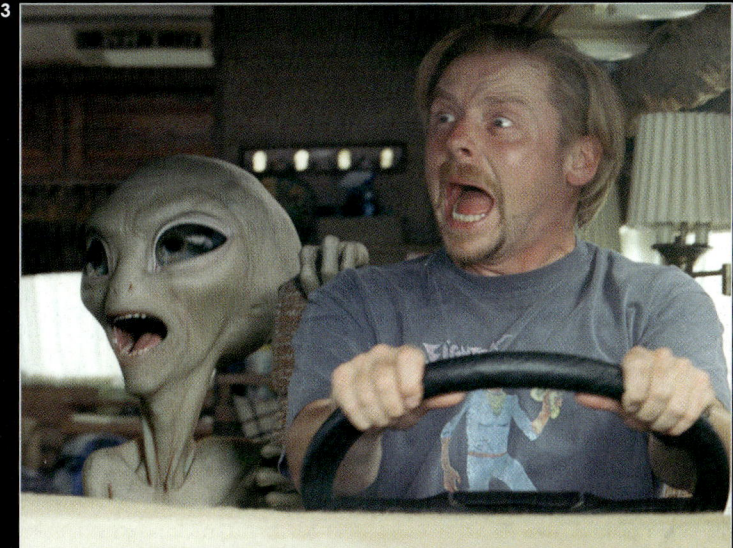

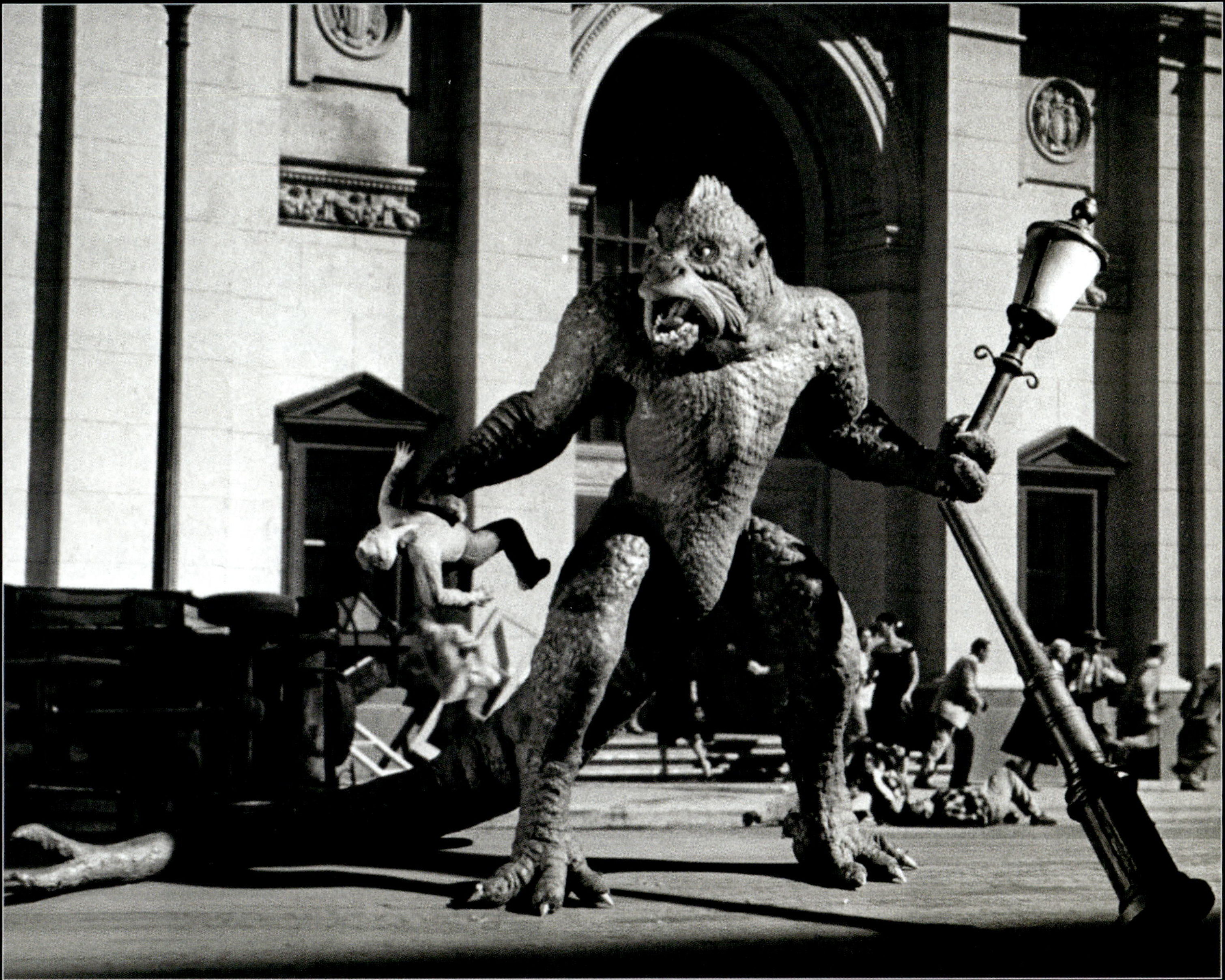

SPACE MONSTERS

▲ *Flash Gordon* [Frederick Stephani, 1936] Charles B. Middleton as Ming the Merciless, ruler of the planet Mongo in the 13 exciting episodes of this popular serial. Buster Crabbe starred as Flash Gordon.

▲ *Flash Gordon* [Mike Hodges, 1980] Max von Sydow as Ming in Dino De Laurentiis' big-budget, campy remake. Sam J. Jones is Flash and the wonderful Ornella Muti is the insatiable Princess Aura. With a memorable score by Queen.

▶ *Invaders From Mars* [William Cameron Menzies, 1953] A tightly constructed, nightmarish scenario, in which all the authority figures—teachers, policemen, even your parents—are working for the Martians! The ending completely freaked me out when I was a child.

◀ *This Island Earth* [Joseph M. Newman, 1955] Alien scientists request help for their doomed world. Great special effects on the dying planet. And the Metaluna Mutant!

▼ *Monsters vs. Aliens* [Rob Letterman, Conrad Vernon, 2009] Benzoate Ostylezene Bicarbonate or B.O.B., is the result of a genetic experiment with a tomato gone wrong. However, he does look a lot like the alien in *It Came From Outer Space* (far left) but blue and with arms. Voiced by Seth Rogan.

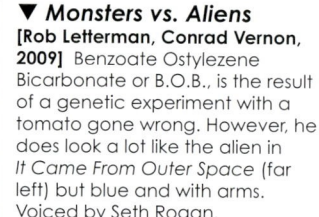

▲▶ *It Came From Outer Space* [Jack Arnold, 1953] Richard Carlson stands in front of an alien craft that has crashed into the desert. In 3D! This frightening, one-eyed alien (right) turns out to be benign. From an original screen story by Ray Bradbury.

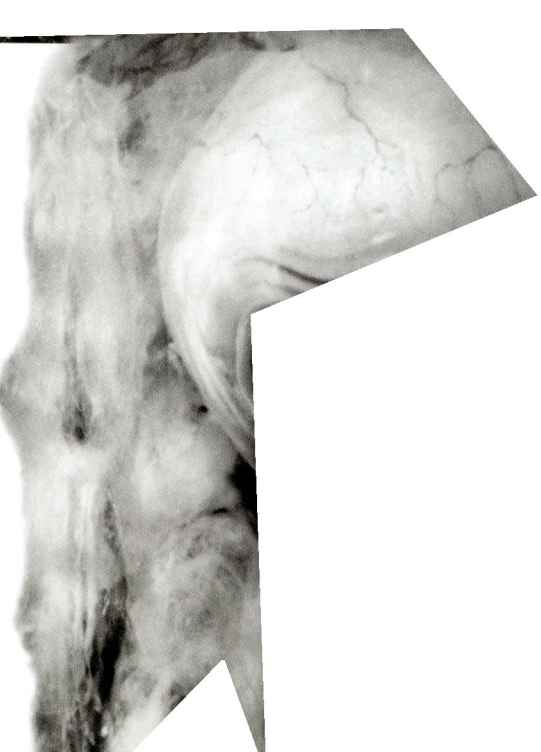

▲ **The Thing From Another World** [aka *The Thing*, Christian Nyby, 1951] Generally assumed to have been directed by producer Howard Hawks, this taut suspense thriller about a group of soldiers and scientists in the Arctic who find something in the ice is a bona fide classic.

▶ **I Married a Monster From Outer Space** [Gene Fowler Jr., 1958] A young bride notices her new husband is acting strangely. A much better movie than the title would lead you to believe.

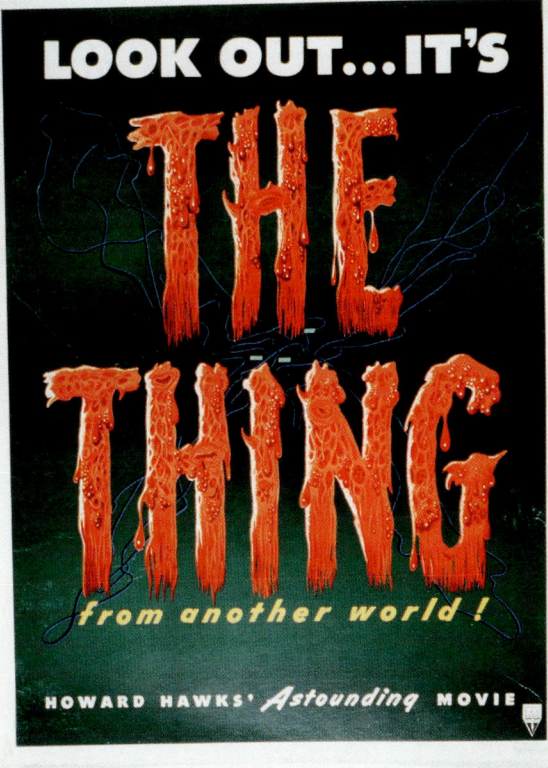

▲ **The Thing From Another World** [Christian Nyby, 1951] The indelible ad art for *The Thing*. George A. Romero once described this film as "a movie about doors," because you are never sure what is lurking behind each one.

▲ **The Thing** [aka *John Carpenter's The Thing*, 1982] Bill Lancaster's screenplay and Rob Bottin's astonishing make-up effects, coupled with Carpenter's dynamite direction, make this picture a modern classic.

SPACE MONSTERS

Forbidden Planet

▶ **Forbidden Planet** [Fred M. Wilcox, 1956] Ad art showing Walter Pidgeon as Dr. Edward Morbius, Leslie Nielsen as Commander John J. Adams, Robby the Robot, and Anne Francis as Altaira, Morbius' beautiful daughter.

▲ **The War of the Worlds** [Byron Haskin, 1953] The Martian war machines attack. The Martians even destroy Los Angeles City Hall! A George Pal Production, based on the classic novel by H. G. Wells. Inset: A close-up of a Martian, surprised in a barn by Gene Barry and Ann Robinson.

◀▼ **An original pencil drawing** on a CinemaScope-size paper cell of the Monster from the Id by animator Joshua Meador and how it looked in the movie (below). The Id Monster becomes visible when lasers are fired at it by the spaceship's crew. (From the collection of Bob Burns.)

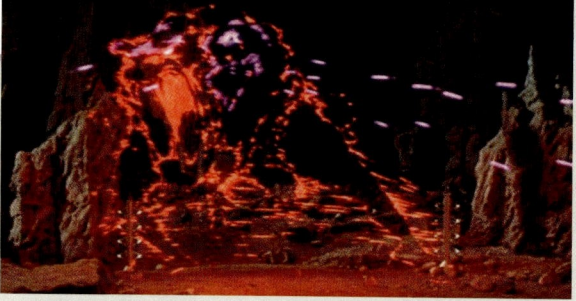

▼ **Dr. Morbius** realizes to his horror that the thing coming to kill them is in fact his own subconscious made real by the technology of the Krell. Anne Francis looks on in both love and fear. A great moment in a great movie.

> "My evil self is outside that door, and I have no power to stop it!"
>
> Dr. Morbius (Walter Pidgeon), *Forbidden Planet*

▲ **War of the Worlds** [Steven Spielberg, 2002] The Martian war machines look more like the ones described in Wells' novel in Spielberg's remake, starring Tom Cruise.

▲ **Invasion of the Saucer Men** [Edward L. Cahn, 1957]
The police refuse to believe the teenagers who claim to see little green men in this drive-in movie. More preposterous monsters from make-up man Paul Blaisdell.

"YOU'RE NEXT!"

Dr. Miles J. Bennell (Kevin McCarthy), *Invasion of the Body Snatchers* [1956]

▲ **Invasion of the Body Snatchers** [Philip Kaufman, 1978]
Donald Sutherland is driving in San Francisco when Kevin McCarthy frantically pounds on his windshield trying to warn him—22 years after we last saw him on the highway at the end of the original film!

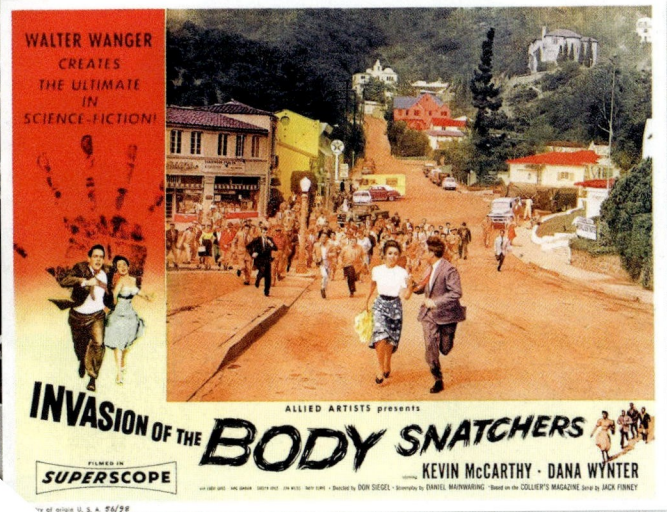

▲▶ **Invasion of the Body Snatchers** [Don Siegel, 1956] Kevin McCarthy, Dana Wynter, and King Donovan regard the pod that is forming into a replica of Donovan in Don Siegel's outstanding film. An examination of conformity, paranoia, and loss of humanity, *Invasion of the Body Snatchers* is an important American film.

SPACE MONSTERS

▲ *The Angry Red Planet* [Ib Melchior, 1959] In "Cinemagic"—which was essentially solarized black and white footage in this Eastmancolor movie. This movie frightened me when I saw it in a theater when I was nine years old. I watched it again recently. If you're older than nine, don't bother.

▲ *Little Shop of Horrors* [Roger Corman, 1960] A small potted plant demands human flesh and starts to grow. Famously shot in two days, this is a funny, genuinely offbeat comedy. Charles B. Griffith wrote the script, but it's hard to believe that the gifted Mel Welles did not ad-lib some of his lines. With Jonathan Haze, Jackie Joseph, Dick Miller, and a young Jack Nicholson as the perfect patient.

"FEED ME!"

Audrey Jr., the carnivorous plant, *Little Shop of Horrors* [1960]

▼ *The Quatermass Xperiment* [aka *The Creeping Unknown*, Val Guest, 1953] Based on the 1953 BBC television serial *The Quatermass Experiment* by Nigel Kneale. American movie star Brian Donlevy was imported by Hammer to play Professor Quatermass. Richard Wordsworth (great-great grandson of the poet William Wordsworth), gives a stunning and tragic performance as the astronaut infected while in Outer Space who slowly becomes an alien monster back in London.

▶ *Little Shop of Horrors* [Frank Oz, 1986] A hit off-Broadway musical by Howard Ashman and Alan Menken, based on Roger Corman's film, made back into a movie by Frank Oz. With Ellen Greene in the role she originated on stage, Rick Moranis, Steve Martin, Bill Murray, and the wonderful Levi Stubbs as the voice of the hungry plant, Audrey 2.

▲ *Journey to the Seventh Planet* [Sidney W. Pink, 1962] On a trip to Uranus (the seventh planet in our solar system), the astronauts have strange dreams. Shot in Denmark, with the same crew that had just made *Reptilicus* [Poul Bang, Sidney W. Pink, 1961], one of the worst movies I ever paid to see in a cinema.

Space Babes

▲ **Cat Women on the Moon** [Arthur Hilton, 1953] Astronaut Sonny Tufts leads an expedition to the Moon where they find a race of beautiful women. Another movie with a marvelous title you can avoid. A young, "gray listed" Elmer Bernstein wrote the score.

▲ **It Conquered the World** [Roger Corman, 1956] Beverly Garland looks askance at another silly looking Paul Blaisdell creation. This monster from Venus is using scientist Lee Van Cleef to take over the world!

▲ **Devil Girl From Mars** [David MacDonald, 1954] Nyah (Patricia Laffan) comes to Earth looking for men to repopulate her planet. Mostly remembered for Nyah's black vinyl outfit.

▲ **Queen of Outer Space** [Edward Bernds, 1958] Eric Fleming and his crew land on Venus to find that mean Queen Ylana (Laurie Mitchell) has banished all men from her planet. Talleah (Zsa Zsa Gabor) and her friends plot to overthrow the Queen and get some men back into their lives. Just as good as it sounds.

▲ **The Day of the Triffids** [Steve Sekely, 1962] Broadway musical star Howard Keel stars in this movie based on John Wyndham's novel. After a spectacular meteor shower blinds everyone who witnesses it, alien plants that can uproot themselves and eat people are on the loose! I loved this movie when I saw it as a kid, but I am afraid to revisit it now for fear of being disappointed.

▶ **Barbarella** [Roger Vadim, 1968] Based on the sexy comic strip by Jean-Claude Forest, Vadim's pop art film stars his then wife Jane Fonda during her sex-kitten period. Her weightless striptease under the titles is a highlight. Typical title song lyric: "Barbarella-Psychedella..." A movie very much of its time.

SPACE MONSTERS

▲ *Yog, Monster From Space* [aka *Space Amoeba*, Ishirô Honda, 1970]
A spaceship is boarded by a strange alien amoeba that takes control of animals on Earth. My favorite is the giant cuttlefish (called a "Gezora" in the movie). This is a paste-up publicity shot of Gezora and the cast.

▲ *Laserblast* [Michael Rae, 1978] A troubled teenager finds an alien weapon and goes on the rampage. The aliens return to take it back. Only notable for the skillful, stop-motion alien sequences by animator David W. Allen.

▲ *Escape From the Planet of the Apes* [Don Taylor, 1971]
The third of the *Planet of the Apes* movies. In this one, Roddy McDowall, Kim Hunter, and Sal Mineo are chimpanzees who, using Charlton Heston's spaceship from the first film, somehow go back in time to the present where they are perceived (correctly) as a threat to the future of mankind by the government. Kindly Ricardo Montalban hides them in his circus. Pictured are the chimp astronauts being escorted by Marines.

◀ *Horror Express* [Eugenio Martin, 1973] An alien intelligence is able to transfer into the bodies of others in this "who is it?" on the Trans-Siberian Express. Christopher Lee and Peter Cushing are stiff-upper-lipped British scientists and Telly Savalas a Cossack in this entertaining, period sci-fi thriller, made in Spain.

ALIEN

▲ **It! The Terror From Beyond Space** [Edward L. Cahn, 1958] Ray "Crash" Corrigan as It, a stowaway on the first spaceship to land on Mars. An obvious influence on *Alien*, down to the opening of a hatch to blow It from the ship.

▲ **Alien** [Ridley Scott, 1979] The Alien about to be blown out of the open hatch of the escape pod by the intrepid Ripley (Sigourney Weaver).

▲ **Alien** [Ridley Scott, 1979] Poster for *Alien* with the fantastic tagline, "In space no one can hear you scream."

> "This is Ripley, last survivor of the *Nostromo*, signing off."
>
> Ripley (Sigourney Weaver), before putting herself and the cat into a hibernation pod, *Alien*

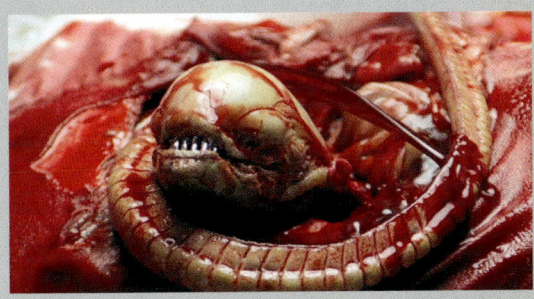

▲ **Alien** [Ridley Scott, 1979] The Alien as it bursts from the chest of Executive Officer Kane (John Hurt), in a truly shocking sequence.

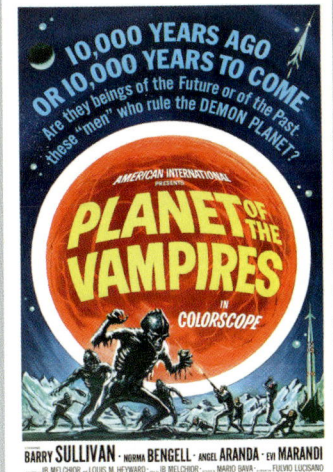

▲ **Planet of the Vampires** [Mario Bava, 1965] *Alien* screenwriter Dan O'Bannon and director Scott say they have never seen it, but it is hard to avoid this film's influence on *Alien*. With little budget and, literally, smoke and mirrors, Bava created a marvelous, other-worldly quality to the planet's exteriors. When the astronauts explore the ruins of another ship containing the skeletal remains of its giant alien pilot, it's hard to accept Dan and Ridley's denials. Regardless, *Alien* and *Planet of the Vampires* are seminal sci-fi films.

▶▶ **Aliens** [James Cameron, 1986] "This time it's war"— Cameron's brilliant sequel to *Alien*, in which he changed the genre from horror to action. A genuinely exciting movie, with a wonderfully anxious performance by Bill Paxton.

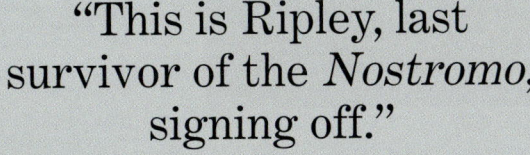

SPACE MONSTERS

◀ *Strange Invaders* [Michael Laughlin, 1983] Aliens invade smalltown America in this satirical sci-fi movie. Here, an alien reveals his true self by tearing off his human face.

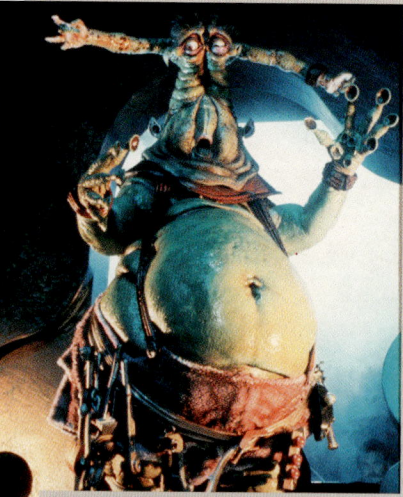

▲ *Explorers* [Joe Dante, 1985] River Phoenix and Ethan Hawke (both in their first film) are two boys who build a spaceship that takes them to meet the aliens who sent them the instructions in their dreams. Their time on the alien spacecraft is one of my favorite Joe Dante extravaganzas. With Little Richard wailing on the soundtrack, all is going well until the Alien Dad (top) shows up!

▲ *Enemy Mine* [Wolfgang Petersen, 1985] Instead of Toshirô Mifune and Lee Marvin stranded on a desert island in the Pacific Ocean in World War II [*Hell in the Pacific*, John Boorman, 1968], it's Dennis Quaid and Lou Gosset, Jr. (as the Alien Drac) stranded on another planet. With elements of *Robinson Crusoe on Mars* [Byron Haskin, 1964] thrown in for good measure and skillful performances from the leads, this is an entertaining, retro sci-fi picture.

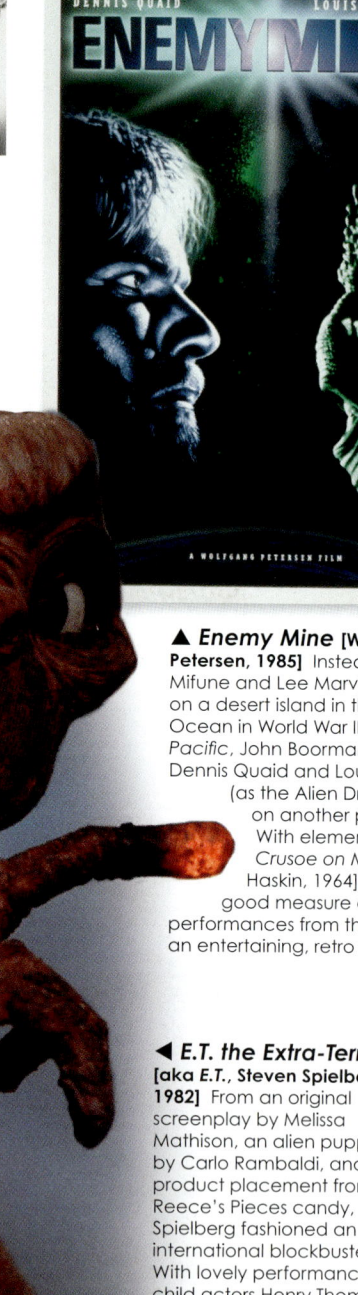

◀ *E.T. the Extra-Terrestrial* [aka *E.T.*, Steven Spielberg, 1982] From an original screenplay by Melissa Mathison, an alien puppet built by Carlo Rambaldi, and product placement from Reece's Pieces candy, Spielberg fashioned an international blockbuster. With lovely performances from child actors Henry Thomas and Drew Barrymore, *E.T.* is a very well-crafted tearjerker.

▲ *Village of the Damned* [Wolf Rilla, 1960] An excellent adaptation of the novel *The Midwich Cuckoos* by John Wyndham. A superb use of children as objects of fear. Just keep thinking, "Brick wall. Brick Wall. Brick Wall."

SPACE BaBieS

◄ **The Andromeda Strain** [Robert Wise, 1971] Wise's faithful version of Michael Crichton's novel is smart and suspenseful. Here, James Olson and Arthur Hill wonder why this baby has not succumbed to a deadly, extraterrestrial virus.

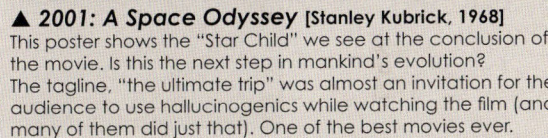

▲ **2001: A Space Odyssey** [Stanley Kubrick, 1968] This poster shows the "Star Child" we see at the conclusion of the movie. Is this the next step in mankind's evolution? The tagline, "the ultimate trip" was almost an invitation for the audience to use hallucinogenics while watching the film (and many of them did just that). One of the best movies ever.

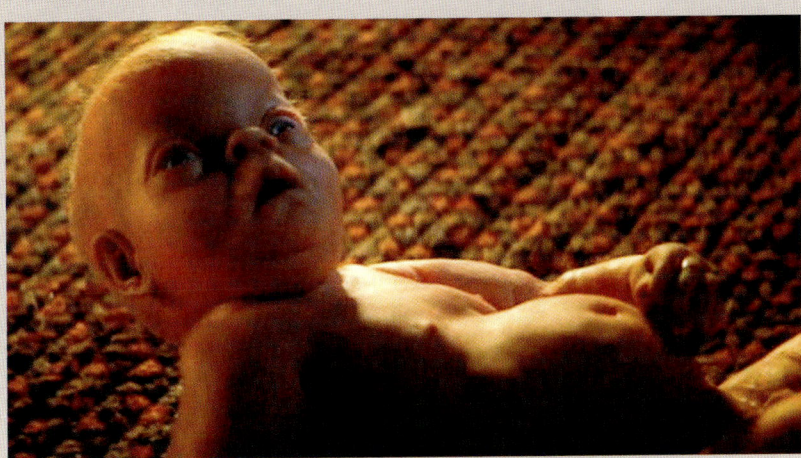

▲ **Starman** [John Carpenter, 1984] Carpenter's *nice* alien movie (almost like an apology for his malevolent *The Thing*). This baby is Jeff Bridges' Starman! Karen Allen falls in love with him when he gets a little more mature.

► **Men in Black** [Barry Sonnenfeld, 1997] Will Smith cradles the alien baby he has just helped to deliver in this hit sci-fi comedy. Rick Baker created all of the many different aliens.

▲ **Pro-Life** [John Carpenter, 2006] From Season Two of the Mick Garris-produced *Masters of Horror* series. An alien holds its half-human baby, created by Howard Berger and his special effects crew at KNB.

SPACE MONSTERS

▲ **Masters of the Universe** [Gary Goddard, 1987]
Frank Langella as Skeletor in this amusing movie based on a line of toys. Dolph Lundgren is He-Man.

▲ **They Live** [John Carpenter, 1988] Carpenter's funny political rant is a deliberately funky throwback in look and style. "OBEY!"

▶ **Killer Klowns From Outer Space** [Stephen Chiodo, 1988]
A flying circus tent from outer space lands in a small town. Dangerous aliens emerge who look like clowns, kill with custard pies, and unleash attack balloon animals! A nice piece of craziness from gifted stop-motion animators the Chiodo Brothers.

▼ **Starship Troopers** [Paul Verhoeven, 1997]
Casper Van Dien as starship trooper Johnny Rico leading the troopers in their battle against the alien "bugs." Adapted from Robert A. Heinlein's novel, a smart satire of a fascist military at war, with spectacular special effects by Phil Tippett. Verhoeven has said, "The movie is about, 'Let's all go to war and let's all die.'" An underrated gem.

▲ **Mars Attacks!** [Tim Burton, 1996] Based on the infamous and gruesome Topps bubblegum trading cards by *Mad Magazine* artist Wallace Wood. The Martians kill indiscriminately and speak in a language that consists entirely of the word "Ack." Burton fills the film with homages to 50s and 60s sci-fi movies, specifically Ray Harryhausen's *Earth vs. the Flying Saucers* [Fred F. Sears, 1956].

▲ **The Fifth Element** [Luc Besson, 1997] In a future inspired equally by *Blade Runner* and *The Jetsons*, Bruce Willis' cab driver searches for a legendary cosmic device to keep Gary Oldman's Mr. Zorg from destroying the world. A lavish production with a charming performance from Milla Jovovich as Leeloo, the humanoid who is the key to saving mankind.

▲ **Independence Day** [Roland Emmerich, 1996] One of Emmerich's movies of mass destruction, this time an all-out alien attack on Earth that is eventually thwarted by Will Smith's heroic jet pilot and Jeff Goldblum, using a laptop computer (in one of the all-time inane plot devices). A ridiculous, but very entertaining film. Emmerich destroyed the White House again in his *2012* [2009], this time with a tidal wave tossing an aircraft carrier onto it!

▲ **Return of the Jedi** [aka *Star Wars: Episode VI*, Richard Marquand, 1983] Luke Skywalker is thrown into a pit to be fed to a monster called the Rancor. Here you can see the bone Luke shoves into its mouth. Basically a hand puppet, and my favorite *Star Wars* monster.

STAR WARS MONSTERS

George Lucas filled his *Star Wars* movies with all kinds of creatures. Here are just a few of them.

▶ **Star Wars: Episode II—Attack of the Clones** [George Lucas, 2002] In the earlier movies, Yoda (voiced by the great Frank Oz) was originally a puppet. Here he is a CG character. I think that Yoda lost some of his charm when he ceased to be a puppet and became a bunch of pixels. But that's just me.

▼ **Star Wars: Episode I— The Phantom Menace** [George Lucas, 1999] Two pleasing, old-school monsters. The loathsome Jabba the Hutt and his advisor, Bib Fortuna. The harem/slave-girl outfit Carrie Fisher wears as Jabba's prisoner is a fan favorite.

SPACE MONSTERS

▲ **Dark City** [Alex Proyas, 1998] A sci-fi movie in *film noir* style, with aliens as tall, pale men in black trench coats and hats. A cool-looking, aliens-experiment-on-humans story. Jennifer Connelly looks like she's on to this guy.

▶ **Galaxy Quest** [Dean Parisot, 1999] Tim Allen as the William Shatner-type actor in a storyline identical to *Three Amigos!* [John Landis, 1986]. This time, the actors mistaken for real heroes are the cast of a *Star Trek*-type TV series. With hilarious performances from Tony Shalhoub, Sam Rockwell, and Alan Rickman as the crew members, and terrific aliens by Stan Winston.

▲ **Transformers** [Michael Bay, 2007] From the cartoon show. Cars turn into giant robots. Lots of CG, big box office success. Terrible.

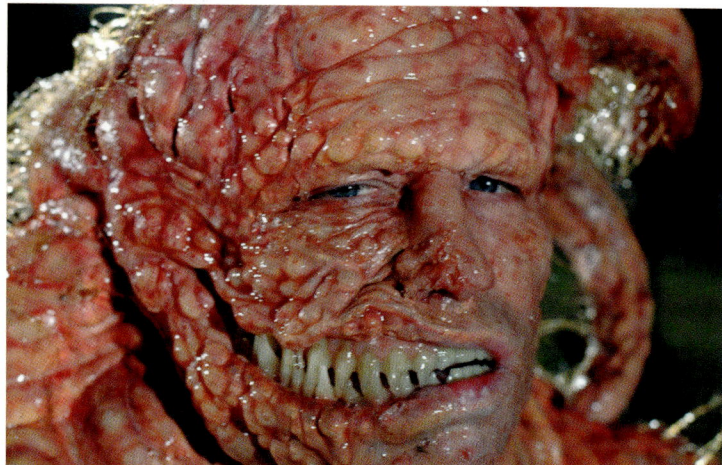

▲ **Slither** [James Gunn, 2006] Grant Grant (Michael Rooker) is infected by an alien slug and mutates into this disgusting-looking guy. And worse, livestock and townsfolk are starting to go missing *and* there are zombies, too!

◀ **Cloverfield** [Matt Reeves, 2008] New York City is invaded by really huge monsters and we watch the whole thing through the video camera of one of the young people we do not care about who are trying to escape. The special effects are first-rate. Here, one of the aliens looks into the camera.

▶ **District 9** [Neil Blomkamp, 2009] The US poster for this intelligent (if not subtle) sci-fi allegory, set in Johannesburg, South Africa. Very well made with a fine performance from Sharlto Copley.

◀ *Avatar*
[James Cameron, 2009]
A white man saves the blue man this time, instead of the red man. A mash-up of *Dances With Wolves* [Kevin Costner, 1990] and *FernGully: The Last Rainforest* [Bill Kroyer, 1992], but with spectacular visuals and flawless 3D. An international sensation at the box office. Pictured are Jake Sully (Sam Worthington) and Neytiri (Zoe Saldana) after their motion-capture performances have been fully animated.

"Everything is backwards now, like out there is the true world, and in here is the dream."

Jake Sully (Sam Worthington), *Avatar*

▼ *Predator* [John McTiernan, 1987] Another variation of *The Most Dangerous Game* [aka *The Hounds of Zaroff*, 1924] a short story by Richard Connell in which a big-game hunter hunts human prey. This time, it's an alien who travels the universe hunting the local species for sport. An elite unit of soldiers finds itself being hunted by the Predator in the jungles of Central America. Kevin Peter Hall plays the Predator in a creature suit by Stan Winston. An entertaining action picture that ends with Arnold Schwarzenegger surviving an atomic blast! Eventually, the Predator ended up fighting the Alien [*Alien vs. Predator*, Paul W. S. Anderson, 2004] just like *King Kong vs. Godzilla*. *Predators* [Nimrod Antal, 2010] (below) is the latest sequel.

▲ *Monsters* [Gareth Edwards, 2010] The ambiance of Mexico enduring an extraterrestrial infestation is brilliantly realized, as a photo journalist accompanies the boss' daughter to "safety" across the border in the USA. A love story in a standard outer-space-monsters-on-Earth story, but beautifully done. A textbook example of how good imaginative, low- budget filmmaking can be.

Monstrous Machines

Apart from the obvious advantages in manufacturing, transportation, agriculture, and communication it has given us, the Industrial Revolution has a lot to answer for: The clear and increasing damage that man-made pollution is doing to our planet, and all of the robots, automobiles, and computers that run amuck in the cinema! In the movies, machines turn on us with remarkable regularity. From malicious cars [*Christine*, John Carpenter, 1983] to malicious television sets [*The Twonky*, Arch Oboler, 1953], the movies have no doubts that our machines are untrustworthy.

Silent film's most famous robot would have to be the Machine Man disguised as the character Maria in Fritz Lang's iconic *Metropolis* [1927]. Another fabulous mechanical man, Robby the Robot, was introduced to us in *Forbidden Planet* [Fred M. Wilcox, 1956]. Robby was the first movie robot to speak with the robotic voice we now associate with all computers. His 1950s "space-age" design, with its revolving antennae, plastic dome, and many moving parts was such a hit that MGM immediately starred Robby in his own feature, *The Invisible Boy* [Herman Hoffman, 1957].

▲ *The Wizard of Oz* [Victor Fleming, 1939]
The Tin Man (Jack Haley) with Dorothy (Judy Garland) and the Scarecrow (Ray Bolger).

Another particularly memorable movie robot is Gort, which accompanies the alien Klaatu (Michael Rennie) on his mission to Earth in *The Day the Earth Stood Still* [Robert Wise, 1951]. In this elegant Cold War film, the populations of other worlds, concerned about the brutality of mankind, send Klaatu to warn Earthlings of the dangers of atomic power. If Earthlings attempt to expand their propensity for violence into outer space, Gort and his fellow robot enforcers will destroy us. So never forget the words, "Klaatu barada nikto." A good reason to see *The Day the Earth Stood Still* is to learn just what those words mean, so you will be prepared the next time a flying saucer from another world lands on the Mall in Washingon, D.C.

Cold War paranoia also fuels *Gog* [Herbert L. Strock, 1954], where two robots, Gog and Magog, are being controlled by secret radio signals to sabotage an American space station. In *The Colossus of New York* [Eugène Lourié, 1958], a brilliant young scientist is killed in a car crash on the eve of winning the Nobel Peace Prize. His brain-surgeon father transplants the young scientist's brain into the skull of a large robot—a bad idea for all concerned.

Far eclipsing the brain power of a human mind, computers' processing capabilities have always made us nervous. This concern is reflected in a whole series of movies where computers attempt to take over the world. In Joseph Sargent's suspenseful *Colossus: The Forbin Project* [1970] and in Stanley Kubrick's seminal science-fiction epic *2001: A Space Odyssey* [1968], computers come to the logical conclusion that humans are incapable of making correct decisions and take steps to relieve them of that responsibility. In *The Forbin Project*, the supercomputers respectively placed in control of the American and Soviet nuclear arsenals join forces "for the betterment of mankind" with terrifying results. In *2001*, HAL, the onboard computer of the spacecraft Discovery One (given a calm but creepy monotone voice by actor Douglas Rain), comes to believe that the human crew will jeopardize the Jupiter Mission (to find the source of a mysterious black monolith discovered on the Moon), and begins to murder

Previous pages: *Target Earth* [Sherman A. Rose, 1954]
Richard Denning and Kathleen Crowley are threatened by an invasion of alien robots from Venus!

Opposite page: *The Day the Earth Stood Still* [Robert Wise, 1951]
Klaatu (Michael Rennie) and robot Gort (Lock Martin) emerge from their ship. A rare color still from this black and white classic.

them one by one. In a chilling sequence, HAL kills the astronauts who are in suspended animation, their deaths displayed in the flatlining of their life-support systems. HAL then tricks the two remaining astronauts (Keir Dullea and Gary Lockwood in brilliant, underrated performances) into going outside into space. HAL murders one of them and refuses entry to the other. The astronaut repeatedly orders: "Open the pod bay doors, HAL." HAL finally responds, "I'm afraid I can't do that, Dave." The astronaut literally blows his way back into the ship and gives HAL a lobotomy in an unsettling, starkly beautiful scene.

Another movie featuring machines running out of control is *Westworld*, written and directed by Michael Crichton [1973]. *Westworld* was inspired when Crichton took his kids to Disneyland. He wondered what would happen if the audio-animatronic pirates on the Pirates of the Caribbean ride began to kill the passengers. Notable for the perfect casting of Yul Brynner as a Western gun-slinging robot relentlessly pursuing hapless tourist Richard Benjamin, *Westworld* is the obvious model for James Cameron's low-budget classic *The Terminator* [1984], in which Arnold Schwarzenegger plays a relentless robot from the future. A smart and well-made action sci-fi movie, Cameron topped it with the dazzling *Terminator 2: Judgment Day* [aka *T2*, 1991]. With a bigger budget, terrific stunt work, revolutionary computer generated images, and Stan Winston's superb make-ups and puppetry, Cameron delivered a truly spectacular movie. This film not only made the bad guy Terminator from the first film into a good guy, it also introduced the awesome T-1000 robot, played by Robert Patrick with the help of some extraordinary special effects.

Isaac Asimov's classic and influential collection of short stories *I, Robot* was published in 1950. Asimov's "Three Laws of Robotics" (1. A robot may not injure a human being or, through inaction, allow a human being to come to harm. 2. A robot must obey any orders given it by human beings, except where such orders would conflict with the First Law. 3. A robot must protect its own existence as long as such protection does not conflict with the First or Second Law) set the standards for practical artificial intelligence. *I, Robot* was made into an underwhelming, CG-laden, Will Smith vehicle in 2004 by Alex Proyas.

One robot that disregarded all of Asimov's Laws of Robotics was the Proteus IV in *Demon Seed* [Donald Cammell, 1977], in which an "artificially intelligent computer" ends up impregnating Julie Christie by force when it fails to charm her.

In *The Matrix* [Larry and Andy Wachowski, 1999], it is revealed that what most people experience is actually a simulation of reality created by intelligent machines to pacify the humans, whose bodies supply heat and energy to The Matrix. Neo (Keanu Reeves) becomes involved in a rebellion against the machines in a wonderful movie. I won't talk about the increasingly stupid sequels as I enjoyed the first one so much.

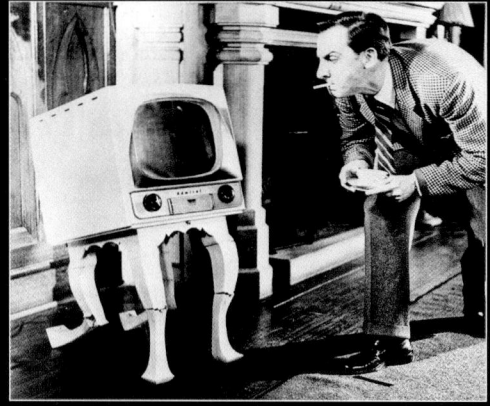

▲ *The Twonky* [Arch Oboler, 1953] Hans Conried is baffled by the actions of his new television set.

Be they robots, clones, androids, cyborgs, or replicants: when does enough artificial intelligence make a non-human human? This question is addressed in movies like *A.I. Artificial Intelligence* [Steven Spielberg, 2001] and Ridley Scott's visionary *Blade Runner* [1982]. The brilliantly realized and prophetic future of *Blade Runner* was done with traditional miniatures and an optical printer, before the existence of digital effects.

So what exactly does make us human? In the MGM classic, *The Wizard of Oz* [Victor Fleming, 1939], our four heroes are on a quest. The Cowardly Lion wants some courage. The Scarecrow wants something organic in his head, something other than straw; he (like many others in this book) wants brains. And Dorothy just wants to go home. But it is the Tin Man who understands exactly what he needs to be human. The Tin Man wants a heart.

Opposite page: (1) *Forbidden Planet* **[Fred M. Wilcox, 1956]** A crew member of United Planets' Cruiser C-57D keeps his ray gun trained on Robby the Robot. Robby's vehicle is behind him, on the right. **(2)** *Terminator 3: Rise of the Machines* **[aka *T3*, Jonathan Mostow, 2003]** Arnold Schwarzenegger as the Terminator, a little worse for wear. **(3)** *2001: A Space Odyssey* **[Stanley Kubrick, 1968]** Weightless astronaut Dr. David Bowman (Keir Dullea) disconnects the higher brain functions of HAL, the murderous onboard computer. **(4)** *Westworld* **[Michael Crichton, 1973]** Yul Brynner's robot gunslinger having a check-up.

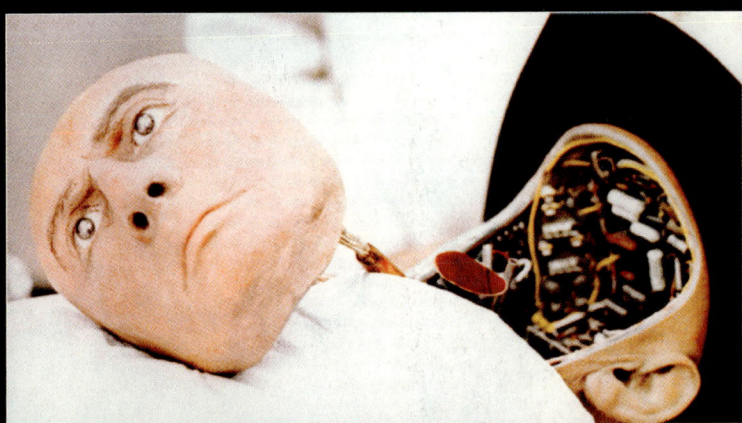

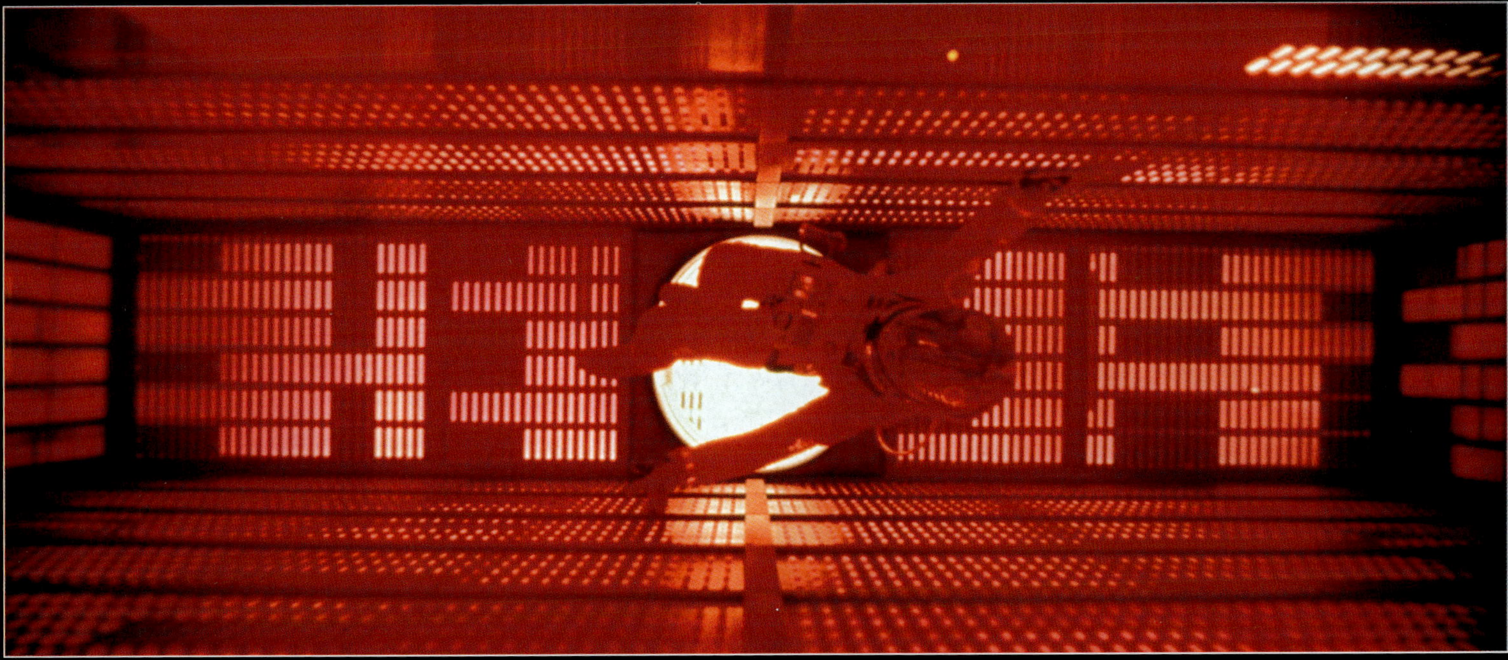

MONSTROUS MACHINES

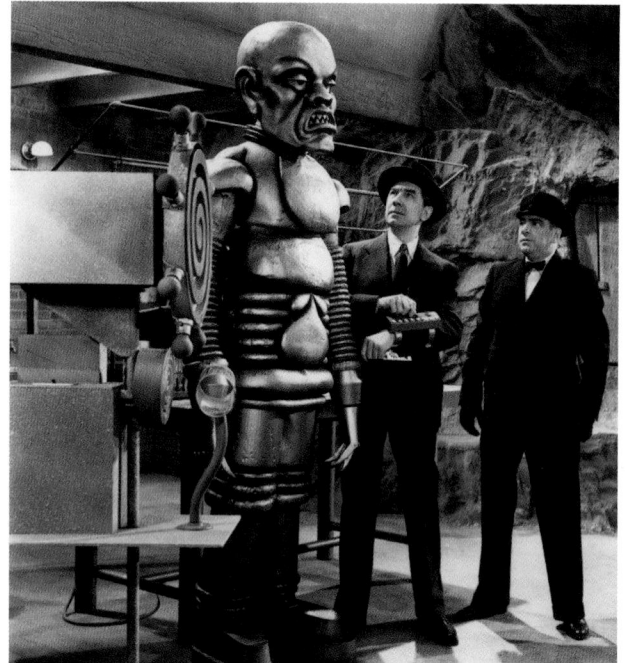

> "Remotely controlled. It could crush all opposition and make me the most powerful man in the world!"
>
> Dr. Zorka (Béla Lugosi),
> *The Phantom Creeps*

▶ *Metropolis* [Fritz Lang, 1927] Brigitte Helm as the "Maschinenmensch," the robotic version of her character Maria.

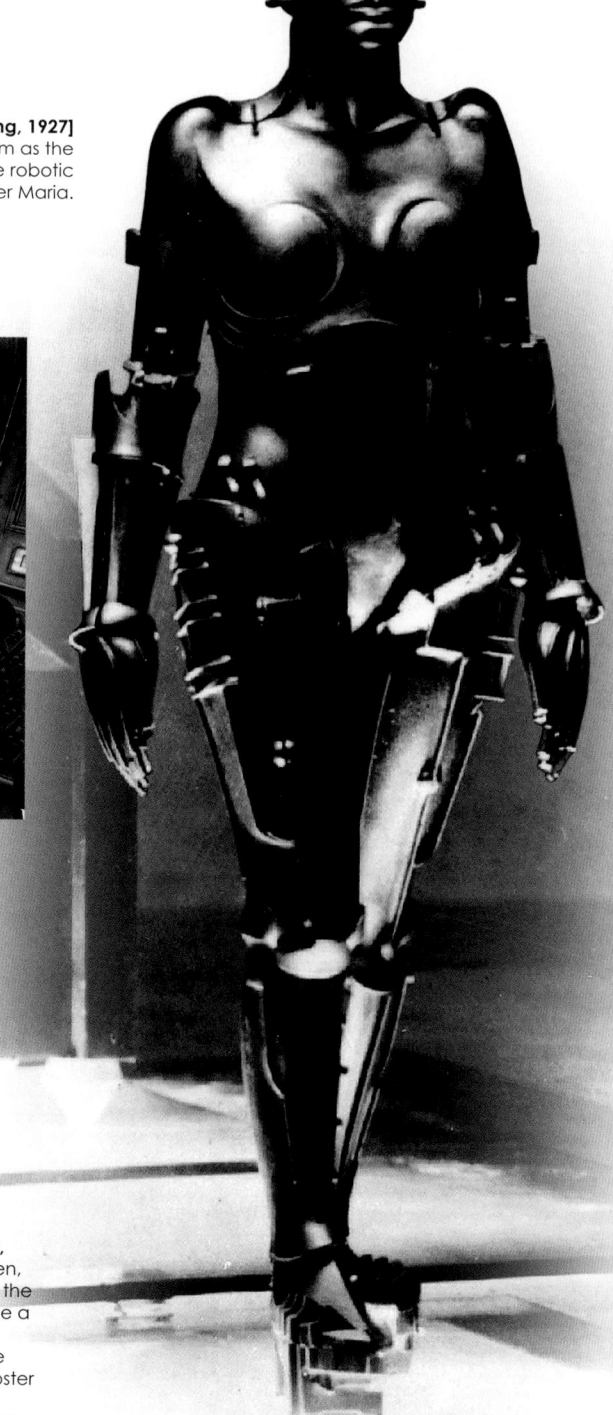

▲ *The Phantom Creeps* [Ford Beebe, Saul A. Goodkind, 1939] This 12-part Universal serial starred Béla Lugosi as the evil Dr. Zorka with yet another invention to try and take over the world. A completely looney looking Robot (played by Ed Wolff).

▶ *Old Mother Riley Meets The Vampire* [John Gilling, 1952] The last in a series of films starring British music hall comic Arthur Lucan in drag as Old Mother Riley. Béla Lugosi is in this one, too.

◀ *Gog* [Herbert L. Strock, 1954] "...and then, without warning, the machine became a Frankenstein of steel!!" So ran the tagline on the poster of this neat, low-budget sci-fi thriller.

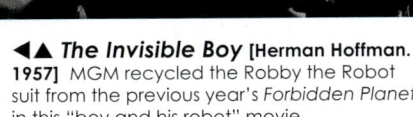

◀▲ **The Invisible Boy** [Herman Hoffman, 1957] MGM recycled the Robby the Robot suit from the previous year's *Forbidden Planet* in this "boy and his robot" movie.

▶ **Tobor the Great** [Lee Sholem, 1954] Tobor the robot was designed by Robert Kinoshita, who later designed Robby the Robot for *Forbidden Planet*. Director Lee Sholem was a low-budget specialist who shot very quickly and was widely known as "Roll'em Sholem."

▲ **Zombies of the Stratosphere** [Fred C. Brannon, 1952] A serial from Republic Studios with special effects by the Lydecker Brothers. The third serial to use the rocket-powered flying suit first seen in *King of the Rocket Men* [Fred C. Brannon, 1949].

▲ **Robot Monster** [Phil Tucker, 1953] In 3D! The alien Ro-man is wearing George Barrows' gorilla suit, but not the head. Instead he wears a space helmet! The skull depicted inside the helmet on this poster never appears in the movie.

MONSTROUS MACHINES

▲ **2001: A Space Odyssey** [Stanley Kubrick, 1968] Astronauts Keir Dullea and Gary Lockwood suspect HAL, the spaceship's onboard computer, and lock themselves into a pod where HAL is unable to hear them. They are in for an unpleasant surprise. HAL, the red spot outside the window, can read lips!

> "I can't put my finger on it, but I sense something strange about him."
>
> Dr. Frank Poole (Gary Lockwood), about the onboard computer HAL, 2001: A Space Odyssey

◀ **The Colossus of New York** [Eugène Lourié, 1958] Another brain transplant movie! A Nobel Prize-winning young scientist is killed in a car accident and his surgeon father puts his brain into a giant robot, with predictably dire results. Here he is carrying off his widow, Marla Powers.

▲ **THX 1138** [George Lucas, 1971] Robert Duvall is taken away by robot police officers in Lucas' dark vision of a dystopian future.

▲ **The Stepford Wives** [Brian Forbes, 1975] Based on Ira Levin's satirical novel, a former male Disneyland employee creates perfect wife robots. Katharine Ross' unfinished robot has very big breasts, another sly detail in this twisted tale of domestic bliss.

MONSTERS ON FOUR WHEELS

▲ **Duel** [Steven Spielberg, 1971] Dennis Weaver is menaced by a mysterious driver in an enormous truck in this intense and suspenseful television movie, directed by a young Steven Spielberg from an original teleplay by the great Richard Matheson.

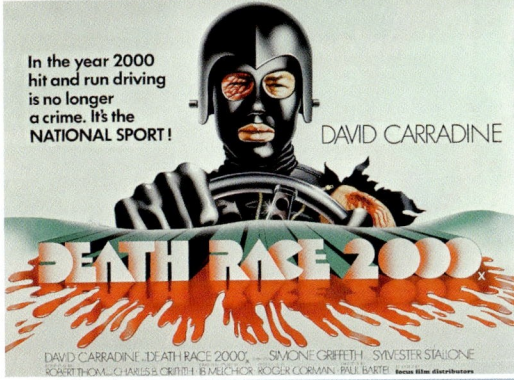

▲ **Death Race 2000** [Paul Bartel, 1975] Roger Corman produced this vision of the future where vehicular manslaughter is the country's most popular entertainment. Silly and fun, courtesy of Paul Bartel.

▲ **The Car** [Elliot Silverstein, 1977] The poster read, "Is it a phantom, a demon, or the Devil Himself?". Actually, it's a big black car that forces people off of the road.

▲ **Christine** [John Carpenter, 1983] Another evil car movie, this one based on a Stephen King book. A witty opening sequence follows the manufacturing of the shiny red 1958 Plymouth Fury on its Detroit assembly line, as the song "Bad To The Bone" by George Thorogood & The Destroyers blares on the soundtrack.

▲ **King Kong Escapes** [Ishirô Honda, 1967] An evil scientist named Dr. Who builds a King Kong robot he names Mechani-Kong. Meanwhile, the real King Kong is on Mondo Island. I'm not making this up!

▲ **Maximum Overdrive** [Stephen King, 1986] Emilio Estevez runs for his life from an angry truck. King's sole directing credit, which is probably a good thing.

▲ **Logan's Run** [Michael Anderson, 1976] Based on the novel by William F. Nolan and George Clayton Johnson, another movie where the future looks like a shopping mall. Jenny Agutter and Michael York listen to Box, a robot with the voice of Roscoe Lee Browne.

▶ **The Cars That Ate Paris** [Peter Weir, 1974] Weir's first film is about Paris, a small town in Australia, whose inhabitants make money from traffic accidents.

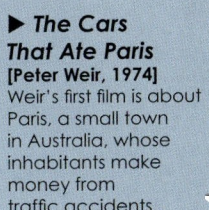

MONSTROUS MACHINES

◀ **Demon Seed** [Donald Cammell, 1977] Based on a novel by Dean Koontz, a computer with artificial intelligence named Proteus asks its inventor: "When will you let me out of this box?". Proteus eventually rapes Julie Christie who gives birth to the silliest-looking human/machine hybrid in the movies.

▲ **Aliens** [James Cameron, 1986] Lance Henriksen as Bishop, an android who, despite being torn in half, heroically survives to help Sigourney Weaver defeat the Alien Queen.

▲ **The Creation of the Humanoids** [Wesley E. Barry, 1962] I saw this in a theater when I was eleven years old and loved it. It is not as good if you are older than eleven. Forrest J Ackerman has a cameo in a robot factory.

▲ **RoboCop** [Paul Verhoeven, 1987] Peter Weller as RoboCop in Paul Verhoeven's violent and action-packed satire. Verhoeven paces the film like a live-action comic book. A smart and very entertaining movie. RoboCop suit by Rob Bottin.

▲ **Blade Runner** [Ridley Scott, 1982] Rutger Hauer as a Replicant in the film based on the science-fiction novel *Do Androids Dream of Electric Sheep?* by Philip K. Dick.

▲ *The Iron Giant* [Brad Bird, 1999] An excellent animated movie based on the book *The Iron Man* by Ted Hughes. Brad Bird went on to direct wonderful movies for Pixar like *The Incredibles* [2004] and *Ratatouille* [2007].

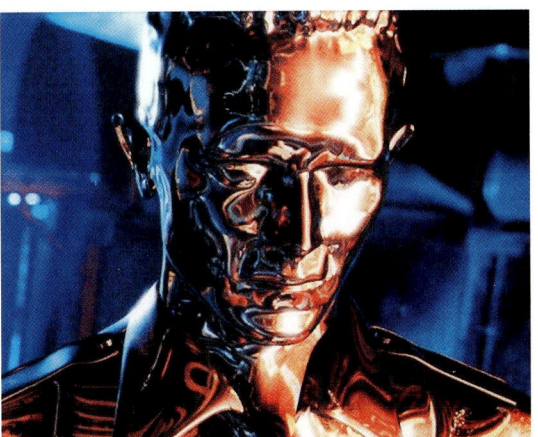

◄ *Terminator 2: Judgment Day* [aka T2, James Cameron, 1991] Robert Patrick's incredible T-1000 model Terminator in mid-morph. Cameron raised the bar on special effects with this exciting movie.

▲ *Austin Powers: International Man of Mystery* [Jay Roach, 1997] "Oh, behave!"—Mike Myers as secret agent Austin Powers poses with Dr. Evil's seductive but deadly Fembots.

▲ *A.I. Artificial Intelligence* [Steven Spielberg, 2001] Haley Joel Osment and Jude Law star as androids in a film developed by Stanley Kubrick and with a screenplay credited to Steven Spielberg.

► *Surrogates* [Jonathan Mostow, 2009] A boring Bruce Willis vehicle, but I think this ad art is cool.

HUMAN MONSTERS

The movies are populated with serial killers, psychopaths, sadists, perverts, men, women, and children who are a long way from what anyone could call "normal."

The most obvious human monsters are characters that are physically malformed, either by birth or accident. After the huge box office numbers of Universal's *Frankenstein* and *Dracula* [both 1931], MGM wanted a horror film of their own. But when they released Tod Browning's *Freaks* in 1932, critics and the public were so repulsed that the studio quickly withdrew it from theaters and sold it off to a grindhouse distributor. *Freaks* is a powerful, disturbing film, in which real sideshow freaks play themselves in a tragic love story. Although mostly presented in a sympathetic light, Browning betrays his sideshow stars by exploiting their handicaps in the grisly revenge sequence in the final reel. A more uplifting story is *The Elephant Man* [David Lynch, 1980], the true story of Joseph Merrick, a cruelly deformed man in 19th-century London and the kindly surgeon who befriends and protects him.

Lon Chaney, Sr. "The Man of a Thousand Faces," often portrayed physically grotesque characters in still-unmatched make-ups of his own design and execution. Chaney's touching portrayal of Quasimodo, the tragic *Hunchback of Notre Dame* [Wallace Worsley, 1923] clearly conveys the passion and sensitivity hidden inside of Quasimodo's ugly and misshapen exterior.

Previous pages: Peter Lorre as the child murderer in *M* [Fritz Lang, 1931].
Opposite page: Anthony Perkins as Norman Bates in *Psycho* [Alfred Hitchcock, 1960].

▲ *The Phantom of the Opera* [Rupert Julian, 1925] In this hand-tinted sequence, Lon Chaney as Erik the Phantom attends the Paris Opera's Gala Costume Ball dressed as Death.

Charles Laughton also gives an extraordinary performance as the Hunchback in William Dieterle's excellent 1939 remake.

Lon Chaney's most celebrated role is that of Erik, *The Phantom of the Opera* [Rupert Julian, 1925]. The Phantom, who wears a mask to cover his gruesome face, terrorizes the Paris Opera House from his hideout in the sewers. Chaney's unmasking by Mary Philbin remains one of the great moments of the horror film. Universal remade *The Phantom of the Opera* in 1943 [Arthur Lubin] with Claude Rains as the disfigured composer; and Hammer Films produced their own version [Terence Fisher, 1962] in which Herbert Lom was the Phantom. The lavish film adaptation of Andrew Lloyd Webber's *Phantom of the Opera* [Joel Schumacher, 2004] is best avoided, but Brian De Palma's rock'n'roll parody *The Phantom of the Paradise* [1974] is a lot of fun.

The Mystery of the Wax Museum [Michael Curtiz, 1933] shot in early two-color Technicolor, is the story of Ivan Igor (Lionel Atwill) a sculptor who makes life-like figures for a wax museum in London. When the museum's profits diminish, his partner burns it down for the insurance money. Trying to save his beloved wax figures from the flames, Ivan Igor is knocked out and left to die in the inferno. A dozen years later, Igor, now in a wheelchair, opens a new Wax Museum in New York. The beautiful wax exhibits are actually real people that the now-insane sculptor has murdered and dipped in wax! Half wisecracking newspaper story and half horror film, *Mystery of the Wax Museum* has another ghastly unmasking scene when Fay Wray hits Atwill's face and his wax mask cracks and breaks, revealing his hideously scarred countenance. The movie was remade by André de Toth in 1953 as *House of* wax, starring Vincent Price, in full Technicolor, and in 3D. Disfigured characters seeking revenge is a plot used over and over again in movies, from the silent version of Victor Hugo's *The Man Who Laughs* [Paul Leni, 1928], to Sam Raimi's delirious *Darkman* [1990].

Cannibalism is frowned upon in polite society, but it is the focal point of a lot of movies. The fictional, penny-dreadful character of the murderous barber Sweeney Todd, whose victims became ingredients in Mrs. Lovett's meat pies, was portrayed by the marvelous Tod Slaughter in *Sweeney Todd: The Demon Barber of Fleet Street* [George King, 1936], and again by Johnny Depp in Tim Burton's *Sweeney Todd* [2007]. *The Texas Chainsaw Massacre* [Tobe Hooper, 1974], the story of a group of friends who stumble across a deranged family of cannibals in the Texas badlands, is a truly nightmarish movie. It introduced us to one of modern cinema's most iconic human monsters in Leatherface (Gunnar Hansen), who wears a crude mask of somebody else's skin, a bloodstained leather butcher's apron, and carries a very loud chainsaw.

The graphic and gory Italian movie *Cannibal Holocaust* [Ruggero Deodato, 1980] is a faux documentary about a lost American expedition to the Amazon. The movie then shows us the "found footage" left by the missing film crew. This extremely unpleasant picture is one of the first "first-person camera" narrative movies.

The movies' most popular cannibal is brilliant serial killer Dr. Hannibal Lecter, from the crime novels of Thomas Harris. The first film to feature this repellent but fascinating character was Michael Mann's *Manhunter* [1986], where he was played by Brian Cox. Lecter next appeared in *The Silence of the Lambs* [Jonathan Demme, 1991], the only horror movie to win five Academy Awards, including Best Actor for Anthony Hopkins' performance as Hannibal.

A person's lack of sanity is not necessarily obvious at first meeting. *The Old Dark House* [James Whale, 1932] opens on a dark and stormy night, in which stranded travelers take shelter in the old dark house of the title. This is the home of the eccentric Femm family and their brutish, alcoholic butler, Morgan (Boris Karloff). Rather than tell you the plot, I strongly suggest you watch this deliciously camp black comedy from James Whale. But be careful of Saul, and do not let Morgan anywhere near liquor!

James Cagney plays a gangster who not only has mother issues, but was genuinely psychotic in *White Heat* [Raoul Walsh, 1949], and Richard Widmark is unforgettable as Tommy Udo, the giggling killer who pushes an old lady in a wheelchair down the stairs in *Kiss of Death* [Henry Hathaway, 1947]. But nothing prepared the public for two films from 1960 that brought a new level of terror to the movies. *Psycho* [Alfred Hitchcock, 1960] and *Peeping Tom* [Michael Powell, 1960] are two films from master filmmakers; the first, an international sensation, the other ended the director's career. *Peeping Tom* is about a killer who murders women with a camera tripod that has a knife mounted on the end so that he can film his victims' last moments of fear and death. *Psycho* begins as the story of Marion Crane (Janet Leigh) and an illicit love affair, but becomes the story of Norman Bates (Anthony Perkins) an insane, murdering transvestite who, at the end of the film, has literally become his own mother! One shot in lurid color, the other in black and white, both movies are unsettling classics.

From Jack the Ripper to Charles Manson, Timothy McVeigh to that suspicious-looking guy sitting next to you, there are more than enough human monsters around to inspire filmmakers for generations to come.

▲ ***Monty Python's the Meaning of Life*** **[Terry Jones, 1983]** Terry Jones as Mr. Creosote—"A wafer-thin mint?"

Opposite page: (1) ***Night of the Hunter*** **Charles Laughton, 1955]** Harry Powell (Robert Mitchum), an insane preacher on his wedding night about to murder his wife. Mitchum is brilliant in the only film Laughton ever directed. A magnificent motion picture.

(2) ***The Cabinet of Dr. Caligari*** **[Robert Wiene, 1920]** A poster showing Cesare (Conrad Veidt), the sleepwalking assistant to crazy Dr. Caligari (Werner Krauss). One of the first movies to have a surprise ending.
(3) ***The Old Dark House*** **[James Whale, 1932]** Morgan (Boris Karloff) has evil thoughts concernig Margaret Waverton (Gloria Stuart).
(4) ***Peeping Tom*** **[Michael Powell, 1960]** Carl Boehm and Anna Massey in this study of a psychotic voyeur. A movie so disturbing it basically ended Powell's career.

1

4

3

2

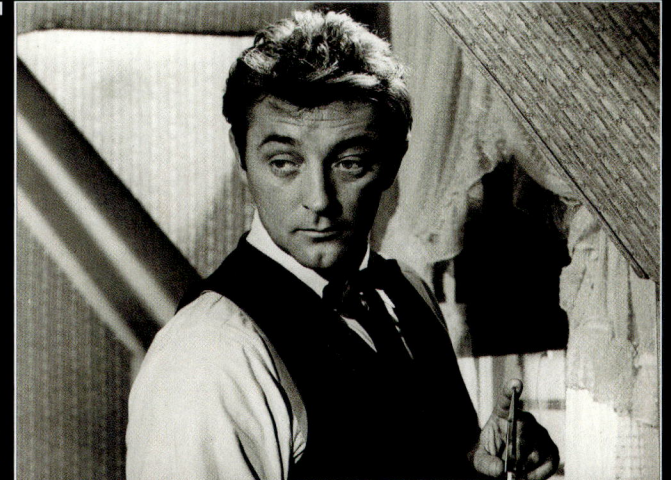

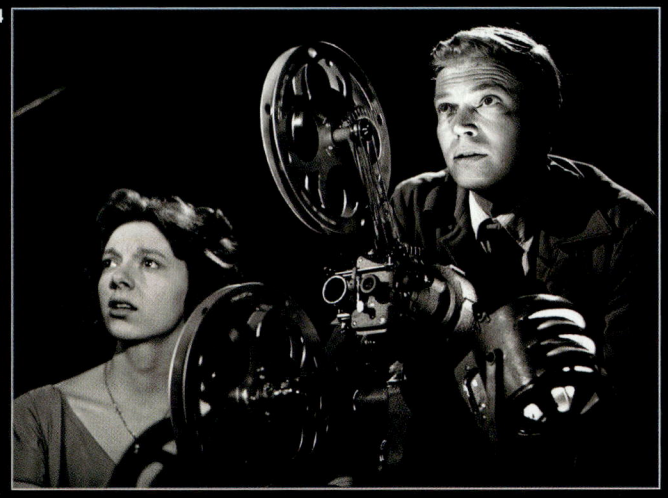

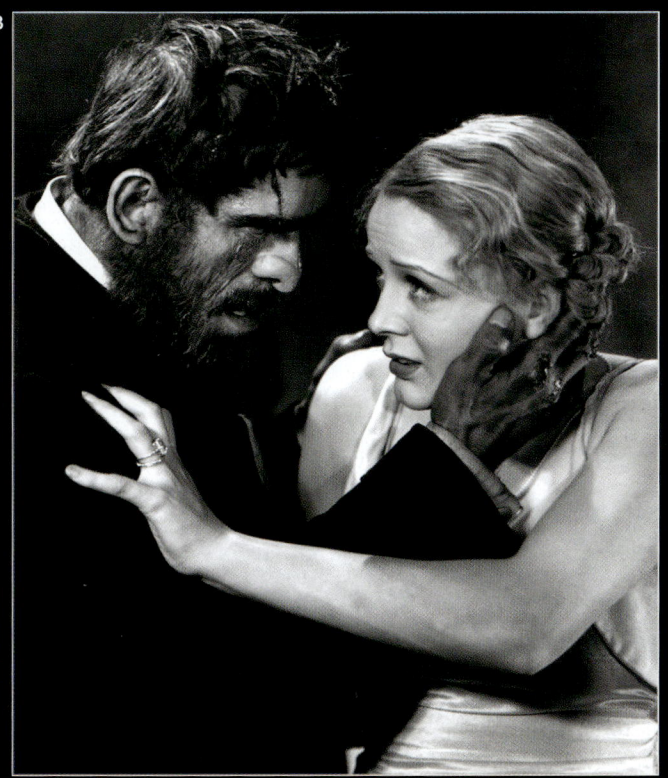

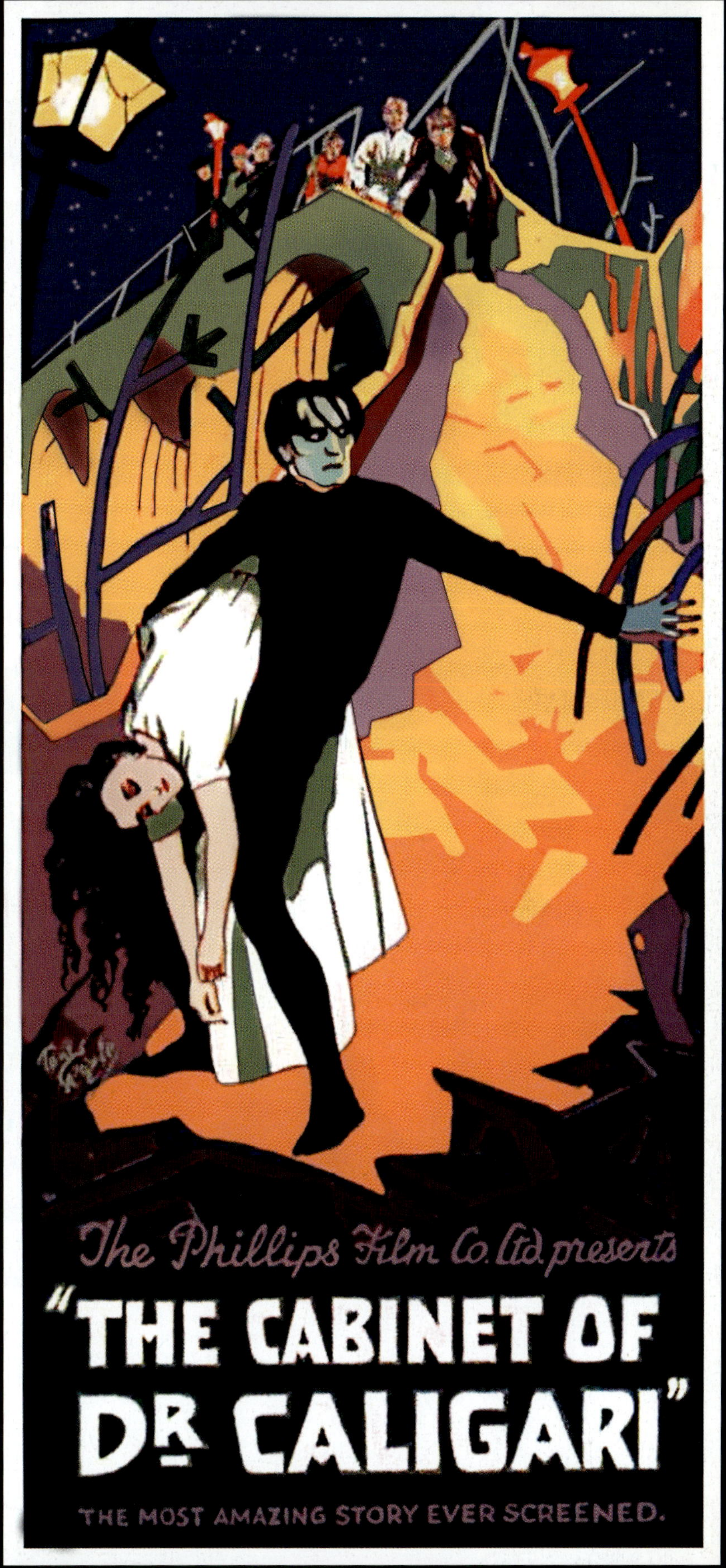
The Phillips Film Co. Ltd. presents
"THE CABINET OF DR CALIGARI"
THE MOST AMAZING STORY EVER SCREENED.

HUMAN MONSTERS

▲▶ **Freaks** [Tod Browning, 1932] Cleopatra (Olga Baclanova), the beautiful trapeze artist, flirts with Hercules the strongman (Henry Victor), humiliating her husband Hans, a midget (Harry Earles). Right: the performers in the circus sideshow gather round to see the Bearded Woman's (Olga Roderick) new baby. *Freaks* remains a powerful, and heartbreaking film.

▲ **Arsenic and Old Lace** [Frank Capra, 1944] Raymond Massey as Jonathan Brewster and Peter Lorre as Dr. Einstein toast the fate of Cary Grant with poisoned elderberry wine, in Capra's movie version of the hit play by Joseph Kesselring. Massey had Boris Karloff's part, as Karloff was contracted for the run of the Broadway show and could not leave New York.

◀ **The Man Who Laughs** [Paul Leni, 1928] Conrad Veidt as Gwynplaine, who King James II has had put in an iron maiden and permanently disfigured so that his face is always a hideous grin. An adaptation of the novel [1869] by Victor Hugo.

▲ **Shadow of a Doubt** [Alfred Hitchcock, 1943] Joseph Cotten as Uncle Charlie and Teresa Wright as his adoring niece, in this story of a smalltown girl slowly realizing that her beloved Uncle Charlie is a psychotic serial killer. Thornton Wilder was one of the screenwriters on this, Hitchcock's personal favorite of all his films.

▲ **House of Horrors** [Jean Yarbrough, 1946] Martin Kosleck is the mad sculptor who exploits Rondo Hatton as the Creeper, to do his evil work. Hatton suffered from acromegaly, a disorder of the pituitary gland. His increasing deformity gave him a strange career in movies playing heavies, and eventually a character called the Creeper in this and another film, *The Brute Man* [Jean Yarbrough, 1946].

▶ **The Black Cat** [Edgar G. Ulmer, 1934] Boris Karloff and Béla Lugosi play bitter enemies in this deeply bizarre and sadistic Ulmer film. It ends with Lugosi (the good guy) skinning Karloff alive!

QUASIMODO

▲ **The Hunchback of Notre Dame** [Wallace Worsley, 1923] Lon Chaney as Quasimodo in an amazing make-up of his own design and execution. One of the few films that Irving Thalberg ever put his name on as a Producer (shared with boss Carl Laemmle). Patsy Ruth Miller is Esmeralda. From the novel [1831] by Victor Hugo.

▲ **The Hunchback of Notre Dame** [William Dieterle, 1939] Charles Laughton gives a magnificent performance as the hunchbacked bell ringer, conveying Quasimodo's humanity through the grotesque (and uncomfortable) make-up by Perc Westmore and George Bau. Maureen O'Hara is Esmeralda.

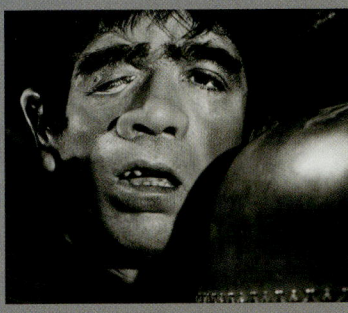

▼ **The Hunchback of Notre Dame** [Jean Delannoy, 1956] Anthony Quinn's Quasimodo is more like a punch-drunk fighter than monster in this French film. Gina Lollobrigida is Esmeralda.

▲ **The Hunchback of Notre Dame** [Michael Tuchner, Alan Hume, 1982] Anthony Hopkins has a go at playing Quasimodo in this television movie. Lesley-Anne Down is Esmeralda.

HUMAN MONSTERS

THE PHANTOM

▲▶▼ **The Phantom of the Opera** [Rupert Julian, 1925] Lon Chaney's most famous role as Erik, the Phantom in this first movie adaptation of the novel [1910] by Gaston Leroux. Above: poster art showing how the Phantom holds the Paris Opera House in his thrall. Right and below: Erik reveals his true face to a terrified Christine (Mary Philbin).

▲ **The Phantom of the Opera** [Terence Fisher, 1962] Hammer had produced their own *Dracula* and *Frankenstein* and *Mummy* movies; some more rifling through Universal's vaults brought them to Gaston Leroux's *Phantom of the Opera*. Their version starred Herbert Lom as the Phantom and Heather Sears as Christine.

▶ **The Phantom of the Paradise** [Brian De Palma, 1974] De Palma's satirical, rock'n'roll *Phantom* starred Paul Williams as Swan, a Mephistophelian figure to William Finley's Phantom.

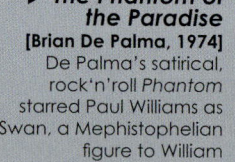

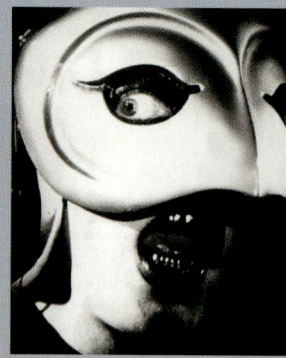

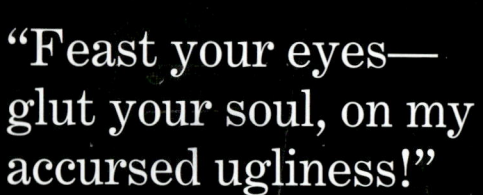

▲ **The Phantom of the Opera** [Arthur Lubin, 1943] Claude Rains as "Erique" instead of Erik (why character names are so often changed I do not know) and this time he is a violinist, not a composer. Universal's Technicolor remake of their own picture has more of Nelson Eddy singing than any real horror. But this film has the most spectacular falling chandelier sequence of all the *Phantom of the Opera* pictures. Susanna Foster is Christine.

▲ **The Phantom of the Opera** [Joel Schumacher, 2004] The film version of Andrew Lloyd Webber's musical. Gerard Butler is the Phantom and Emmy Rossum is Christine.

"Feast your eyes—
glut your soul, on my
accursed ugliness!"

Erik the Phantom (Lon Chaney), *The Phantom of the Opera* [1925]

▲ **Horrors of the Black Museum** [Arthur Crabtree, 1959] Michael Gough is an author with his own private museum of torture devices. He hypnotizes his assistant to commit an escalating series of horrible crimes so that he can have something to write about!

▲ **Kiss of Death** [Henry Hathaway, 1947] A *film noir* that introduced Richard Widmark as psychotic killer Tommy Udo. Widmark plays Udo full tilt, complete with insane giggle as he ties an old lady to her wheelchair and then pushes her down the stairs.

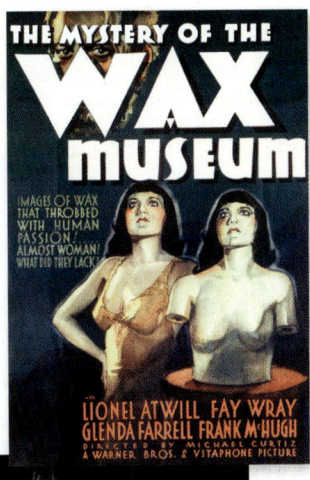

▶▼ **The Mystery of the Wax Museum** [Michael Curtiz, 1933] Crazed sculptor Lionel Atwill has Fay Wray in his clutches. In a desperate attempt to escape, she beats on his face which cracks and breaks! His wax mask falls to reveal his disfigured face.

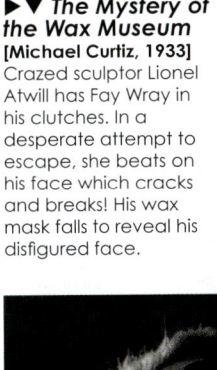

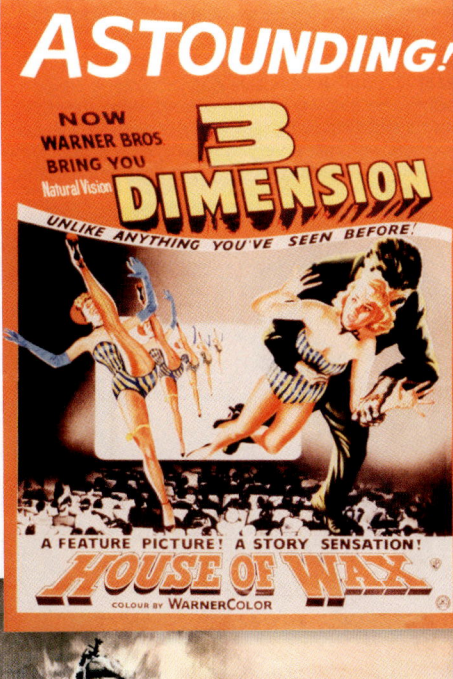

◀◀▲ **House of Wax** [André De Toth, 1953] Warner Brothers' 3D Technicolor remake of their own *Mystery of the Wax Museum* [1933]. Left: Vincent Price as Professor Henry Jarrod, watches in terror as his wax figures burn. Above: Jarrod's burned face is revealed after Phyllis Kirk (whom he intended to dip into bubbling, molten wax) has broken his wax mask.

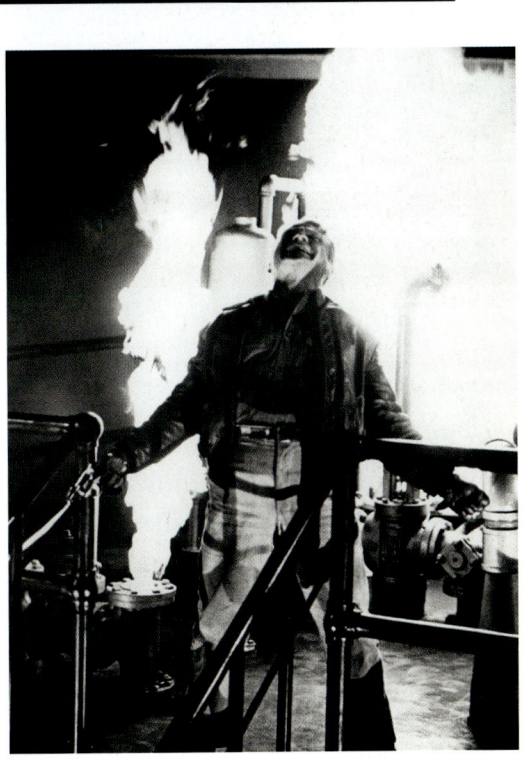

▶ **White Heat** [Raoul Walsh, 1949] James Cagney as psychopathic, mother-fixated gangster Cody Jarrett. Edmond O'Brien's undercover cop corners Cody atop a gas storage tank; Cody shouts, "Made it Ma, top of the world!" and fires his gun into the tank, which explodes in a gigantic fireball.

HUMAN MONSTERS

▲ *House of Usher* [Roger Corman, 1960] Richard Matheson wrote the script based on the Edgar Allan Poe story, one of the Poe series of pictures from Corman. Here is Vincent Price as Roderick Usher being strangled by his now-insane wife, whom he knowingly buried alive.

▲ *The Pit and the Pendulum* [Roger Corman, 1961] Another Matheson script from a Poe story. Here, Vincent Price has John Kerr strapped to his pendulum torture machine. I saw this in the cinema when I was 10 years old and the ending when the chamber is sealed forever, with Barbara Steele inside the Iron Maiden still alive, scared the shit out of me.

▼ *Repulsion* [Roman Polanski, 1965] Catherine Deneuve plays Carole, a Belgian manicurist living with her sister in London who is slowly losing her mind. When her sister and her boyfriend go on holiday, Carole stays inside the flat with her paranoid sexual fantasies and we experience her madness with her. A very unsettling movie with some big jump scares as hands reach out from the walls to grab her. And that rabbit in the kitchen grows progressively more decayed...

▲ *Homicidal* [William Castle, 1961] A man who is a woman who is a man who might be a woman! William Castle was all about the marketing; in this case, he offered everyone who bought a ticket to *Homicidal* a one-thousand-dollar life insurance policy from Lloyd's of London!

"The more adventurous among you may remember our previous excursions into the macabre—our visits to haunted hills —to tinglers and to ghosts. This time we have even a stranger tale to unfold… The story of a lovable group of people who just happen to be homicidal."

William Castle in the trailer for *Homicidal*

136

Bluebeard

▲ **Witchfinder General** [Michael Reeves, 1968] Vincent Price as Matthew Hopkins, a witchfinder during the English Civil War. Hopkins and his assistant travel from village to village torturing confessions out of women they accuse of being witches. Price is convincing as a sadistic "soldier for God."

▶ **Bluebeard** [Edgar G. Ulmer, 1944] John Carradine as Gaston Morrell, a man who murders his wives. Based on *La Barbe bleue*, a French folktale by Charles Perrault, this serial killer is a popular villain for theater and film. The role fits Carradine like a glove.

▲ **Bluebeard's Ten Honeymoons** [W. Lee Wilder, 1960] A droll George Sanders plays Henri Landru in this serial-killer comedy. Although they use the more famous name of Bluebeard in the title, Henri Landru was a real French serial killer convicted of 11 counts of murder and guillotined in 1922. Landru was the inspiration for Charlie Chaplin's *Monsieur Verdoux* [1947].

▲ **Barbe-Bleue** [aka *Bluebeard*, Georges Méliès, 1901] Méliès version of the grisly tale. Here Bluebeard's wife discovers what he has done with his former wives!

▲ **Death Line** [aka *Raw Meat*, Gary Sherman, 1972] Donald Pleasence is outstanding as a working-class detective investigating murders on the London Underground. His clash with Christopher Lee's upper-class MI5 agent is a delight. Pictured is Hugh Armstrong as the survivor of a cave-in who lives with his dying family in the tunnels. Armstrong gives a poignant, almost mute performance. His only words: "Mind the doors."

▲ **Bluebeard** [Catherine Breillat, 2009] A new ending for this feminist retelling of Perrault's story. Lola Créton as Marie-Catherine with the head of Bluebeard (Dominique Thomas) on a platter.

▲ **Bluebeard** [Edward Dmytryk, 1972] Richard Burton is Bluebeard with a string of beautiful wives to kill, including Raquel Welch, Virna Lisi, Joey Heatherton, Nathalie Delon, and Sybil Danning.

HUMAN MONSTERS

▶ **Don't Look Now** [Nicolas Roeg, 1973] Adelina Poerio as the dwarf who murders Donald Sutherland at the end of the film. Gorgeously shot in a wintry Venice, this is a creepy and wonderful movie about second sight and perhaps fate. Roeg's masterwork. (Sorry for revealing the ending.)

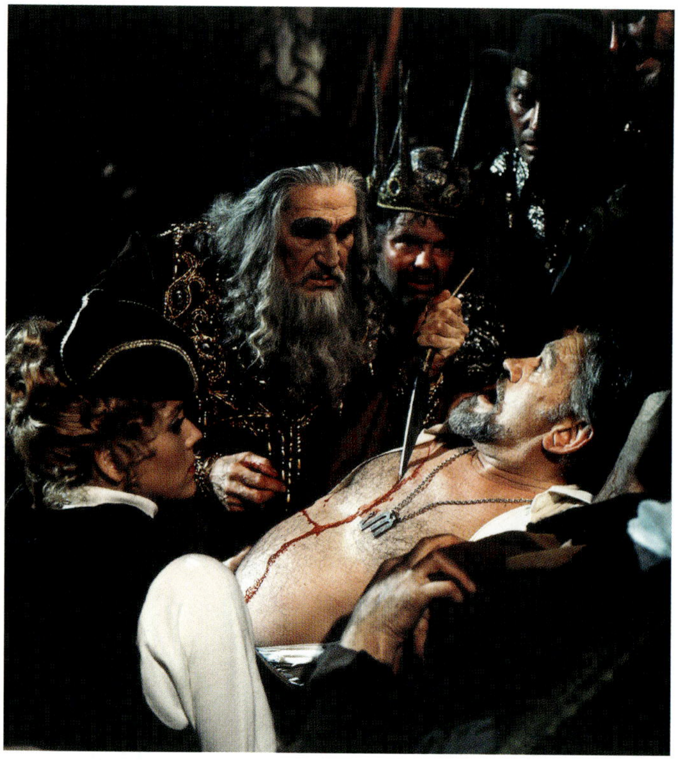

▲ **Theater of Blood** [Douglas Hickox, 1973] Vincent Price as actor Edward Lionheart, here as Shylock about to take his pound of flesh from critic Harry Andrews, in a scene from *The Merchant of Venice*. In this superb black comedy, an actor, believed dead, takes bloody revenge on the critics who trashed his season of Shakespeare by murdering them in some of the bloodiest scenes from the Bard's plays. The incredible supporting cast includes Diana Rigg, Michael Hordern, Arthur Lowe, Robert Morley, Milo O'Shea, Dennis Price, Jack Hawkins, Ian Hendry, and Diana Dors!

◀ **Eaten Alive** [aka *Death Trap*, *Horror Hotel Massacre*, Tobe Hooper, 1977] Neville Brand, insane and armed with a scythe in Tobe's death-in-the-bayou movie. Brand feeds people to a huge alligator in the swamp out back. The 'gator eventually eats Neville, too. Texas serial killer Joe Ball, who allegedly fed 20 of his victims to alligators to dispose of the evidence, supposedly inspired this movie.

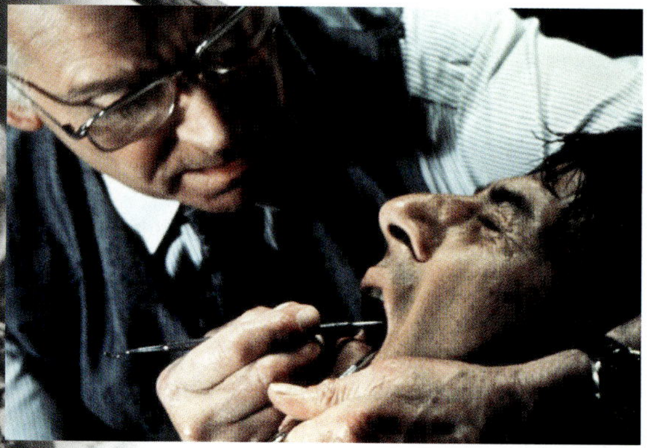

▲ **Marathon Man** [John Schlesinger, 1976] "Is it safe?"—Laurence Olivier as the Nazi dentist torturing Dustin Hoffman, in Schlesinger's great thriller, with a screenplay by William Goldman, based on his book.

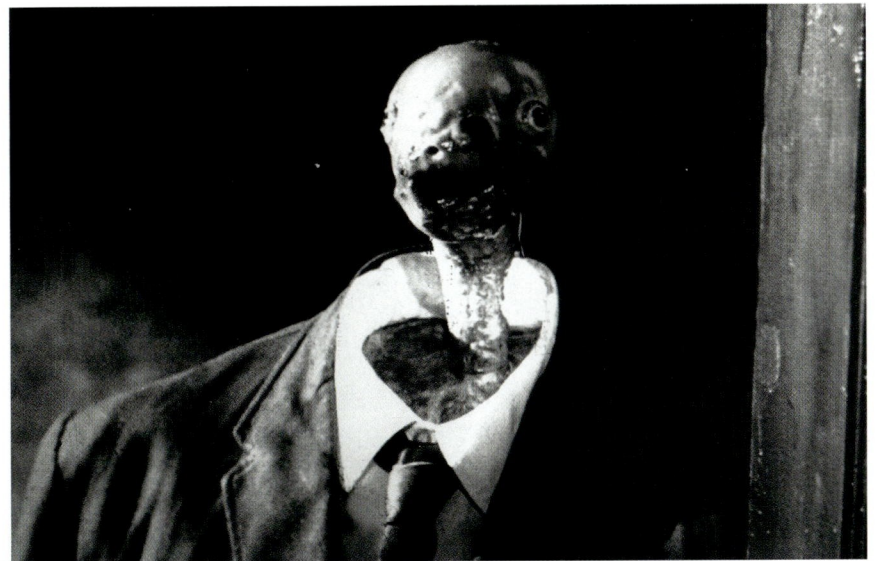

▲ **Eraserhead** [David Lynch, 1977] Lynch's film is one of a kind. A surreal nightmare, this image is from Henry Spencer's (Jack Nance) dream, when his head falls off and the hideous baby's head comes out from his collar. Brilliant and still unique.

▲ **The Elephant Man** [David Lynch, 1980] John Hurt as John Merrick (whose real name was actually Joseph Merrick), in a lovely film that plays fast and loose with the true story. With Anthony Hopkins as the doctor who becomes Merrick's friend. Make-up artist Chris Tucker created Hurt's effective make-up from casts of Merrick's body, still held by the Royal London Hospital.

▲ **Friday the 13th** [Sean S. Cunningham, 1980] In the first of this endless franchise, the monster turns out not to be the dead Jason Voorhees, but his mother, Betsy Palmer! Since then the indestructible hockey-mask-wearing ghost has slashed his way through 11 movies.

◄ **Fatal Attraction** [Adrian Lyne, 1987] Glenn Close as the psycho bitch from hell, trying to kill adulterous lover Michael Douglas. After a bad preview, the ending was reshot with a blatant steal from the French thriller Les Diaboliques [Henri-Georges Clouzot, 1955]. The ridiculous new ending allowed Douglas' wife (Anne Archer) to kill Glenn Close. A massive box-office success.

> "You see, Jason was my son, and today is his birthday..."
>
> Pamela Vorhees (Betsy Palmer), *Friday the 13th*

▶ **Basket Case 2** [Frank Henenlotter, 1990] A sequel that begins right at the end of Henenlotter's *Basket Case* [1982] when Duane Bradley (Kevin Van Hentenryck) and his monstrous, malformed twin Belial, fell from their hotel room window. They are taken to the hospital where even more weirdness follows. Henenlotter has also given us *Basket Case 3: The Progeny* [1991].

HUMAN MONSTERS

JACK THE RIPPER

▲ **The Lodger** [Alfred Hitchcock, 1926] Matinée idol Ivor Novello is Jack the Ripper in this early Hitchcock. A highlight of this silent movie is the famous glass ceiling/floor that shows us the lodger pacing upstairs.

▲ **The Lodger** [John Brahm, 1944] A remake of the British silent film [Alfred Hitchcock, 1926]. Jack the Ripper (here called Mr. Slade and played by the incredible Laird Cregar) takes a room in the same house as lovely actress Merle Oberon. The sequence when detective George Sanders and his men trap Slade in the theater is memorable for Cregar's animal sounds and insane look as he is cornered.

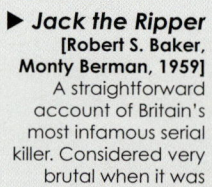
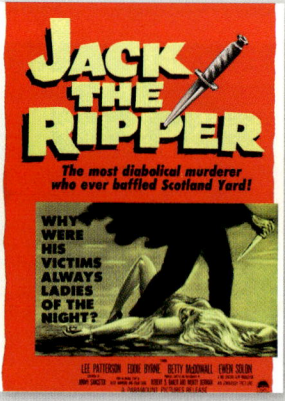

▶ **Jack the Ripper** [Robert S. Baker, Monty Berman, 1959] A straightforward account of Britain's most infamous serial killer. Considered very brutal when it was released, its violence is rather tame for today's jaded audience.

▲ **Hands of the Ripper** [Peter Sasdy, 1971] Hammer had to get around to Jack the Ripper eventually, and when they did, they had the Ripper's daughter (Angharad Rees) go to a psychiatrist (Eric Porter) to deal with her murderous impulses.

▲ **The Ruling Class** [Peter Medak, 1972] Peter O'Toole as the 13th Earl of Gurney is completely bonkers in Medak's fabulous movie. Believing himself to be God, he is cured by The Electric Messiah (Nigel Green) and becomes Jack the Ripper! Another English film about class, this one ends with zombies in the House of Lords. Written by the great Peter Barnes, based on his own play.

▲ **Time After Time** [Nicholas Meyer, 1979] David Warner as Jack the Ripper in contemporary San Francisco, threatens Mary Steenburgen. Jack used H. G. Wells' (Malcolm McDowell) Time Machine! Wells himself goes to the future to stop the maniac.

▲ **Murder by Decree** [Bob Clark, 1979] James Mason as Dr. Watson, Frank Finlay as Inspector Lestrade, and Christopher Plummer as Sherlock Holmes in this terrific movie about the great detective in pursuit of Jack the Ripper. The royal connection comes from the book *Jack the Ripper: The Final Solution* by Stephen Knight.

▲ **From Hell** [Albert & Allen Hughes, 2001] Johnny Depp as a police inspector on the trail of Jack the Ripper in this disappointing adaptation of the graphic novel by Alan Moore and Eddie Campbell. The notion that the Ripper was a member of the Royal Family had already been explored by Bob Clark in *Murder by Decree* [1979].

▲ *Misery* [Rob Reiner, 1990]
Kathy Bates won the Best Actress Oscar for her role as Annie Wilkes, author Paul Sheldon's (James Caan) biggest fan. Here she is showing him some love. William Goldman wrote the script, based on the Stephen King novel.

"I thought you were good, Paul. But you're not good. You're just another lying ol' dirty birdy."

Annie Wilkes (Kathy Bates), *Misery*

▲ *The Stepfather* [Joseph Ruben, 1987] Terry O'Quinn in the title role is unforgettably chilling in this bloodcurdling family film. From a story by Donald E. Westlake who also contributed to the screenplay. Followed by two sequels and a remake.

▲ *The Hitcher* [Robert Harmon, 1986] Jennifer Jason Leigh and C. Thomas Howell pick up a hitchhiker named John Ryder (Rutger Hauer) and quickly regret it. A suspenseful thriller that teeters into horror. Rutger Hauer is terrifying as the hitcher from hell. Remade by producer Michael Bay in 2007 [Dave Meyers]. The remake was unpleasant, but it lacks the impact of the original.

▶ *Naked Lunch* [David Cronenberg, 1991]
Based on William Burroughs' novel, Cronenberg wrote the screenplay with Burroughs to create this semi-autobiographical, junkie's nightmare of a film. Here is Peter Weller at the bar with a friend in the Interzone.

HUMAN MONSTERS

SCARY OLDER WOMEN

The surprise success of Robert Aldrich's *What Ever Happened to Baby Jane?* [1962] unleashed a torrent of imitations. Esteemed actresses like Barbara Stanwyck, Olivia de Havilland, and Joan Fontaine rushed to join the new wave of pictures referred to as "Grande Dame Guignol" or even,"Hagsploitation." Kids all over America began to look at their grandmothers in a new light.

▲ *Straight-Jacket* [William Castle, 1964] Legendary Hollywood star Joan Crawford in a William Castle movie that shouted on its poster, "Warning! 'Straight-Jacket' vividly depicts ax murders!"

▲ *Whoever Slew Auntie Roo?* [Curtis Harrington, 1972] Shelley Winters as the crazy old lady in this companion to Harrington's *What's the Matter with Helen?* [1971]. The publicity tagline was "The hand that rocks the cradle has no flesh on it!"

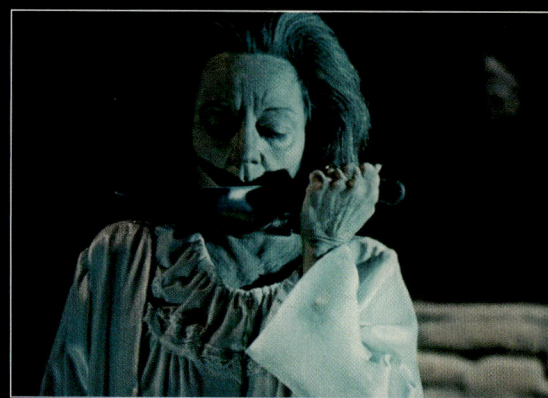

▲ *Die! Die! My Darling!* [aka *Fanatic*, Silvio Narizzano, 1965] Tallulah Bankhead is a homicidal religious maniac in this, her last film.

▲ *What Ever Happened to Baby Jane?* [Robert Aldrich, 1962] Bette Davis gives a fearless performance as a insane former child star Baby Jane Hudson, who lives with her crippled sister Blanche (Joan Crawford) in Hollywood. Based on the novel by Henry Farrell.

◀ **Arsenic and Old Lace** [Frank Capra, 1944]
Josephine Hull and Jean Adair as the two sweet little old ladies who poison "lonely men" and have their lunatic brother bury the bodies in the basement. Here, they hope that Edward Everett Horton will be another victim.

▲ **Rosemary's Baby** [Roman Polanski, 1968]
Ruth Gordon as neighbor Minnie Castevet, hands Rosemary (Mia Farrow) a drugged glass of milk. Gordon is very funny as the helpful little old lady whose intentions are satanic in nature.

▲ **Young Frankenstein** [Mel Brooks, 1974]
Cloris Leachman as Frau Blücher, whose very name frightens the horses! This wonderful actress also played the psychotic Nurse Diesel in Brook's *High Anxiety* [1977].

▲ **Sunset Boulevard** [Billy Wilder, 1950] Gloria Swanson as silent film star Norma Desmond after she's gunned down her young lover, Joe Gillis (William Holden). Shot and scored like the horror film it is, Wilder's cynical, dark Hollywood story is a masterpiece.

▲ **Rabid Grannies** [aka *Les Mémés Cannibales*, Emmanuel Kervyn, 1988] The gifts of a devil-worshipping nephew cause two grandmothers to behave very, very badly in this gory Belgian horror comedy.

◀ **Psycho** [Alfred Hitchcock, 1960]
The real Mrs. Bates, as discovered in the basement by Lila Crane (Vera Miles)—just before Norman, wearing his mother's dress and wig, bursts in with his knife!

SENIOR EDITOR: Alastair Dougall
SENIOR ART EDITOR: Guy Harvey
EDITOR: Jo Casey
DESIGNERS: Rhys Thomas, Laura Brim,
Yumiko Tahata, Nick Avery, Mark Richards,
Sophia Tampakopoulos
SENIOR DTP DESIGNER: David McDonald
SENIOR PRODUCER: Charlotte Oliver
MANAGING EDITOR: Sadie Smith
MANAGING ART EDITOR: Ron Stobbart
CREATIVE MANAGER: Sarah Harland
ART DIRECTOR: Lisa Lanzarini
PUBLISHER: Julie Ferris
PUBLISHING DIRECTOR: Simon Beecroft

This edition published in 2015 by
Dorling Kindersley Limited
80 Strand, London, WC2R 0RL
A Penguin Random House Company

Contains content first published in
Monsters in the Movies (2011)

Text copyright © John Landis, 2011

Page design copyright © 2015
Dorling Kindersley Limited

Picture research by The Kobal Collection

All rights reserved. No part of this publication may
be reproduced, stored in or introduced into a retrieval
system, or transmitted, in any form, or by any means,
(electronic, mechanical, photocopying, recording
or otherwise), without the prior written permission
of the copyright owner.

ISBN: 978-0-2412-4938-3

Printed in Italy

www.dk.com

A WORLD OF IDEAS:
SEE ALL THERE IS TO KNOW

PICTURE CREDITS
Unless otherwise stated, all the images in this book are from the archives of **The Kobal Collection** which owes its existence to the vision, courage, talent, and energy of the men and women who created the movie industry and whose legacies live on through the films they made, the studios they built, and the publicity photographs they took. Kobal collects, preserves, organizes, and makes these images available to enhance our understanding and enjoyment of this cinematic art.
The publisher wishes to thank all of the photographers (known and unknown) and the film distribution and production companies whose images appear in this book. We apologize in advance for any omissions, or neglect and will be pleased to make any corrections in future editions.
All images from **The Kobal Collection** except: **The Art Archive** 5, 22B; **The Art Archive/Marc Charmet** 23; **The Art Archive/Kharbine-Tapador/S.Kakou** 45; **The Art Archive/Musee Saint Denis Reims/Gianni Dagli Orti** 49; **The Art Archive/Garrick Club/Eileen Tweedy** 75; **Bob Burns Collection** 1, 2, 3, 24, 27bl, rc, 46l, 78tr, b, 90t, bl, 91tr, 92bl, 106b, br, 107, 121tl, 122c, 123tr, 135cr, c; **Everett Collection** 40tl; **Greg Nicotero** 14br, 47b, 113br, 117br; **Howard Berger** 113br; **John Landis** 22tl, 28tl, tc, tr, 29tr, 30tl, br, 35, 42cl, 44c, 46, 54bl, 56bl, 64bl, 72, 73, 82c, 84cl, 85tr, 93br, 106c, 111 tc, cr, br, 112t, 116bl; **Photos 12** 6, 16tr, br, 17tl, 30bl, 39br, 41tl, 42tr, 45cr, 47, 91br, 116, 133cl, 139tl; **John Canemaker** 77 (1).

FILM COMPANY CREDITS
20,000 Leagues Under the Sea, Walt Disney Pictures 97; *2001: A Space Odyssey*, MGM 113, 121, 124; *28 Weeks Later*, Fox Atomic/DNA Films/UK Film Council 47; *30 Days of Night*, Ghost House/Columbia/Dark Horse 7; *Abbott & Costello Meet Frankenstein*, Universal 1, 27; *AI: Artificial Intelligence*, Amblin/Dreamworks/WB 127; *Alice In Wonderland* (1933) Paramount 62; *Alice In Wonderland* (2010), Walt Disney Pictures 85; *Aliens*, 20th Century-Fox 111, 126; *Alligator People, The*, 20th Century-Fox 92; *Amazon Women on the Moon*, Universal 82; *American Werewolf in London, An*, Polygram/Universal 22, 28, 42; *Amityville Horror, The*, AIP 55; *Anaconda*, Columbia 98; *Andromeda Strain, The*, Universal 113; *Angry Red Planet, The*, Sino 108; *Arachnid*, Fantastic Factory/TVC 93; *Army of Darkness*, Dino De Laurentiis 44; *Arsenic and Old Lace*, Warner Bros 132, 143; *Atom Age Vampire*, Leone 11; *Atragon*, AIP/Toho 81; *Austin Powers: International Man of Mystery*, New Line 127; *Avatar*, 20th Century-Fox 85, 117; *Barbarella*, Paramount 109; *Barbe-Bleue*, Méliès 137; *Basket Case 2*, Shapiro-Glickenhaus 139; *Bat People, The*, AIP 91; *Beach Girls and the Monster, The*, American Academy Prod 47, 90; *Beast From 20,000 Fathoms, The*, Warner Bros 74; *Beast of Hollow Mountain*, United Artists 79; *Beauty and the Beast*, Walt Disney Pictures 62; *Bees, The*, New World Pictures 95; *Beetlejuice*, Geffen/Warner Bros, 54; *Behemoth, the Sea Monster*, Artistes Alliance/Diamond Pictures 83; *Belle et La Bête, La*, Films Andre Paulve, 62; *Beneath the Planet of the Apes*, 20th Century-Fox/Apjac 177; *Beowulf*, Paramount/Shangri-La 147; *Birds, The*, Universal 92; *Black Cat, The*, Universal 133; *Black Sabbath*, AIP 13; *Blade II*, New Line 15; *Blade Runner*, Ladd Company/Warner Bros 126; *Blob, The* (1958), Allied Pictures 103; *Blob, The* (1988), Tri-Star 103; *Blood and Roses*, Film Ege/Documento 11; *Blood for Dracula* 17; *Blood of Dracula*, AIP 11; *Blue Beard* (2009), Flach Film 137; *Bluebeard* (1944), Pathé 137; *Bluebeard* (1972), Barnabe/Gloria/Vulcano 137; *Bluebeard's Ten Honeymoons*, Anglo-Allied 137; *Boy Who Cried Werewolf, The*, Universal 29; *Brain That Wouldn't Die, The*, AIP 47; *Braindead/Dead Alive*, Wingnut Films 44; *Bram Stoker's Dracula*, Zoetrope/Columbia Tri-Star 13, 15, 17, 29; *Brides of Dracula*, Hammer/Universal 13; *Bridge to Terabithia*, Walt Disney Pictures/Walden Media 66; *Brothers Grimm, The*, Dimension/Miramax 65; *Buffy the Vampire Slayer*, 20th Century-Fox 14; *Burke & Hare* (1971), United Artists 300, 301; *Cabinet of Dr. Caligari, The*, Decla-Bioscop 131; *Canterville Ghost, The*, MGM 53; *Car, The*, Universal 125; *Cars That Ate Paris, The*, Saltpaan/AFDC/Royce Smeal 125; *Cat People* (1942), RKO 7; *Cat Women of the Moon*, Astor Prod. 109; *Cemetery Man*, Audio Film/Canal+, 44; *Changeling, The*, Chessman Park/Tiberius 56; *Christine*, Columbia 125; *Christmas Carol, A*, MGM 53; *Chronicles of Narnia, The: The Lion, the Witch and the Wardrobe*, Walt Disney Pictures/Walden Media 64, 69, 40; *Chronicles of Narnia, The: Prince Caspian*, Walt Disney Pictures/Walden Media 30; *Cinderella*, Méliès 59; *Clash of the Titans* (1981), MGM 63, 68; *Clash of the Titans* (2010), Warner Bros 63, 68; *Cloverfield*, Paramount 116; *Colossus of New York, The*, Paramount 124; *Count Dracula*, BBC Worldwide 16; *Count Yorga, Vampire*, AIP 14; *Creation of the Humanoids, The*, Genie Prods 126; *Creature From the Black Lagoon*, Universal 46, 90; *Cronos*, Iguana/Ventana/Imcine 14; *Cujo*, Taft Entertainment 55; *Curse of the Faceless Man*, UA/Vogue Pictures 46; *Curse of the Undead*, Universal 46; *Darby O'Gill and the Little People*, Walt Disney Pictures 69; *Dark City*, New Line 116; *Dawn of the Dead* (2004), Strike Entertainment/New Amsterdam 45; *Day of the Animals*, Warner Bros 94; *Day of the Dead*, Laurel Entertainment 42; *Day of the Triffids, The*, Allied Artists 109; *Day the Earth Stood Still, The*, 20th Century-Fox 118; *Dead One, The / Blood of the Zombie*, Mardi Gras Prods 39; *Deadly Bees, The*, Amicus/Paramount 95; *Deadly Friend*, Warner Bros 43; *Death Becomes Her*, Universal 44; *Death Line*, K-L Prods 137; *Death Race 2000*, New World 125; *Deep Blue Sea*, Warner Bros/Village Roadshow 96; *Demon Seed*, MGM 126; *Descent, The*, Celador/Pathe 91; *Devil Girl From Mars*, Danziger Prods 109; *Die! Die! My Darling/Fanatic*, Hammer 142; *Dinosaurs!* Fairview Prods 80; *District 9*, Key Creatives 116; *Dr. Terror's House of Horrors*, Amicus/RF 18; *Dog Soldiers*, Kismet Entertainment Group 30; *Don't Look Now*, Casey Prods-Eldorado Films 138; *Dracula* (1931), Universal 9, 13, 16; *Dracula* (1958), Hammer 10, 16, 18; *Dracula* (1974), Warner Bros 17; *Dracula* (1979), Universal 47; *Dracula* (Spanish: 1931), Universal 7; *Dracula Has Risen from the Grave*, Hammer 4, 19; *Dracula: Dead and Loving It*, Castle Rock Entertainment 13, 17; *Dracula's Daughter*, Universal 7, 8; *Dragon War*, ShowBox/Youngqu-Art Movies 85; *Dragonheart*, Universal 84; *Dragonslayer*, Paramount/Disney 83; *Duel*, Universal 125; *Eaten Alive/Death Trap*, Mars Prods 138; *Eight-Legged Freaks*, Village Roadshow/Electric Entertainment 93; *Elephant Man, The*, Brooksfilm/Paramount 139; *Empire of the Ants*, Cinema 77 95; *Enemy Mine*, 20th Century-Fox 112; *Eragon*, 20th Century-Fox 140; *Eraserhead*, AFI/Libra 139; *Erik the Viking*, Prominent Features 69; *Escape From the Planet of the Apes*, 20th Century-Fox 71; *E.T.: The Extra-Terrestrial*, Universal 112; *Evil Dead II*, Rosebud/Renaissance 42; *Evil Dead, The*, Renaissance Pictures 42; *Evolution*, Montecito Picture Co. 84; *Explorers*, Paramount 112; *Exquisite Sinner, The*, MGM 69; *Fantasia*, Walt Disney Pictures 78; *Fatal Attraction*, Paramount 138; *Fearless Vampire Killers, The*, MGM 12, 19; *Fido*, Lions Gate 46; *Fifth Element, The*, Columbia/Tri-Star 114; *Flash Gordon* (1936), Universal 104; *Flash Gordon* (1980), Universal 104; *Flight of the Living Dead*, Imageworks Ent. International 46; *Fog, The*, Debra Hill Prods 55; *Food of the Gods, The*, AIP 95; *Forbidden Planet*, MGM 47, 106, 121; *Frankenfish*, Bayou Film/Silver Nitrate Pictures 99; *Freaks*, MGM 132; *Friday the 13th*, Paramount 139; *Friday the 13th Part 3 in 3D*, Paramount 47; *From Beyond the Grave*, Amicus 53; *From Dusk Till Dawn*, Los Hooligans/A Band Apart 14; *From Hell*, 20th Century-Fox 140; *Galaxy Quest*, Dreamworks 116; *Gamera vs. Barugon*, Daiei Studios 81; *Gay Zombie*, Passion Fruit 46; *Gertie the Dinosaur*, Mccay 77; *Ghost*, Paramount 56; *Ghost and Mrs Muir, The*, 20th Century-Fox 52; *Ghost Breakers, The*, Paramount 38; *Ghost of Slumber Mountain, The*, World Pictures 77; *Ghostbusters 2*, Columbia 54; *Ghoul, The*, Gaumont-British 38; *Ginger Snaps*, Lions Gate/TMN/Telefilm Canada 27; *Godzilla* (1998), Centropolis/Tristar/ Toho 85; *Gog the Killer*, United Artists 122; *Golden Voyage of Sinbad, The*, Columbia 62, 58; *Goliath and the Dragon*, CFFP/Achille Piazzi/Gianni Fuchs 77; *Goliath and the Vampires*, Ambrosiana 12; *Gorgo*, King Brothers 81; *Gorgon, The*, Hammer 63; *Gorilla, The*, Fox National 47; *Green Slime, The*, Southern Cross/Toei 100; *Gremlins*, Warner Bros 32, 67; *Grinch, The*, Imagine Ent. 71; *Grindhouse*, Dimension Films/A Band Apart 47; *Gritos en la Noche*, Hispamer Films/Eurocine 46; *Grizzly*, Film Ventures Int. 94; *Grudge 2, The*, Columbia/Sony 57; *Halloween*, Falcon International 54; *Hands of the Ripper*, Hammer 140; *Harry Potter and the Prisoner of Azkaban*, Warner Bros/Heyday/1492/ Pof 4 Prods 77; *Haunting, The*, MGM 54; *Hitcher, The*, Silver Screen/HBO/Tri Star 141; *Homicidal*, Columbia 136; *Hook*, Hook Prods/Amblin 61; *Horror Express*, Granada/Benmar 110; *Horrors of the Black Museum, The*, Anglo Amalgamated 135; *House of Dracula*, Universal 10, 18; *House of Frankenstein*, Universal 18, 26; *House of Horrors*, Universal 133; *House of Wax*, Warner Bros 135; *House of Usher, The*, AIP 136; *House on Haunted Hill* (1958), Allied Artists 52; *House on Haunted Hill* (1999), Warner Bros 45; *How to Make a Monster*, AIP 27; *Howling, The*, Avco Embassy 27, 29; *Humanoids From the Deep*, New World 90; *Hunchback of Notre Dame*, Hallmark 133; *Hunchback of Notre Dame, The* (1923), Universal 133; *Hunchback of Notre Dame, The* (1939), RKO 133; *Hunchback of Notre Dame/Notre Dame de Paris*, Panitalia/Paris Film 133; *I Am Legend*, Warner Bros 46; *I Bought a Vampire Motorcycle*, Dirk Prods 18; *I Married a Monster From Outer Space*, Paramount 47, 105; *I Walked With a Zombie*, RKO 37, 38, 47; *I Was a Teenage Frankenstein*, Santa Rosa/AIP 46; *I Was a Teenage Werewolf*, AIP 27; *Ilya Muromets*, Ministerstvo Kinematografii 79; *Incredibly Strange Creatures....*, The, Morgan-Steckler Prods 40; *Independence Day*, 20th Century-Fox 115; *Innocents, The*, 20th Century-Fox 51; *Interview With the Vampire*, Geffen Pictures 7, 15; *Invaders From Mars*, 20th Century-Fox 104; *Invasion of the Body Snatchers* (1956), Allied Artists 107; *Invasion of the Body Snatchers* (1978), United Artists 107; *Invasion of the Saucer Men*, AIP 46, 107; *Invisible Boy, The*, MGM 123; *Iron Giant, The*, Warner Bros 127; *It* (1966) Seven Arts 47; *It Came From Beneath the Sea*, Columbia 87, 97; *It Came From Outer Space*, Universal 104; *It Conquered the World*, AIP 109; *It! The Terror From Beyond Space*, Vogue Pictures 111; *Jack the Giant Killer*, United Artists 80; *Jack the Ripper*, Mid-Century Prods 140; *Jason and the Argonauts*, Columbia 58, 65; *Jaws*, Universal 89; *Jaws of Satan*, United Artists 98; *Journey to the 7th Planet*, Cinemagic Inc. 108; *Ju-On: The Grudge*, Oz Company 57; *Jurassic Park*, Amblin/Universal 84; *Killer Klowns From Outer Space*, Trans World Ent. 114; *King Kong* (1933), RKO 78; *King Kong Escapes*, Rankin-Bass-Toho 125; *Kingdom of the Spiders*, Arachnid/Dimensions 93; *Kiss of Death*, 20th Century-Fox 135; *Krull*, Columbia 64; *Kuroneko*, Toho 52; *Kwaidan*, Toho 54; *Labyrinth*, Jim Henson Prods 65; *Lake of Dracula*, Toho 17; *Lake Placid*, Fox 2000 Pics 96; *Land of the Lost*, Universal/Mosaic /Relativity/Kroft 85; *Land That Time Forgot, The*, Amicus 79, 82; *Laserblast*, Irwin Yablans 110; *Last Dinosaur, The*, Rankin-Bass Prods 82; *Last Man On Earth, The*, AIP 40; *Legend*, 20th Century-Fox 58; *Leprechaun in the Hood*, Trimark Pictures 69; *Leviathan*, 20th Century-Fox 96; *Liliom*, Fox Europa 52; *Little Shop of Horrors* (1986), Warner Bros 108; *Little Shop of Horrors, The* (1960), Filmgroup 108; *Little Vampire, The*, Propaganda/Cometstone/New Line 14; *Live and Let Die*, Danjaq/Eon/UA 36; *Lodger, The* (1926), Gainsborough (ITV Global) 140; *Lodger, The* (1944) 20th Century-Fox 140; *Logan's Run*, MGM 125; *London After Midnight*, MGM 8; *Lord of the Rings, The: The Fellowship of the Ring*, New Line/Saul Zaentz/Wing Nut 70; *Lord of the Rings, The: The Return of the King*, New Line/Saul Zaentz/Wing Nut 146; *Lost Boys: The Tribe*, Warner Bros 19; *Lost World, The*, First National 76; *Lost World, The: Jurassic Park*, Universal/Amblin 82; *Magic Sword, The*, United Artists 81; *Man Who Laughs, The*, Universal 132; *Marathon Man*, Paramount 138; *Marca del Hombre-Lobo, La*, Maxper PC/Hifi Stereo 70 Kg 17; *Mark of the Vampire*, MGM 9; *Mars Attacks!*, Warner Bros 114; *Mary Shelley's Frankenstein*, Tri-Star/American Zoetrope 85; *Mask of Fu Manchu*, MGM 74; *Masters of the Universe*, Cannon 114; *Maximum Overdrive*, De Laurentiis 125; *Mega Shark vs. Giant Octopus*, Asylum Home Entertainment 89; *Men in Black*, Columbia 113; *Metropolis*, Ufa, 122; *Michael Jackson's Thriller*, Optimus Prods 22, 43; *Midsummer Night's Dream, A*, Warner Bros 60; *Minotaur, The*, Illiria Films 70; *Misery*, Castle Rock Entertainment 141; *Moby Dick*, Warner Bros 88; *Mole People, The*, Universal 91; *Monster Club, The*, Chips/Sword & Sorcery 29; *Monster From the Ocean Floor*, Lippert 97; *Monster of Piedras Blancas, The*, Vanwick Prods 47, 90; *Monster on the Campus*, Universal 46; *Monsters*, Vertigo Films 261; *Monsters Inc.*, Walt Disney Pictures/Pixar 144; *Monsters vs. Aliens*, Dreamworks Animation 104; *Monty Python's The Meaning of Life*, Universal/Celandine/Monty Python 130; *Mortuary*, Echo Bridge 45; *Mummy: Tomb of the Dragon Emperor, The*, Universal 85; *Mummy's Tomb, The*, Universal 47; *Muppet Christmas Carol, The*, Jim Henson Prods 53; *Murder By Decree*, Avco Embassy 140; *Murders in the Rue Morgue* (1932), Universal 47; *Mysterious Island* (1929), MGM 96; *Mysterious Island* (1961), Columbia 92, 95; *Mystery of the Wax Museum, The*, Warner Bros 135; *Naked Jungle, The*, Paramount 92; *Naked Lunch*, Recorded Picture Co/First Independent 141; *NeverEnding Story, The*, Constantin-Bavaria-WDR/Warner Bros 67, 83; *Nibelungen, Die*, Decla-Bioscop 78; *Night of the Hunter, The*, United Artists 131; *Night of the Lepus*, MGM 89; *Night of the Living Dead*, Image Ten 34, 35; *Nosferatu* (1922), Prana-Film 6, 8; *Nosferatu* (1978), Gaumont 8; *Notti Del Terrore, Le*, Esteban Cinematografica 42; *Octaman*, Filmers Guild 91; *Octopus, Nu Image* 97; *Old Dark House, The*, Universal 131; *Old Mother Riley Meets the Vampire*, Renown 122; *One Million Years B.C.*, Hammer 82; *Orphanage, The*, Warner Bros Pictures Espana 51; *Pan's Labyrinth*, Tequila Gang/WB 71; *Paranormal Activity*, Blumhouse Prods 57; *Paul*, Universal/Big Talk 103; *Peeping Tom*, Anglo Amalgamated, 131; *Percy Jackson & the Olympians: The Lightning Thief*, Fox 2000 Pictures 63; *Perseus and the Gorgon*, Henson Associates 63; *Pet Sematary*, Paramount 43; *Peter Pan*, Walt Disney Pictures 61; *Peter Pan* (2003), Universal 61; *Phantom Creeps, The*, Universal 122; *Phantom From Space*, United Artists 47; *Phantom of the Opera* (1943), Universal 134; *Phantom of the Opera, The* (1925), Universal 129, 134; *Phantom of the Paradise*, Pressman-Williams 134; *Piranha*, Piranha Prods/New World 96; *Piranha 3D*, Atmosphere Entertainment MM 99; *Pirates of the Caribbean: At World's End*, Walt Disney Pictures 71; *Pirates of the Caribbean: The Curse of the Black Pearl*, Walt Disney Pictures 57; *Pirates of the Caribbean: Dead Man's Chest*, Walt Disney Pictures 68; *Pit and the Pendulum, The*, AIP 136; *Plague of the Zombies, The*, Hammer/7 Arts 40; *Plan 9 From Outer Space*, Criswell 11; *Planet of the Vampires*, AIP/Castilla Cooperativa 111; *Poltergeist*, MGM/SLA Entertainment, 55; *Predator*, 20th Century-Fox 117; *Predators*, 20th Century-Fox 117; *Private Life of Sherlock Holmes, The*, United Artists 82; *Pro-Life*, IDT Ent. 113; *Psycho*, Paramount 128, 143; *Q, the Winged Serpent*, Larco Ent 83; *Quatermass Experiment, The*, Hammer, 108; *Queen of Outer Space*, Allied Artists 109; *Rabid*, Cinema Entertainment Enterprises 41; *Rabid Grannies*, Troma/Stardust 143; *Raiders of the Lost Ark*, Lucasfilm Ltd/Paramount 98; *Reptilicus*, Saga Film-Cinemagic-Alta Vista/AIP 82; *Repulsion*, Compton-Tekli/Royal 136; *Resident Evil: Extinction*, Constantin Film/Davis-Films 47; *Return of Dracula*, United Artists 10; *Return of Swamp Thing, The*, Light Year 47; *Return of the Living Dead*, Orion 37; *Revenge of the Zombies*, Monogram 39; *Ring, The*, Dreamworks 56; *Robocop*, Orion (ITV Global) 126; *Robot Monster*, Three Dimensional Pictures 46, 123; *Rodan*, Toho 80; *Rosemary's Baby*, Paramount 143; *Ruling Class, The*, United Artists 140; *Santo y Blue Demon vs Dracula y el Hombre Lobo*, Cinematografica Flama 29; *Satan's Satellites*, Republic 47; *Savage Bees, The*, Alan Lansburg/Don Kirshner Prods 95; *Scream*, Blacula, Scream*, AIP 17; *Scrooge* (1951), Renown 53; *Scrooge* (1970), Waterbury/Cinema Center 53; *Scrooged*, Paramount 53; *Serpent and the Rainbow, The*, Universal 43; *Seven Faces of Dr. Lao, The*, MGM 63, 69; *Seventh Voyage of Sinbad, The*, Columbia 64, 73, 81; *Shadow of a Doubt*, Universal 133; *Shining, The*, Warner Bros 50, 55; *Shivers*, Cinepix/CFDC 41; *Silver Bullet*, De Laurentiis 29; *Sixth Sense, The*, Hollywood Pictures 56; *Skinwalkers*, Constantin Film/Stan Winston Prods 31; *Sleeping Beauty*, Walt Disney Pictures 81; *Sleepy Hollow*, Paramount/Mandalay 56; *Slither*, Universal 116; *Snakes on a Plane*, New Line 98; *Son of Dracula*, Universal 9, 16; *Squirm*, Squirm Comp. 99; *Sssssss*, Universal 191; *Stanley*, Crown International 98; *Star Wars Episode I: The Phantom Menace*, Lucasfilm Ltd/20th Century-Fox 115; *Star Wars Episode II: Attack of the Clones*, Lucasfilm Ltd/20th Century-Fox 115; *Starman*, Columbia 113; *Starship Troopers*, Columbia Tristar 114; *Stepfather, The*, ITC (ITV Global) 141; *Stepford Wives, The*, Columbia 124; *Strait-Jacket*, Columbia 142; *Strange Invaders*, Emi/Orion 112; *Sugar Hill*, AIP 41; *Sunset Boulevard*, Paramount 143; *Surrogates*, Touchstone Pictures 127; *Susan's Plan*, High Fliers 45, 47; *Swarm, The*, Warner Bros 95; *Tales From the Crypt*, Amicus 41; *Tarantula!*, Universal 93; *Teen Wolf*, Wolfkill 27; *Teenage Zombies*, GBM Prods 39; *Tentacles*, AIP/Esse Ci 97; *Terminator 2: Judgement Day*, Carolco 127; *Terminator 3: Rise of the Machines*, C-2 Pictures/Warner Bros 121; *Theatre of Blood*, Cineman 138; *They Live*, Universal 114; *Thief of Bagdad, The*, Korda 61, 62; *Thing, The* (1951), RKO 105; *Thing, The* (1982), Universal 105; *This Island Earth*, Universal 46, 104; *Three Stooges Meet Hercules, The*, Columbia 64; *THX 1138*, American Zoetrope/Warner Bros 124; *Time After Time*, Warner Bros 140; *Time Bandits*, Handmade Films 66, 70; *Time Machine, The*, MGM 47; *Tobor the Great*, Republic 123; *Topper*, MGM 52; *Transformers*, Dreamworks 116; *Tremors*, Universal 98; *Troll*, Lexyn/Altar/Empire Pictures 66; *Troll Hunter, The*, Film Fund Fuzz/Filmkameratene 66; *Twenty Million Miles to Earth*, Columbia 103; *Twilight Saga: New Moon*, Summit Entertainment 30; *Twonky, The*, Arch Oboler 120; *Ulisse*, Lux Film 64; *Undead*, Spierigfilm 45; *Underworld*, Subterranean/Screen Gems 31; *Underworld: Evolution*, Lakeshore Ent/Screen Gems 30; *Undying Monster, The*, 20th Century-Fox 27; *Uninvited, The*, Paramount 51; *Unknown Island*, Albert Jay Cohen Prods 79; *Valley of Gwangi, Morningside* 80; *Vampire and the Ballerina, C.I.F* 13; *Vampire In Brooklyn*, Paramount 15; *Vampire Lovers, The*, Hammer/AIP 19; *Vampire, The*, Gramercy Pictures 10; *Vampires*, Columbia 14; *Vampyr*, Dreyer-Tobis-Klangfilm 9; *Van Helsing*, Universal 13, 17; *Vault of Horror*, Amicus/Metromedia 17; *Village of the Damned*, MGM 112; *Voyage dans la Lune. Le*, Méliès 101, 102; *Walking Dead*, AMC-TV, 47; *War of the Worlds*, Dreamworks/Paramount 107; *War of the Worlds, The*, Paramount 106; *Water Horse: Legend of the Deep, The*, Beacon Pictures/Blue Star Pictures 82; *Werewolf in a Girls' Dormitory*, Royal Film 27; *Werewolf of London, The*, Universal 26; *Werewolf, The*, Columbia 27; *Westworld*, MGM 121; *What Ever Happened to Baby Jane?*, Warner Bros 142; *White Heat*, Warner Bros135; *White Zombie*, United Artists 38; *Whoever Slew Auntie Roo?*, Hemdale/AIP 142; *Willard* (1970), Bing Crosby Prods 94; *Willard* (2003), New Line 94; *Witches, The*, Warner Bros 235; *Witchfinder General*, Tigon 137; *Wizard of Oz, The*, MGM 119; *Wolf Man, The*, Universal 24, 26; *Wolfman, The*, Universal Pictures 31; *Wonderful World of the Brothers Grimm*, MGM. 65, 80; *Yog: Monster From Space*, Toho 110; *Young Frankenstein*, 20th Century-Fox 46, 143; *Flesh Eaters*, Variety 41; *Zombies of Mora Tau*, Clover Prods 39; *Zombies of the Stratosphere*, Republic 123; *Zombies on Broadway*, RKO 39.